Organizational Develo
Innovation, and Econ(

This edited collection comprehensively explores Economy 5.0, focusing on critical aspects such as organizational development, intellectual capital, soft agent dynamics, and agility. Through in-depth analysis, real-world case studies, and forward-looking perspectives, the book provides readers with practical insights into the challenges and opportunities that define contemporary organizations and skills that can be applied in different cultural and organizational contexts. The overarching goal is to empower individuals to thrive in the dynamic economic landscape of Economy 5.0 by promoting sustainable practices, fostering future-proof skill sets, encouraging ethical leadership, and inspiring innovative solutions. It addresses issues and trends that are universally relevant in today's globalized world, offering a multidisciplinary perspective that will make it valuable to researchers, academics, practitioners, and students in the fields of organizational development, management, innovation, sustainability, and ethical leadership.

Elżbieta Jędrych is a Professor of Economics at the University of Vistula, Poland.

Agnieszka Rzepka is a Professor in the Department of Economics and Economic Management, Faculty of Management, Lublin University of Technology, Poland.

Routledge Studies in Management, Organizations and Society

This series presents innovative work grounded in new realities, addressing issues crucial to an understanding of the contemporary world. This is the world of organized societies, where boundaries between formal and informal, public and private, local and global organizations have been displaced or have vanished, along with other nineteenth century dichotomies and oppositions. Management, apart from becoming a specialized profession for a growing number of people, is an everyday activity for most members of modern societies.

Similarly, at the level of enquiry, culture and technology, and literature and economics, can no longer be conceived as isolated intellectual fields; conventional canons and established mainstreams are contested. *Management, Organizations and Society* addresses these contemporary dynamics of transformation in a manner that transcends disciplinary boundaries, with books that will appeal to researchers, students and practitioners alike.

Recent titles in this series include:

Innovation Management and the Law
An Institutional Approach
Alexander Styhre

Strategic Management and Drivers of Success
The Growth, Adaptation, Resilience, and Competition Framework
Surja Datta and Tobias Kutzewski

Management, Conflict Resolution and Strategy
Coping with Stress at Work
Magdalena Kraczla and Anna Wziątek-Staśko

Organizational Development, Innovation, and Economy 5.0
Challenges in the Digital Era
Edited by Elżbieta Jędrych and Agnieszka Rzepka

Organizational Development, Innovation, and Economy 5.0

Challenges in the Digital Era

Edited by
Elżbieta Jędrych
and Agnieszka Rzepka

Routledge
Taylor & Francis Group
NEW YORK AND LONDON

First published 2025
by Routledge
605 Third Avenue, New York, NY 10158

and by Routledge
4 Park Square, Milton Park, Abingdon, Oxon, OX14 4RN

Routledge is an imprint of the Taylor & Francis Group, an informa business

Library of Congress Cataloging-in-Publication Data
Names: Jędrych, Elżbieta, editor. | Rzepka, Agnieszka, editor.
Title: Organizational development, innovation, and Economy 5.0 : challenges in the digital era / edited by Elżbieta Jędrych and Agnieszka Rzepka.
Description: New York, NY : Routledge, 2025. |
Series: Routledge studies in management, organizations and society | Includes bibliographical references and index.
Identifiers: LCCN 2024018916 | ISBN 9781032817248 (hardback) | ISBN 9781032819693 (paperback) | ISBN 9781003502272 (ebook)
Subjects: LCSH: Organizational change. | Technological innovations. | Management. | Sustainable development.
Classification: LCC HD58.8 .O733 2025 | DDC 658.4/06—dc23/eng/20240612
LC record available at https://lccn.loc.gov/2024018916

ISBN: 978-1-032-81724-8 (hbk)
ISBN: 978-1-032-81969-3 (pbk)
ISBN: 978-1-003-50227-2 (ebk)

DOI: 10.4324/9781003502272

Typeset in Galliard
by codeMantra

Contents

Tables

Contributors

Grażyna Bartkowiak is a professor at the Naval Academy in Gdynia's Faculty of Humanities and Social Sciences. She specializes in psychological and social aspects of human functioning in the work environment and human resources management.

Justyna Bagińska is an assistant professor at the Department of Tourism and Recreation at the Wrocław Business University of Applied Sciences. Tour leader, translator, author, and co-author of scientific papers in Polish and English on rail transport, transport accessibility, socio-economic aspects of tourism, a broad range of cultural tourism, and recently also the psychology of sport.

Justyna Berniak-Woźny works at the University of Innovation Technology and Management in Rzeszow and is an experienced lecturer and business trainer in marketing communication and CSR. Her current research interests range across business ethics, corporate social responsibility (mostly from a marketing and HR perspective), university social responsibility, and business education for sustainability.

Ryszard Borowiecki is a professor at Krakow University of Economics, where he served as Rector from 2002 to 2008. He is also a researcher with 54 years of experience and is the author, co-author, and/or scientific editor of more than 600 works in the fields of corporate management, economic analysis and diagnostics, and corporate development.

Piotr F. Borowski is a professor at the Vistula University in Warsaw. He is the author of over 150 articles in national and international scientific journals and monographs, including 28 articles indexed in the Web of Science and Scopus. His research focuses on the management of companies in the energy sector, taking into account the requirements of zero-emission economies, CO_2 emissions reduction, and innovative solutions classified as green innovation.

Magdalena Czerwińska is a professor at the Lublin University of Technology. She is the author of over 50 papers. She specializes in knowledge management, health, information technology acceptance models, and health information.

Marta Drozdowska is a professor at the University of Business in Wrocław. Her research interests include the sectoral and territorial cooperation of travel agencies, city tourism, cultural tourism, sustainable development, and B2C customer relationship management tools. She has published nearly 50 scientific papers, mostly in international journals.

Arif Erkol holds a PhD in management from the University of Economics and Business in Poznań. Dr Erkol is a serial entrepreneur. He specializes in managing EU projects and providing consulting for the internationalization of universities. His interests include ed-tech, aviation, higher education, internationalization, and EU projects. He is co-author of two books and several articles.

Agnieszka Faron is a professor at Vistula University in Warsaw. Her research focuses on entrepreneurship and management. She is the author or co-author of numerous papers. She is actively engaged in working with the business environment through research and education.

Jan Fazlagić is a professor at the University of Economics in Poznań as well as a lecturer at the Vistula University in Warsaw. During his 21 years of scientific activity, he wrote 75 articles in peer-reviewed journals as well as 16 monographs. His research interests include intellectual capital in organizations, education, management in education and local government, and knowledge management.

Hubert Gąsiński is a professor at WSB MERITO University in Warsaw in the Department of Entrepreneurship and Innovation. He specializes in the banking system and the use of quantitative methods in the practical management and forecasting of economic phenomena.

Paulina Graczyk is a lecturer at the Wrocław University of Economics and Business. She is writing her dissertation on culinary heritage as a factor in the sustainable development of the region. As a lecturer, she focuses on issues such as food conservation and reducing food waste. Her charity ran a Ghanaian school for four years, supporting children's education and renewable energy development.

Izabela Gruszka is a professor at the University of Economics and Business in Wrocław. She has authored or co-authored numerous scientific papers. Her research interests are related to the study of the competitiveness of cities and regions in the tourism market, the assessment of urban area absorption capacity, and the commercialization of tourist qualities.

Dariusz Ilnicki is a professor and researcher at the Institute of Geography and Regional Development (the University of Wroclaw). His research interests are focused on the geography of services and spatial management. His research into new services, spheres of influence, and functional relationships between cities and their surroundings is quantitative and supported by data from geographic information systems.

Elżbieta Jędrych is a professor of management at Vistula University in Warsaw, Poland. She holds a PhD in economics and specializes in management sciences. The author of more than 120 scientific papers and expert analyses on industrial practice, she specializes in human resources and social capital management as well as the management of employee development, motivation, and rewards.

Magdalena Kaczkowska-Serafińska is a professor and HR manager at Vistula University in Warsaw. She is the author of 20 papers, including scientific publications on the multifaceted management of employees. Her scientific interests include employee job satisfaction, employee commitment, generation Y, intercultural differences among employee expectations, competence management, and implementing changes in organizations.

Barbara Karlikowska works at the Institute of Finances at Vistula University. She is an author and co-author of many scientific works in the field of risk management.

Dariusz Klimek works on a research team at the Department of Management Systems and Innovation at Lodz University of Technology. He specializes in sustainable business management and industrial policy. He is the author of more than 70 scientific publications. In the past, he has managed large industrial companies in Poland as well as abroad.

Agnieszka Knap-Stefaniuk is a professor at the Jesuit University Ignatianum in Krakow. Her teaching and research interests include contemporary management, especially human resource management, intercultural management, and multiculturalism, as well as various challenges related to managing culturally diverse teams of employees. She is the author of about 70 publications in the field of people management, with particular emphasis on workplaces with culturally diverse employees and managers.

Maria Kocot is a professor at the University of Economics in Katowice. Her research interests relate to knowledge and information management, the development of the knowledge economy, and economic information technology. Her latest research included modern business management methods.

Juliusz Kotyński is a professor of economic sciences and has been lecturing and conducting research studies at Vistula University in Warsaw since 1999. He is the author of many books, papers, and studies on the theory of international economics and finance, economic and financial policies, globalization and regional economic integration, risk management, and financial mathematics.

Agnieszka Krugiełka is a professor at the Institute of Logistics at the Faculty of Engineering Management at Poznań University of Technology. Her research interests include human resources management, knowledge management, and corporate social responsibility, especially in the area of the internal customer. She also specializes in team management from the perspective of the team leader and inter-generational team management.

Artur Kwasek is a professor at the University of Technology and Economics in Warsaw, working in the Department of Management and Logistics. He specializes in management with the use of new ICT technologies, open and active education, e-learning and combining science with business practice.

Małgorzata Leśniak-Johann is currently an assistant professor at the Wrocław Business Academy in Applied Sciences. In her work, she combines teaching students and cooperation with entities involved in the development of Lower Silesia in the spheres of entrepreneurship, tourism and recreation, and protection of the natural environment by implementing joint projects. She is the author of publications on political and economic geography, tourism, and management in naturally valuable areas. Her special scientific interests are related to the issue of sustainable development.

Wojciech Maciejewski is an assistant professor in the Department of Entrepreneurship and Social Innovation of the Uniwersytet Komisji Edukacji Narodowej in Cracow, Poland. His research interests concern entrepreneurship, entrepreneurial features, issues of entrepreneurship education, factors of success and failure of enterprises, decision issues, and factors affecting the success of business ventures.

Ewa Mazur – Wierzbicka is a professor at the Department of Human Capital Management at the University of Szczecin. Author of more than 150 scientific publications. Her scientific interests include: corporate social responsibility (CSR), business ethics, human resource management, diversity management, change management in organizations, coaching and mentoring, sustainable development, quality of life, and human capital management.

Radosław Miśkiewicz is a professor at the University of Szczecin. He professionally combines business and research activities; hence, his scientific interests pertain to the organizational structures of metallurgical enterprises, knowledge transfer and management, and the integration of metallurgical enterprises in terms of the transfer of innovative technologies. He has an impressive academic record that includes more than 140 papers.

Krzysztof R. Nowakowski is a professor at Vistula University in Warsaw. He is the author of 33 articles and scientific papers, four books, 12 articles in collective publications, and 17 texts that are published in scientific journals. His research interests include international relations, economic sociology and economic policy, global marketing, international human resource management, and the cultural diversity of organizations involving Asian capital (Korean, Japanese, and Chinese in particular).

Zbigniew Olesiński is a professor at the Vistula University in Warsaw and specializes in inter-organizational management, inter-organizational networks, clusters, and globalization problems. He has participated in or managed 11 research programs and 13 EU research grants. He is also the author or co-author of 206 publications, including 14 books.

Mariana Petrova is a professor at St. Cyril and St. Methodius University of Veliko Tarnovo, Bulgaria, and a professor of economics and management at ISMA, Riga, Latvia. She specializes in IT process, project, and service management, digital solutions in business and management, smart economics and innovation, and smart data analysis in economics. Mariana has published more than 200 papers. She has served as an editor in chief, managing editor, and member of the editorial board for numerous journals.

Kamila Pihur is a graduate of the University of Social Sciences and Humanities in Wrocław. Currently, she works as a research and development consultant at the Wrocław Business Academy in Applied Sciences. In her work, she combines the fields of psychology, trainer and facilitator of the Design Thinking method in problem solving for business

Marlena Plebańska is a professor at Vistula University who was one of the precursors of Polish e-learning and specializes in knowledge management, e-learning, and design thinking. She is the author of more than 100 scientific publications as well as dozens of popular science publications in the field of e-education, with nearly 20 years of experience in designing e-learning solutions and knowledge management in many Polish enterprises, schools, and non-governmental organizations.

Sultan Ramazanov is a professor with a Ph.D. in technical sciences and a Ph.D. in economic sciences. Distinguished activist of the Science and Technology Center in Ukraine. He is a professor in the Department of Information Systems in Economics at Kyiv National Economic University, Ukraine. He is a mathematics, cybernetics, and environmental economics expert in designing and developing integrated information systems for managing complex objects with AI. He has published over 500 academic and scientific papers, including 45 monographs and 14 teaching aids and textbooks.

Agnieszka Rzepka is a professor at Lublin University of Technology in the Faculty of Management in the Department of Economics and Economic Management. A specialist in inter-organizational management, intellectual capital, self-management, and SMEs, her current research focuses on teal organizations. In addition to 140 papers, she has written seven proprietary and collective monographs.

Monika Sak-Skowron works in the Department of Enterprise Management at the John Paul II Catholic University of Lublin. Her scientific interests are employee competence, strategic management, and relationship management.

Łukasz Skowron is a professor at the Lublin University of Technology. His teaching and research interests include marketing, business and marketing research, business performance management, customer behavior, customer relationships, satisfaction, loyalty, motivation, artificial intelligence in business solutions, and strategic management. He has written or co-written four books and 80 articles and reviews.

Ludmiła Stemplewska is a professor at Vistula University with more than 25 years of work experience at various companies that operate on international markets. She is the author and co-author of eight books and 50 scientific articles that are published in Poland as well as abroad.

Anna M. Wiśniewska works at Vistula University, Warsaw. She has also worked as a certified internal auditor as well as a lecturer on business financing issues, the basics of management, and crisis management since 2014. She is the author of publications on age management, ethics in business, and SME financing, as well as management in medical tourism.

Jacek Witkowski works at the Lublin University of Technology and deals with the issues of environmental management at the local level and the development of entrepreneurship based on the pro-ecological use of natural resources. Author of over 40 scientific publications.

Agata Włodkowska is a professor at Vistula University, Warsaw, and an expert in the field of political science. Her key research areas concern international relations and security in post-Soviet areas, the foreign and security policies of the Russian Federation and the post-Soviet states, the foreign policy of Poland, and the feminist approach to international relations. She is a co-author and coordinator of the project *Women in Polish Political Science.*

Introduction

Agnieszka Rzepka and Elżbieta Jędrych

The rapid advancements in super-automation and artificial intelligence, coupled with the imperative to maintain ecological equilibrium, have underscored the significance of developing organizations, intellectual capital, business enterprises, soft factors, agility, creativity, and innovations.

A group of authors, having collaborated for years on comprehensive research spanning Europe and the globe, and recognized for their work with Routledge, have taken on the task of offering a fresh perspective on solving the challenges faced by contemporary society and the modern economy, often referred to as Society 5.0 and Economy 5.0.

The first part of the monograph is dedicated to identifying trends in the evolution of modern organizations to confront these challenges. Of particular importance is the recognition of the growing role and importance of factors such as self-management, cultural diversity, and data updates. The next section delves into the primary soft factor – intellectual capital, while the third section deals with the contextual factors shaping business development, which encompasses the growing role and significance of soft management factors, including intellectual capital, and the previously described trend of organizational development. The fourth part conducts a comprehensive analysis of the aforementioned soft factors. The fifth one zeroes in on the concepts of agility and creativity, which are pivotal in discerning the manifestations of soft factors and the strategies for their assimilation into organizations. Lastly, part six represents a culmination of prior discussions and showcases the practical application of managerial principles laid out in the preceding parts of the monograph.

DOI: 10.4324/9781003502272-1

1 Organizational development

Developmental factors in organizations

Ryszard Borowiecki, Czerwińska Magdalena, Radosław Miśkiewicz, and Zbigniew Olesiński

Introduction

Today (the third decade of the 21st century), the role and significance of service-oriented companies is growing substantially. These types of organizations encounter entirely new challenges that call for the organizations' internal transformations. As changes are developed and implemented successfully in one organization, they serve as benchmarks for their traditional counterparts. By identifying and analyzing the key developmental factors, we can determine the direction and speed of such changes within organizations (particularly those that cooperate with one another).

Unveiling managerial mechanisms of evolution toward Society 5.0 and Economy 5.0

As we enter the third decade of the 21st century, we are observing noteworthy transformations in the operations of societies and economies, especially in developed nations. Across scientific, political, economic, and social dialogs, the impending era is synonymous with sustainable development and is commonly termed "Society 5.0" and "Economy 5.0." This era anticipates the advancement of governance systems, with one of its enduring models being expounded in Integral Theory.

In 2014 (Laloux, 2014), Frederic Laloux's "Reinventing Organizations: A Guide to Creating Organizations Inspired by the Next Stage of Human Consciousness" was published, drawing inspiration from the work of Jenny Wade (1996) and Ken Wilber (1996). Ken Wilber provided a foreword to Laloux's book in which he elucidated the concept of Integral Theory and clarified the essence of the theory (which posits humanity's transition into the post-modern [teal] era after the postmodern era) as per Lyotard's concept that was formulated as early as 1967 (Lyotard, 2016). Lyotard's theory was intended to succeed the Modernist era, which reached its peak during the Industrial Age (orange) around 1492 in Europe (shortly after the Modernist agrarian age [amber]).

DOI: 10.4324/9781003502272-2

Table 1.1 Criteria for consumer choice on different types of markets

Type of economy	*Market type*	*Key criterion for consumer choice*	*Purchases based on*
Agrarian	Commodity	Availability	Reliability and availability of supplies
Industrial (industrial)	Goods	Price	Affordability of quote
Services (industrial)	Services	Quality	Obtaining evidence of excellent product quality
Feelings (post-industrial)	Feelings	Authenticity	Compatibility with one's image

It is characteristic that organizational and management models from different eras (spanning from purple to teal) persist in today's societies, interact with each other, and undergo evolution. In the foreword that was mentioned earlier, Wilber explained that, within contemporary Western societies, the pluralistic postmodern phase encompasses approximately 20% of the population (green), with mythic (amber) constituting 40%–50%, and 10% belonging to the magical (purple) stage (Laloux, 2014).

The concept of mutual interaction among organizations and social relationships in various eras quickly garnered a fitting response in Polish publications. The notion of teal organizations specifically piqued the interest of Blikle (2017). Other authors have derived inspiration from the concept of organizational development stages and the developmental stages of civilization (culture). An illustrative instance is a collaborative effort that Glinka and Koster authored entitled "New Directions of Organization and Management" (Glinka & Kostera, 2016). Of particular significance within the outlined context is their work, "Management in the Experience Market."

Table 1.1 presents the evolution of the market over the course of history; the distinct stages of this evolution are similar to Laloux's concept.

In the same text on the market of feelings, the authors singled out the stages of development of the competition market (as presented in Table 1.2).

In her 2018 book titled *Inter-organizational Relations and Intellectual Capital as Factors for the Development of Micro and Small Enterprises*, Agnieszka Rzepka scrutinized the escalating significance of inter-organizational cooperation (Rzepka, 2018). Through her research, she highlighted the characteristics of a company's operations, its management framework, and its business profile in the context of evolving business environments. The study's findings culminated in the inference that, presently, inter-organizational cooperation plays a pivotal role in the advancement of teal organizations.

Table 1.2 Stages of development of the competition market

Stages of market development	*Product*	*Competition's offer*	*Customer needs*	*Price*	*Fee charged for*
Commodity market	Commodity (extracted or harvested)	Unbalanced	Not relevant	Market	Value of unbalanced substance
Market of goods	Goods (produced by manufacturers with value added)	Some variation	Considered (generally)	Market plus	Value of separated tangible object
Service market	Personalized service	Greater variation	Quite important	Premium minus	Value of manufacturer's activities
Market for feelings	Feelings (arranged, theatrical, experienced by individual)	High variation	Essential needs of individuals	Premium	Value of customer feelings in market of manufacturer's involvement
Transformation market	Transformation (moving toward transformation): goal is to achieve potential of uniqueness	Full variation	Key (self-fulfillment of needs of individual)	Premium plus	Value of benefits that customer will gain, from selling time to consuming product

Role and importance of innovation

To temporarily enhance a company's market position amid ongoing changes, strategies such as workforce downsizing, salary reductions, relaxing occupational health and safety standards, overlooking environmental protection norms, and engaging in questionable financial practices (particularly those pertaining to taxes as well as loans and other expenditures) are frequently employed. These measures are all of a short-term nature and fail to address the company's liquidity situation in the long run; they merely sustain liquidity over a certain period.

The pathway toward enhancing a company's market stance lies in the adoption of novel techniques and technologies, along with the introduction of appealing new products into the market.

Innovation can stem from creative ideas generated by a company's employees, but their implementation generally carries significant risks. Therefore, acquiring an innovative enterprise can be a prudent choice. If a novel product gains traction in the market, the purchasing company can integrate it into their operations. Presently, market observation and the emulation of successful solutions from other innovation endeavors are paramount. Throughout the entire innovation process, it is crucial for companies that seek novel solutions to foster collaboration with their surrounding counterparts (ideally within networks of inter-organizational cooperation).

In a paper titled "The Bagel Economics" (published a few years ago), Kate Raworth advocated for a radical reduction in land utilization by residents.

With the perspective gained over these years, it is now enticing to explore an alternative vision. Instead of drastically cutting consumption, the focus should shift toward fundamentally transforming consumption.

First and foremost, it is noteworthy to highlight the role and significance of advancements in computer science and artificial intelligence. These advancements enable remote communication, thereby reducing the carbon footprint associated with travel. Additionally, they curtail paper consumption, consequently contributing to forest preservation. Artificial intelligence also streamlines the processing of raw materials and energy consumption. Recycling also presents substantial opportunities by facilitating material reuse.

Innovation also deserves consideration, as it provides an additional pathway toward reducing energy consumption, decreasing the use of raw materials, and promoting recycling.

It is important to consider systematically improving the longevity of used items, including extending the lifespans of apartments, furniture, household appliances, vehicles, clothing, and other commodities.

Significant changes are on the horizon in the energy sector that involve the progress of photovoltaics, wind turbines, heat pumps, and energy-storage facilities.

Areas of development of contemporary organizations in 5.0 economic age

When we analyze the functioning of different organizations, fundamental differences become readily apparent. Of particular significance are the organizational structure and the operations of employee teams in companies that leverage modern technology (especially computer technology). Similarly, organizations that are engaged in promotion, marketing, research, or artistic endeavors showcase distinct features. Within such organizations, there is a notable presence of employees who are attuned to present challenges and are prepared to contribute to innovative projects.

In today's landscape, organizations collaborate with one another in order to achieve market success, giving rise to the challenge of establishing connections between organizations of diverse types.

From the adopted research standpoint, we have "red," "amber," "orange," "green," and "teal" organizations. While operating within a network, individual organizations naturally gravitate toward the practices that they have mastered. In the realm of goods markets, for instance, agrarian organizations that supply traditional products like grains or potatoes hold dominance. In a seamless manner, fostering a relationship between the employees of a consulting firm (teal) and those of an agrarian company (amber) requires mutual consideration and tolerance. However, it appears plausible that, in the domain of promoting and marketing the products of the agrarian company, the incorporation of behavior models that are advocated by the consultancy firm (teal) is achievable (perhaps through the establishment of a marketing team within the agrarian company).

The notion of marketing a consulting firm within an industrial organization can be embraced in a similar manner. Such companies typically view the market as a commodities market and tailor the advice that is provided by the consulting firm to align with their operations (see Table 1.2). As the experience market develops (see Tables 1.1 and 1.2), both agrarian and industrial companies try to adapt to the requirements of the modern market.

When a consulting company operates within networks of agrarian or industrial organizations, there tends to be a disposition to accommodate conventional organizational practices. However, this inclination may inadvertently curtail the innovative potential of the consulting firm. Conversely, if a manufacturing entity (like a bakery) is situated amid service companies (such as catering establishments), this context can exert an influence on modernizing the traditional company. Catering firms can offer a substantial array of innovative products, including diverse varieties of bread.

This progression could be amplified if catering enterprises become integral to the experience market (where catering is merely one facet of a broader sector), such as a tourism market that specializes in event organization. This dynamic might propel the bakery to explore novel types of breads, bake loaves of bread during various events with audiences, or create opportunities for individuals to partake in the baking process, among other possibilities.

Management in interstate networks

The considerations in the previous sub-section focused mainly on organizations that operate in local environments, in which both benchmarking and outsourcing are much easier to carry out since the interested parties operate under essentially similar conditions (in a district or municipality). These organizations are well-acquainted with the cultural dynamics of collaboration and the prevalent norms and customs within a given environment.

In the context of interregional, national, and international cooperation, the landscape becomes more intricate. While an organization's operations are rooted in local conditions, community leaders (namely, companies that are endowed with production and capital prowess, innovative manufacturing, and skilled teams) endeavor to forge connections with counterparts from other regions and countries. Such collaboration is facilitated through collective involvement in industry associations and joint participation in trade shows, exhibitions, and conferences.

Contemporary management in global context

In an increasingly globalized world, establishing networks with a global reach is of paramount importance. Achieving the functioning of these networks necessitates endorsements from macro-regional, micro-regional, and local networks. While limited, incidental impacts can garner acceptance relatively easily, broader and more substantial impacts tend to trigger heightened contention and countermeasures. Consequently, this prompts adjustments to the influence that is exerted by emerging global networks, ultimately resulting in a diminution of their effect.

Certain segments of local and micro-regional networks remain isolated, a circumstance that often engenders social tensions.

The formation of local and micro-regional networks with global networks is the result of isolationist and cooperative tendencies.

Creating new relationships requires a nuanced understanding of how to structure them in accordance with the utilization of emerging information and knowledge as well as the development of specific behaviors. Consequently, we are dealing with developing the ability to comprehend the flow of information and goods at this stage.

This complexity deepens when such comprehension demands a revision of the prevailing norms and value systems. Information that generally holds less relevance to the present standards and values can be tolerated, causing minimal disturbance to existing systems due to the influx of new goods.

It is evident that matters become intricate when a significant shift in perception is needed, altering the value that is attributed to the information or goods at hand. For instance, products and their use that challenge social norms (like women's clothing) or modify behavior in public spaces heighten this complexity. The same holds true for the acceptance of innovative standards of value, which encompass the utilization of such items as smartphones and laptops.

A more significant challenge emerges when the importance of the norms and values that form the bedrock of traditions or religious beliefs within certain systems is diminished.

When constructing global networks, the newly established relationships strive for acceptance within local communities, such as academia or urban contexts known for their innovative approaches. These locales often exhibit a willingness to embrace innovation due to factors like high-income dynamics and social empowerment.

The process of adaptation can span months, years, or even decades. In certain instances, this transition may lead to social tensions that counterbalance economic gains and result in the rejection of certain behaviors.

The most prominently evident issues are the escalating social tensions within sizable segments, particularly when these tensions stem from breaches of core customary values, interpersonal norms, faiths, traditions, and patriotism. Presently, these tensions are conspicuously pronounced in areas that concern the social status of women along with their professional conduct and public behavior, among other aspects. From the perspective of the science of management and quality, these tensions give rise to distinct challenges in fostering inter-organizational relationships, spanning various levels of relationships such as local and micro-regional contexts. In social dynamics, this gives rise to specific pressures on prevailing political connections.

Through political choices, the establishment of inter-organizational relationships can be influenced to a certain degree. The interactions between nations and blocs of nations hold particular significance in this context. This becomes even more crucial when these interactions involve groups from diverse civilizational spheres that encompass value systems that have evolved gradually over extended periods and are relatively resistant to rapid changes.

One example of a political nature could be found in a situation in which a political party's trajectory has been steadily shifting toward the right. This evolution could be marked by a sequence of internal upheavals, each following a familiar pattern whereby the complacent party establishment seeks to harness the energy of right-wing radicals in order to mobilize the electorate. However, such a strategy often leads to unintended consequences. The radicals eventually gain ascendancy within the party, pulling it further to the right. Over time, these once-radical ideas become mainstream, firmly embedding themselves within the establishment. Next, however, another wave of radicalism begins to emerge on the right flank. Following the election, the radicals often gravitate toward the center, aligning themselves with the demands of the governing body. This dynamic opens the door to the potential emergence of another faction of radicals in subsequent elections. This phenomenon highlights not only the pulsation of individual perspectives but also the fluctuations of specific group ideologies.

It should be noted that not only the opinions of individual social groups are subject to pulsation but also those of individual organizations; hence, constant change that is also at the intersection of "tectonic plates" that determine the temporary boundaries of the social, political, and economic behaviors of individual civilizations.

It is important to acknowledge that the fluctuations extend not just to the viewpoints of distinct social groups but also to those of organizations. This dynamic leads to continuous shifts at the crossroads of "tectonic plates," which define the temporary boundaries of social, political, and economic behaviors within individual civilizations.

Recommendations

The development of superautomation and artificial intelligence, coupled with the imperative of environmental preservation (including the curbing of CO2 emissions), has sparked discussions regarding the escalating significance of what are often termed "soft management factors." These factors encompass knowledge, human capital, social capital, relational capital, multiculturalism, trust, and other elements that foster the decentralization of organizational structures. They contribute to the amplified role and relevance of self-management, the cultivation of inter-organizational connections, and the stimulation of creativity and innovation—all working toward environmental protection.

Given this backdrop, it is prudent to foster inter-organizational collaboration that is bolstered by artificial intelligence. Such collaboration can facilitate the emergence of environmentally friendly technologies like photovoltaics, heat pumps, and energy storage, thus driving advancements that align with ecological well-being.

Summary

After years of comprehensive international research, the authors of this chapter have discerned a trend that is characterized by continuous, advantageous, and innovative transformations within the operations of contemporary societies. This trend is commonly denoted as Society 5.0, and it corresponds with the modern economic paradigm known as Economy 5.0. However, these favorable and innovative changes perpetually contend with challenges that are rooted in historical legacies (such as conventional agriculture or traditional industries that emerged from the coal and steel era).

The widespread adoption of valuable innovative approaches that is inherent to Economy 5.0 holds the potential to progressively mitigate the environmental impact that is associated with traditional agro-industrial economies. Simultaneously, the advancement of the service economy will usher in economies that are centered on experience and transformation. These changes will collectively enhance the operational landscape of those societies that are steadily progressing toward the ideals of Society 5.0.

References

Blikle, A. (2017). *The doctrine of quality: Teal. A thing about turquoise self-organization.* Gliwice: Onepress Publishing House.

Glinka, B., & Kostera, M. (2016). *New directions of organization and management: Organization, contexts, and processes of management.* Warsaw: Wolters Kluwer.

Laloux, F. (2014). *Reinventing organizations: A guide to creating organizations inspired by the next stage of human consciousness.* Nelson Parker: BC: Nelson Parker.

Lyotard, J.-F. (2016). *La condition postmoderne: Rapport sur le savoir.* Les Ed. de Minuit.

Rzepka, A. (2018). *Relacje międzyorganizacyjne i kapitał intelektualny jako czynnik rozwoju mikro i małych przedsiębiorstw; Studium na przykładzie wybranych przedsiębiorstw polskich i gruzińskich.* Warsaw: Difin.

Wade, J. (1996). *Changes of mind: A holonomic theory of the evolution of consciousness.* Albany: State University of New York Press.

Wilber, K. (1996). *A brief history of everything.* Boston: Shambhala Publications.

2 Navigating sustainable development

Challenges and imperatives for European Economy 5.0

Juliusz Kotyński

Introduction

The evolution of contemporary organizations, encompassing their transformation, diverse forms of employment and governance structures, and the outcomes they achieve depend to a large extent on the competence and capabilities of their managers. Additionally, its trajectory is profoundly intertwined with the geopolitical landscape in the world and the actions undertaken by politicians, international organizations, and major powers. Their readiness and ability to formulate and execute strategic decisions that are intended to uphold worldwide peace amidst emerging challenges like Russia's aggression against Ukraine, as well as their agility in reshaping national economies to foster sustainable development within an era of global warming, assume paramount importance. Moreover, grappling with imminent perils to Earth's biosphere and humanity, which are progressively palpable across diverse countries and continents, adds to the complexity.

The roster of threats and opportunities concerning the sustainable development of Society 5.0 and Economy 5.0, propelled by the integration of new technologies, digitalization, and artificial intelligence within the context of international cooperation and globalization, has proven to be much lengthier than initially anticipated during the 2021–2022 timeframe. Successfully addressing these threats, which travers both global and regional realms, stands as a pivotal facet of the objectives that undergird the establishment of Society 5.0 and Economy 5.0, or what is colloquially referred to as the "Emerald Economy" (Kotyński, 2022). This term encapsulates a green economy interwoven with innovation, democracy, pro-social economic practices, as well as a purple economy that embraces the cultural and civilizational dimensions of development. Characteristics such as global and regional security, resilience against shocks, and the enduring political and financial stability of economies—be it at the national, regional, or global level—emerge as defining attributes of the Emerald Economy.

DOI: 10.4324/9781003502272-3

The cultivation of these attributes is incumbent upon a governance approach deeply rooted in democratic principles and the rule of law.

This study places its focus on these overarching macroeconomic, geopolitical, and social determinants, alongside the ensuing challenges. It draws conclusions pertinent to sustainable development and the evolutionary pathway of managerial mechanisms within contemporary organizations, as they navigate their journey toward embracing the principles of Society 5.0 and Economy 5.0. This alignment bears significance not solely within the bounds of Europe but also across the multipolar global landscape.

A new paradigm for sustainable development: charting the course toward Industry 5.0 and Economy 5.0

Evaluating a nation's economic and social advancement merely based on fluctuations in gross domestic product (GDP) output has been widely critiqued by politicians and experts for its one-sidedness and limited scope. However, owing to statistical and pragmatic reasons, real GDP growth endures as a commonly utilized yardstick. Extensive literature on this matter exists (Kołodko, 2013; Kotyński, 2020), though we won't delve into it here. Nevertheless, it's noteworthy to highlight, drawing on the analysis of Elżbieta Mączyńska (2021), that conflating GDP growth with sustainable, well-rounded, and harmonious socio-economic advancement is an error. The foundations of such progress encompass not only economic growth but also social and ecological advancements. Solely pursuing economic growth, without substantial strides in social and environmental spheres, constitutes unchecked economic expansion that hampers societal well-being. Thus, a need exists for a coherent terminological framework in this context. In the mid-1990s, Ignacy Sachs (2000) introduced the proposition that the term "development" should be reserved exclusively for scenarios wherein advancements occur across three dimensions: economic, social, and environmental. This comprehensive perspective on sustained and harmonious socio-economic progress resonates throughout the literature on economics and management theory, as well as empirical investigations within the domains of the information society, Industry 4.0 (Götz, 2021), Economy 4.0, and their evolution toward Economy 5.0 and Society 5.0.

Sachs' delineation of these three dimensions serves as the foundational pillars of Economy 5.0, and can be further divided into distinct subsets that have been given varying definitions across scholarly works. Among the essential components of Economy 5.0 and Society 5.0, human development assumes a distinct role whose key factors are interdependently connected with one other. Gauging their progression is feasible, albeit limited, especially when placed in the context of historical backdrop, through empirical studies. The current situation is largely shaped by the decisions made by policymakers presently at power, with many of these decisions presenting challenges due to their questionable optimality (United Nations Development Programme, 2019, 2020). These decisions undergo scrutiny through normative analysis, a forward-looking and long-term approach that places increased emphasis on the ramifications of climate change and environmental degradation, both of which pose significant threats to humanity. Research on the transition process toward Industry 5.0 and Economy 5.0 takes diverse trajectories, encompassing countries in Central and Eastern Europe, including the four Visegrad Group nations (Éltető et al., 2022). The term "Industry 5.0" was initially introduced on social media by Rada in 2015 (Rada, 2019). His approach, which has garnered widespread support, emphasizes the imperative of waste reduction, advocating for the promotion of a circular economy and directing attention toward the technological facets of advancement.

Additionally, an expert consortium known as ESIR (Expert group on the economic and societal impact of research and innovation), operating under the auspices of the European Commission's Directorate-General for Research and Innovation, has unveiled its perspective on the evolution from European Industry 4.0 to Industry 5.0. This vision is encapsulated in the publication titled "Industry 5.0- A Transformative Vision for Europe" (European Commission, 2022). This paper stated that Europe confronts a threefold mandate: safeguarding, preparing, and undergoing transformation as it aspires to forge a better future following one of history's deadliest pandemics. Furthermore, Europe endeavors to tackle head-on the paramount challenge humanity has ever encountered: the tandem issues of climate change and the collapse of biodiversity. This daunting task revolves around reconfiguring human existence to enable 8 billion people to coexist sustainably and harmoniously, all within the confines of our planet's finite resources and ecosystems. Europe possesses the potential to guide the global community, but to achieve this role of leadership it becomes imperative to prioritize internal unity, present a cohesive voice, and advocate for a substantial transformation of the global economy (European Commission, 2022). In another publication by the European Commission regarding the new paradigm of industrial transformation (European Commission, 2022a), authored by experts from The Policy Learning Platform, it was stated The requirement for a fresh industrial paradigm, surpassing the confines of Industry 4.0, has intensified over time due to the escalating intricacies and urgent economic and societal predicaments. These encompass challenges such as climate change and the precipitous decline of biodiversity, along with issues like resource scarcity and global disruptions like the COVID-19 pandemic and more recently, the conflict in Ukraine. These intricate challenges extend beyond the scope of conventional industrial approaches for effective resolution. Likewise, fostering resilience within our existing economy and its transformation to withstand forthcoming shocks and pressures necessitates a more ambitious approach than merely striving to restore the previous status quo (European Commission, 2022a).

However, the three primary elements of Industry 5.0 and Economic Development 5.0 outlined earlier—namely sustainability, human development, and shock resilience—are not entirely novel in comparison to the scrutiny of Industry 4.0 and contemporary organizations. This is particularly evident when contrasted with the concept of the Emerald Economy (conceived as a facet of sustainable development), which encompasses a green economy interwoven with innovation, democracy, and pro-social economic frameworks, alongside a purple economy that also factors in cultural and civilizational aspects of progress. These concepts were also explored in a monograph authored by Rzepka et al. (2023), which additionally presents an illustrative diagram of the emerald economy, differentiating its attributes and foundational principles (Kotyński, 2022, p. 22). Presently, however, this diagram requires supplementation to underscore the significance of building resilience against both external and internal shocks, often referred to as "anti-fragility" and as defined by Taleb (Taleb & Siara, 2015). This augmentation is imperative, alongside the transformation of the external security infrastructure at the levels of countries, regions, and the global stage. Such transformations are indispensable for fostering survival, sustainable development, and the necessary adaptability in times marked by challenges and uncertainties. This adaptation is equally pertinent to contemporary strategies for managing modern organizations.

This particular factor, underpinning the necessity for European unity, cohesion, and collaborative leadership to counter unforeseeable crises and external threats at various turning points in world history (Kukliński et al., 2012; Mandelbrot, 1982), is also echoed in the referenced paper from the European Commission's study.

Liberal democracy vs. authoritarianism and 21st-century neo-imperialism: implications for international security policy

The idealistic ideas of liberal democracy underlying the European Union and supported by the United States of America, especially during the presidency of Joe Biden, whose strategy formulated in 2021 envisaged taking up the fight against autocracy on the international scene (Brands, 2021), are not shared by the leaders of many new or emerging powers with emerging market economies, nor are they implemented in the economic and social practice of all EU Member States, which are part of the Euro-Atlantic civilization. On the contrary, on various continents there has been a deterioration of democracy and an increase in authoritarian, nationalist, and neo-imperialist tendencies, as well as a regression of globalization in its form over the last 30 years. The concept of modern neo-imperialism adopted here by the author (Kotyński, 2021) has a meaning different from "new imperialism," understood as colonialism of the nineteenth and early 20th century (Kagarlicki, 2022). In the current era of deep political and economic transformations and rivalries between old and new powers, with different cultural, political, religious and moral traditions, different levels of socio-economic development and different demographic situation, *on the global stage, the tendency towards authoritarianism and political neorealism, manifested in the pursuit of politics from the position of hard power (hard power)* and the pursuit of a balance of power between the powers (*balance of power*), advocated by, among others, Zbigniew Brzeziński (2013) and Henry Kissinger (2014).

In my perspective (Kotyński, 2021), within the realm of contemporary powers, we can categorize states that adhere to the principles of liberal democracy. These principles encompass the autonomy of the judiciary from executive influence, respect for civil liberties, tolerance, and human rights. The neo-imperialistic tendencies of such states are defensive in nature, aligned with participation or leadership in democratic collective security systems, such as the North Atlantic Treaty Organization (NATO). On the other hand, there exist authoritarian states whose neo-imperialism takes on an expansionist, offensive character. This approach is coupled with the pursuit of global or regional hegemony, thereby endangering the equilibrium of the power structure and global security. Additionally, these states employ cutting-edge technologies and artificial intelligence (AI) for comprehensive surveillance and the indoctrination of their own populace. Furthermore, they employ these technologies for the tracking and manipulation of other governments and societies. Overall, the concept of a balance of power and the utilization of hard power to ensure security and deter potential aggression from adversaries continue to hold sway globally, overshadowing the Kantian and Wilsonian ideals of striving for enduring peace. However, the application of these principles should be accompanied by agreements aimed at stabilizing the international order and averting nuclear catastrophes, as well as fostering broader international alliances, as emphasized by the President of the United States of America, Joe Biden. The pessimistic (or rather realistic) viewpoint expressed by the editors and co-authors of the esteemed handbook on international relations and European integration remains relevant, asserting that nationalism, an enduring reminder of current realities, maintains significant sway in global politics. Convincing arguments indicate that the 21st century will be characterized by the prevalence of Realism. Despite the efforts of federalists to rekindle idealism's fervor, Europe remains both united by common interests and divided by distinct national agendas (Schmidt & Dunne, 2008). Within the emerging geopolitical landscape, the European Union has the potential to stand as one of the cornerstones of global security, alongside NATO. To realize this role, it must garner the backing of both the populations and governments of its Member States, fostering suitable institutional and political reforms. These reforms should aim at further integration, cohesion, and the advancement toward a democratic, sustainable, and technologically advanced Economy 5.0. Additionally, bolstering shared defense capabilities would contribute to strengthening its position. Following Great Britain's exit from the European Union, a noticeable lack of political consensus has emerged in nations under conservative-authoritarian leadership. This disunity has considerably weakened Europe's stance in the face of the unfolding challenges of the 21st century (Kleer, 2020). Moreover, this issue extends to instances where Member States are disregarding their international human rights commitments and encountering delays in tackling the grave repercussions of climate change. These developments pose a substantial threat to the Earth's biosphere as the Anthropocene era begins.

Impact of the COVID-19 pandemic and the Russian invasion of Ukraine on international cooperation, globalization and the prospects for economic development 5.0

The emergence of the COVID-19 pandemic in 2020 and subsequent years triggered a global economic downturn, impacting multiple nations, including China. Concurrently, factors such as Brexit and the policy direction of former US President Donald Trump, known for his anti-multilateral stance (Góralczyk, 2022), ushered in a new phase of globalization characterized by regression, termed deglobalization. This shift resulted in the disruption or scaling down of numerous global value chains. Interestingly, insights from UNCTAD's expert analyses revealed that the decline in international trade during 2020 was comparatively milder for nations within regional trade blocs, showcasing their enhanced resilience to unique shocks (Nicita & Saygili, 2021). Following the economic rebound in 2021 and the restoration of foreign direct investment to $1.6 trillion globally, a subsequent drop emerged in trade volume, economic collaboration, and an increase in inflation due to the Russian incursion into Ukraine in 2022. Mrs. Rebeca Grynspan, Secretary-General of UNCTAD, highlighted in her preface to the United Nations Conference on Trade and Development's yearly report that the convergence of the Ukrainian conflict and the pandemic's aftermath has profoundly restructured the global investment environment. Beyond its immediate consequences, this conflict has sparked a cost-of-living crisis that is impacting billions around the globe. Escalating energy and food costs are putting pressure on real incomes and worsening debt difficulties. Heightened uncertainty and investor aversion to risk might considerably limit global foreign direct investment (FDI) in the current year. The outcome holds immense importance for development prospects, given the ongoing need for investment in productive capacity, Sustainable Development Goals (SDGs), and climate change mitigation and adaptation. However, investment trends vary: while global FDI improved in 2021, industrial investment lags, particularly in impoverished nations. SDG investment is growing but falls short of 2030 targets. Climate change mitigation investment, especially in renewables, thrives in developed countries, but adaptation investment lags considerably (United Nations Conference on Trade and Development, 2022).

These phenomena have occurred in years reminiscent of threats known from ancient and medieval times, stemming from global climate change, environmental degradation, deforestation, greenhouse gas emissions, and pollution of air, land, and water (Burchard-Dziubińska et al., 2020; Popkiewicz et al., 2018). The acceleration of these processes in this century necessitates new development strategies and immediate adaptation measures to address the beginning of an era characterized by water shortages, changing landscapes, pandemics, migration for sustenance, and the flight from conflict to more developed regions, akin to the dynamics of the early Middle Ages that contributed to the fall of the Roman Empire (Frankopan, 2018; Harper, 2016), as well as other empires in more recent history (Deutsch, 1979; Kagarlicki, 2022).

A significant challenge for international governance in an era of significant political and economic transformation is the rise of autocratic and neo-imperial tendencies among regional and global powers in the 21st century. This is occurring within a framework of evolving political, economic, and military alliances centered around the United States of America and the People's Republic of China. The Russian Federation has aligned itself with China, aiming to restore its former power, which was constrained in the 19th century as a "prisoner of nations." This ambition persisted through the Concert of Powers following the Congress of Vienna (1815) and continued through the tsarist, Stalinist, and Putin eras marked by authoritarianism, terror, and lawlessness (Gabuev, 2022).

The hegemonic aspirations of the People's Republic of China, driven by authoritarian leadership and rapid economic growth after 1989, have led to the renaissance of its former power. With substantial domestic potential and the benefits of globalization, China now extends its ambitions beyond the Greater China area, even venturing into space (Góralczyk, 2018). The People's Republic of China (PRC) alongside Russia, Kazakhstan, Kyrgyzstan, and Tajikistan established a regional integration grouping known as the Shanghai Cooperation Organization (SCO) through the Intergovernmental Agreement on Security and Economic Cooperation on June 15, 2001 (Fredholm, 2012). China became a member in 2001, followed by Uzbekistan and later as observers, Mongolia, Iran, India, and Pakistan. By

2017, India and Pakistan had become formal members of the SCO. Subsequently, Armenia, Azerbaijan, Cambodia, Nepal, Sri Lanka, and Turkey were granted "partner in dialog" status. China is also the instigator and leader of a new Partnership and Free Trade Agreement, with the participation of 15 East Asian and Pacific nations of diverse sizes, economic systems (often authoritarian), and stages of development. Collectively, including China, these countries contribute to 30.5% of global GDP (United Nations Conference on Trade and Development, 2022).

The Regional Comprehensive Economic Partnership (RCEP), effective from January 1, 2022, has been identified by UNCTAD as a new "center for global trade gravity," albeit somewhat prematurely (United Nations Conference on Trade and Development, 2021). This recognition follows unsuccessful endeavors to execute the Chinese Belt and Road Initiative (16+1), initially announced in Warsaw in 2012 and involving 16 Central and Eastern European countries (Johnson, 2022).

The armed aggression of the Russian Federation against Ukraine, initiated on February 24, 2022, following the prior annexation of Crimea in 2014 and years of military actions in eastern Ukraine, has transformed into a comprehensive and criminal conflict with the objective of absorbing a neighboring sovereign nation (Von Der Leyen, 2022). This assault shattered the illusion of Russia's potential for peaceful economic and political collaboration with European Union and NATO member countries, ushering in a new Cold War era that holds the potential to escalate into a broader international confrontation, particularly imperiling nations in Russia's proximity. The current third decade of the 21st century is marked by a pronounced accumulation of international conflicts and threats to the security of both Europe and the global community (Haass, 2022). Under these conditions, conducting conventional trade with Russia under Putin's authoritarian regime, characterized by energy manipulation and hybrid warfare against competitors and partners, along with outright aggression, terrorism, and war crimes, has become untenable for EU and NATO nations. Western sanctions imposed on Russia, coupled with restrictions on energy resources (such as oil, gas, and coal), technologies, and strategic goods, have concurrently contributed to elevated prices of fuels, energy, metals, fertilizers, and food on the global market. This has led to a substantial surge in inflation across the USA, Europe, and including Poland (World Bank, 2022).

Projections from IMF experts, as outlined in a report for the G20 meeting in Bali, Indonesia in November 2020, point to the persistence and deepening of global challenges (International Monetary Fund & Group of Twenty, 2022). Similar conclusions and recommendations for enhancing economic policies are echoed by various other experts. For instance, Gudmundsson's assessment underscores that the worldwide economic growth faces a complex array of hurdles, spanning from Russia's encroachment into Ukraine to rising interest rates aimed at taming inflation, and persistent disruptions stemming from the pandemic, such as China's lockdowns and supply chain interruptions. Despite these multifaceted impediments, the anticipation of additional policy measures remains to counteract high inflation and facilitate economic stabilization (Gudmundsson, 2022).

Notes on the future and recommendations for supporting the development of the 5.0 economy in Europe and the world

Even if the conflict between the Russian Federation and Ukraine doesn't escalate to involve other nations in the upcoming years, the priority for Poland and fellow European Union countries located on NATO's eastern and northern flank will encompass not only establishing a sustainable Economy 5.0 but also transforming their economic and managerial systems toward a quasi-war economy. This shift is driven partly by the necessity of increased defense spending, surging inflation, deteriorating terms of trade (particularly in 2022–2023 after Russia's aggression on Ukraine), and mounting internal and external deficits that impact the current account balances of major global economies (International Monetary Fund, 2022a, 2022b).

In tandem, many countries will strive for greater self-reliance and reduced globalization following the "post-Cold War era of hyperglobalization" observed in prior decades (Rodrik & Walt, 2022). Nonetheless, such intentions warrant cautious consideration. Accelerated growth in domestic industrial production, including armaments and renewable energy, along with reinforcing regional cooperation in these sectors, is crucial in the current context. However, simultaneously transitioning the economy and energy infrastructure toward green Economy 5.0, prioritizing environmental preservation and climate change adaptation, while prudently leveraging European Union reconstruction and development funds, remains equally imperative. Yet, it's imperative to heed the caution shared by Posen (2022), discouraging a return to protectionism and autarky.

Posen's perspective extends to the notion that embarking on a spiral of protectionism and trade conflicts would constitute a detrimental course for both the global economy and the European Union. In a previous work (Kotyński, 2019, p. 34), I highlighted that "over time, adopting isolationist strategies and limiting collaborations with developing nations could potentially trigger a surge in inflation or even stagflation within developed economies. This, in turn, might diminish their global competitiveness and subsequently result in the loss of higher-paying employment opportunities, elevated debt levels, and worsened financial conditions."

Additionally, such an approach could prompt efforts to rectify the situation through additional constraints on imports and deliberate devaluation of their currency, potentially setting off a cycle of currency conflicts. It is worth recalling that in the early years of the current century, Kenneth S. Rogoff (2003) emphasized the significant role of international competition and deregulation, as well as the policies of governments and banks, in restraining inflation during the acceleration of globalization processes in the last decade of the 20th century. Rogoff warned against the risks of deglobalization after the Russian invasion of Ukraine (Rogoff, 2022a) and in his latest work, cautioning that "the era of perpetually low inflation will not return quickly. As the world enters a new era of persistent inflation, central banks, including the Fed, must be better isolated from political pressures to fulfill their mandate—especially at a time when the world economy is still suffering from seismic shocks" (Rogoff, 2022b). These recommendations are applicable to the monetary policy of other central banks, including the European Central Bank and the National Bank of Poland.

On a global scale, one can anticipate energy, food, and health crises, alongside the potential for recession and stagflation in the mid-2020s. This crisis may impede efforts to combat the effects of global warming, including the transition away from coal. Growing economic and social challenges could lead to currency depreciation in non-euro area EU countries and lower real income levels for their citizens, potentially giving rise to social unrest and political changes involving a return to democratic principles and the rule of law, as well as reinforcing populist and authoritarian trends.

Currently, governments and companies are compelled to explore and implement innovative solutions for energy conservation and the replacement of fossil fuels with zero-emission energy sources. Over the longer term, the process of globalization is likely to revive, albeit with a different structure, in which China will occupy a central role for much of the world. Economic relations between the more tightly integrated Euro-Atlantic West and the East and South are expected to be reconfigured in the collective interest, building on revised foundations, despite the growing rivalry between the 21st-century space superpowers. This concept of "decoupling" (separation) of globalization, as previously described (Eppinger et al., 2021), in the context of shifting global interdependence, is articulated, among others, by Ian Bremmer (2022), the president of the "Eurasia Group."

However, if the European Union, influenced by certain members, adopts a looser concept of cooperation, Germany may assume the role of an autonomous leader and mediator in economic and political relations between the United States and China, as evidenced by the meeting between the Chancellor of the Federal Republic of Germany, Olaf Scholz, and the leaders of China on November 4, 2022. Scholz was accompanied by a significant group of entrepreneurs. According to news agencies (Reuters, AFP, or TVN24), the Chinese leader emphasized that "China and Germany should cooperate with each other, especially in times of change and turmoil, for the sake of global peace," while Scholz stressed the need for "face-to-face meetings during challenging times when the Russian invasion of Ukraine threatens the rule-based global order." He also expressed his intention to "further develop economic cooperation with China, even though both countries hold 'different points of view'" (Olaf Scholz, 2023).

In a New Year's essay published in Foreign Affairs, Olaf Scholz (2023) presented his political doctrine of augmenting Germany's role in global politics and averting a new Cold War amid the tectonic shifts of the multipolar world. He emphasized Germany's active commitment to upholding and promoting a global order rooted in the principles of the UN Charter. Germany's democratic foundations, security, and economic well-being are inextricably linked to adherence to universally accepted regulations. Consequently, Germany is resolute in its pursuit of safeguarding European security, uniting forces within the European Union, and advocating collaborative solutions to address global challenges. This strategic trajectory is vital for Germany to navigate the intricate geopolitical divisions that characterize the contemporary era (Scholz, 2023).

The G20 meeting in Bali in November 2022, featuring the leaders of China and the United States, showcased their shared aim to sidestep armed confrontation and maintain cooperation on issues pivotal to global peace and sustainable development. Irrespective of the future trajectory of international political and economic relations, a proactive stance and transformative organizational management are essential to attaining the goals of Economy 5.0. This must be pursued with governmental support and the utilization of cutting-edge technologies.

Within the evolving geopolitical landscape, the European Union could aspire to become a democratic political and economic force by garnering the backing of its member states' populations and governments for the necessary institutional and political reforms that deepen Union integration and cohesion. Simultaneously, this would facilitate the transformation toward a democratic, green, and modern Economy 5.0, bolstered by enhanced defense capabilities. Strengthening Poland's position within the European Union and NATO would also contribute to significant financial improvement and heightened foreign direct investment flow to Poland and other Central and Eastern European countries, echoing calls from historians (Davies, 2022), political scientists, and economists (Götz et al., 2023).

Up until now, in EU countries where conservative-authoritarian governments have held sway, there has been resistance to deeper integration and empowering EU institutions, despite societies and authorities previously embracing the democratic political and economic-financial principles enshrined in the Treaty of Lisbon, including the adoption of the euro (Götz et al., 2021). This also extends to disregard for international human rights commitments by certain countries, encompassing refugee treatment and efforts to mitigate climate change's effects that imperil the biosphere and global life.

Such a scenario could change if proponents of civil liberties, liberal democracy, and European solidarity regain power in these nations. This transition could unlock substantial development opportunities for European countries and enterprises, including those in Poland, fostered by the EU Recovery and Development Plan and the extraordinary "The Future Generation of the EU" package (European Commission, 2022b).

References

Brands, H. (2023, April 19). The emerging Biden doctrine: democracy, autocracy, and the defining clash of our time. Foreign Affairs. https://www.foreignaffairs.com/articles/united-states/2021-06-29/emerging-biden-doctrine.

Bremmer, I. (2022). Globalization isn't dead. *Foreign Affairs*. https://www.foreignaffairs.com/world/globalization-isnt-dead.

Brzeziński, Z. (2013). *Strategic vision. America and the crisis of global power*. Kraków: Wydawnictwo Literackie Sp. z o.o.

Burchard-Dziubińska, M., Prandecki, K., & Prognoz, K. (Eds.) (2020). *Zmiana klimatu: skutki dla polskiego społeczeństwa i gospodarki*. Polska Akademia Nauk, Komitet Prognoz „Polska 2000 Plus" PAN.

Davies, N. (2022). *Mała Europa. Szkice polskie*. Warszawa: Znak.

Deutsch, K. W. (1979). *Tides among nations*. London: Collier Macmillan Publishers.

Éltető, A., Sass, M., & Götz, M. (2022). The dependent Industry 4.0 development path of the Visegrád countries. *Intersections, 8*(3), 147–168. https://doi.org/10.17356/ieejsp.v8i3.980.

Eppinger, P., Felbermayr, G. J., Krebs, O., & Kukharskyy, B. (2021). Decoupling global value Chains. *SSRN Electronic Journal*. https://doi.org/10.2139/ssrn.3848341

European Commission. (2022a). *Industry 5.0*. Research and Innovation. https://research-and-innovation.ec.europa.eu/research-area/industrial-research-and-innovation/industry-50_en

European Commission. (2022b). *Recovery Plan for Europe*. European Commission. https://ec.europa.eu/info/strategy/recovery-plan-europe_pl. Accessed 2.11.22.

European Commission, Directorate-General for Research and Innovation, Renda, A., Schwaag Serger, S., Tataj, D. (2022). *Industry 5.0, a transformative vision for Europe: Governing systemic transformations towards a sustainable industry*. Brussels: Publications Office of the European Union. https://data.europa.eu/doi/10.2777/17322.

Frankopan, P. (2018). *Jedwabne szlaki: nowa historia świata*. Warszawa: Wydawnictwo WAB.

Fredholm, M. (2012). *The Shanghai cooperation and Eurasian geopolitics*. Stockholm: Stockholm International Program for Central Asian Studies.

Gabuev, A. (2022). China's new vassal: How the war in Ukraine turned Moscow into Beijing's junior partner. *Foreign Affairs*. https://www.foreignaffairs.com/china/chinas-new-vassal

Góralczyk, B. (2018). *Wielki Renesans [The great renaissance]*. Warsaw: DIALOG.
Góralczyk, B. (2022). Rola i miejsce UE w tworzeniu ładu międzynarodowego. In Niżnik J. (ed.), *Polska w Europie jutra. Polityka europejska Polski w kontekście zmian międzynarodowych XXI wieku* (pp. 49–56). Warszawa: Polska Akademia Nauk.
Götz, M. (2021). *Clusters, digital transformation and regional development in Germany*. New York: Routledge. https://doi.org/10.4324/9781003005506
Götz, M., Jankowska, B., & Talouni, Z. (2023). Reflections on FDI in an post-communist country in the context of EU membership: Retrospectives and prospects. *Post-Communist Economies, 35*(2), 134–153. https://doi.org/10.1080/14631377.2022.2137325
Götz, M., Nowak, B. E., & Orłowski, W. M. (2018). Poland and the Euro zone. Three possible scenarios and their consequences. *Studia Europejskie-Studies in European Affairs, 3*, 203–219.
Gudmundsson, T. (2022, November 13). *Slowing global economic growth is increasingly evident, high-frequency data show*. IMF. https://www.imf.org/en/Blogs/Articles/2022/11/13/slowing-global-economic-growth-is-increasingly-evident-high-frequency-data-show?utmmedium=email&utmsource=govdelivery.
Haass, R. (2022). The dangerous decade. A foreign policy for a world in crisis. *Foreign Affairs*, September/October
Harper, K. (2016). *Los Rzymu. Klimat, choroby i koniec imperium*. Warsaw: Napoleon V.
Hübner, W. (2016). *Asia of the 21st century and the renaissance of the Silk Road. Tradition shaping the future*. Warszawa: Vistula Academy of Finance and Business.
International Monetary Fund. (2022a). *External sector report. Pandemic, war, and global imbalances*, August.
International Monetary Fund. (2022b). *Countering the cost-of-living crisis*. World Economic Outlook 2022, October.
International Monetary Fund & Group of Twenty. (2022). *G-20 Report on Strong, Sustainable, Balanced, and Inclusive Growth*, November.
Johnson, I. (2022). Has China lost Europe? *Foreign Affairs*. https://www.foreignaffairs.com/articles/china/2022-06-10/has-china-lost-europe.
Kagarlicki, B. (2022). *Od imperium do imperializmu. Państwo i narodziny cywilizacji burżuazyjnej*. Sieradz: Wydawnictwo Glowbook.
Kissinger, H. (2014). *World Order: Reflections on the character of nations and the course of history*. New York: Penguin Press HC.
Kleer, J. (2020). *Zmierzch Europy*. Warszawa: Wydawnictwo Naukowe PWN.
Kołodko, G. W. (2013). *Dokąd zmierza świat: Ekonomia polityczna przyszłości*. Warszawa: Prószyński i S-ka.
Kotyński, J. (2019). Transformacje globalne i tendencje do spowolnienia rozwoju gospodarki światowej. In Kotyński, J. (Ed). *Dilemmas of sustainable development of the Polish economy and finance in the global environment*. Warsaw: Vistula Academy of Finance and Business in Warsaw.
Kotyński, J. (2020). Szanse i zagrożenia dla trwałego rozwoju Polski w epoce zmian globalnych In Kleer, J., & Prandecki, K. (Eds.), *Zmieniający się świat a globalizacja*. Warszawa: Komitet Prognoz „Polska 2000 Plus".
Kotyński, J. (2021). Demokracja i kapitalizm w Europie i na świecie. In Niżnik, J., Barcz, J., & Truszczyński, J. (Eds.), *Polska w Europie jutra. Polityka europejska*

Polski w kontekście zmian międzynarodowych XXI wieku (pp. 75–82). Warszawa: Polska Akademia Nauk, Komitet Prognoz "Polska 2000 Plus".

Kotyński, J. (2022). Components of Economy 4.0 as factors for sustainable development. Chapter 2. In Rzepka, A., Olesiński, Z., & Jędrych, E. (Eds.), *Self management, entrepreneurial culture, and economy 4.0: A contemporary approach to organizational theory development*. London: Routledge, Taylor & Francis Group.

Kukliński, A., Pawłowski, K., & Swianiewicz, J. (2012). *The turning points of world history. Financial and methodological interpretations*. Piastów: Rewasz.

Mączyńska, E. (2021). Unia Europejska wobec nierówności ekonomicznych. In: Niżnik, J., Barcz, J., & Truszczyński, J. (Eds.), *Polska w Europie jutra. Polityka europejska Polski w kontekście zmian międzynarodowych XXI wieku*. Warszawa: Polska Akademia Nauk, Komitet Prognoz „Polska 2000 Plus".

Mandelbrot, B. (1982). *The fractal geometry of nature*. New York: W.H. Freeman.

Nicita, A., & Saygili, M. (2021). Trade agreements and trade resilience during COVID-19 pandemic. *UNCTAD Research Paper No. 70*, UNCTAD/SER.RP/2021/13.

Popkiewicz, M., Kardaś, A., & Malinowski, S. (2018). *Nauka o klimacie*. Katowice: Sonia Draga Sp. z o.o.

Posen, A. (2022). The end of globalization? What Russia's war in Ukraine means for the world economy. *Foreign Affairs, 17*.

Rada, M. (2019). *Industry 5.0 experts rising*. Medium. https://michael-rada.medium.com/industry-5-0-experts-rising-556253a641a3.

Rodrik, D. & Walt, S.M. (2022), How to build a better order. Limiting Great Power Rivalry in an anarchic world. *Foreign Affairs*, September/October.

Rogoff, K. (2003). Globalization and global disinflation. *Economic Review-Federal Reserve Bank of Kansas City, 88*(4), 45–80.

Rogoff, K. (2022a). *The long-lasting economic shock of war*. IMF. https://www.imf.org/en/Publications/fandd/issues/2022/03/the-long-lasting-economic-shock-of-war

Rogoff, K. S. (2022b). The age of inflation: Easy money, hard choices. *Foreign Affairs, 101*, 120.

Rzepka, A., Olesiński, Z., Jędrych, E., & Prachowski, J. (2023). *Self-management, entrepreneurial culture, and economy 4.0: A contemporary approach to organizational theory development*. New York: Routledge.

Sachs, I. (2000). *W poszukiwaniu nowych strategii rozwoju*. Warszawa: Wydawnictwo Naukowe PWN.

Schmidt, B. C., & Dunne, T. (2008). Realizm. In Baylis, J., Smith, S., & Owens, P. (Eds.), *Globalizacja Polityki Światowej: Wprowadzenie do stosunków międzynarodowych* (p. 221). Kraków: Wydawnictwo Uniwersytetu Jagiellońskiego.

Scholz, O. (2023). Nach der Zeitenwende. In Deckers, D., *Facetten der Gegenwart* (pp. 280–286). Frankfurt am Main: Brill Schöningh https://doi.org/10.30965/9783657790791_030.

Taleb, N. N., & Siara, O. (2015). *Antykruchość: O rzeczach, którym służą wstrząsy*. Warszawa: Kurhaus.

United Nations Conference on Trade and Development. (2021, 15 December). *Asia-Pacific partnership creates new 'center of gravity' for global trade*. A new center of gravity: The regional comprehensive economic partnership and its trade effects (UNCTAD/DITC/INF/2021/5).

United Nations Conference on Trade and Development. (2022). *World Investment Report 2022.* UNCTAD World Investment Report (WIR). https://doi.org/10.18356/9789210015431.

United Nations Development Programme. (2019). *Human Development Report 2019.* https://doi.org/10.18356/838f78fd-en.

United Nations Development Programme. (2020). UNDP-HDR.-2020-Dimension-1-Status-of-human -development.xlsm.

Von Der Leyen, U. (2022). Speech by President von der Leyen at the European Parliament Plenary on the Russian aggression against Ukraine. https://ec.europa.eu/commission/presscorner/detail/en/SPEECH_22_1483. Accessed 23 June.

World Bank. (2022, October). *A World Bank Report: Commodity markets outlook. Pandemic, war, recession: Drivers of aluminum and copper prices.* International Bank for Reconstruction and Development/World Bank. https://openknowledge.worldbank.org/bitstream/handle/10986/38160/CMO-October-2022.pdf.

3 Sustainable development and transition from Economy 4.0 to Economy 5.0

Marta Drozdowska, Izabela Gruszka, and Dariusz Ilnicki

Introduction

The term "Economy 4.0" (Industry 4.0) was initially coined in 2011 at a trade fair in Hannover as a promotional slogan for the German economy, which was built upon advanced and innovative technologies (Majstorović et al., 2018). Swiftly, Economy 4.0 (also recognized as the Fourth Industrial Revolution) emerged as the paramount concept that characterized the economic progress of the 21st century. It was rooted in profoundly dynamic technological advancement, encompassing Big Data analysis, robotics, and the employment of artificial intelligence (AI) or digital-physical systems as well as the utilization of cloud computing, machine learning, and other sophisticated solutions (Ahsan & Siddique, 2022; Mourtzis et al., 2022). Unquestionably, the contemporary technologies that were introduced in Concept 4.0 wielded a positive influence on production efficiency and the genesis of novel business models. Among the advantages that Economy 4.0 bestowed upon businesses were enhanced efficiency, heightened potential for innovation, greater control over production, augmented labor productivity, accelerated time-to-market, and refined supply chains (Ching et al., 2022).

In 2017, the European Commission initiated a discussion on an alternative developmental concept—an extension of the Economy 4.0 framework. Economy 5.0 was designed to address the shortcomings of Economy 4.0, which stemmed from an excessive reliance on digitalization and modern technologies that were primarily aimed at boosting enterprise revenues. Concurrently, it aimed to offer a solution for the crisis that was prompted by the COVID-19 pandemic and its economic aftermath. The core tenets of Economy 5.0 encompassed human orientation, sustainability, and resilience (Breque, De Nul, & Petridis, 2021). Its objective was to synergize precise and potent machinery with individuals' critical and creative thinking, all while furnishing sustainable solutions for environmental preservation (Maddikunta et al., 2022).

DOI: 10.4324/9781003502272-4

This study aims to discern the socio-economic attributes within the economies of individual European Union countries that influence sustainable development. These attributes are the foundation for their seamless transition from Economy 4.0 to Economy 5.0. The research employs the World Economic Forum's Global Competitiveness Indicator 4.0 (GCI 4.0) along with the values that are associated with each sustainable development goal (SDG). The specifically chosen GCI 4.0 and SDG components were compared and aligned in order to answer the question of which European Union nations have embarked on trajectories toward Economy 5.0.

Literature review

Economy 5.0 operates under the fundamental premise that the evolution of an industry that is rooted in digitalization and technology (as fostered by Economy 4.0) must be seamlessly intertwined with a commitment to the principles of social equity and sustainable progress. A cornerstone of Economy 5.0 is its emphasis on the role of research and innovation in delivering contemporary sustainable technological solutions that serve humanity and the planet (Huang et al., 2022). Of significant note is the extension of the innovation process, which encompasses not only the production units but also the personnel within companies. Innovations that are centered around the well-being of employees yield manifold advantages: they acknowledge their challenges, requirements, and aspirations and devise fitting solutions, thereby enhancing long-term working conditions (Orso et al., 2022).

According to Xu et al., the primary challenges that confront Economy 5.0 include the following:

- social diversity and acceptance;
- measuring environmental and social value;
- process integration;
- interdisciplinarity and complexity;
- eco-friendly innovation policy with agility and result orientation;
- combining productivity and investment (Xu et al., 2021).

A particularly crucial distinction in the perception of Economies 4.0 and 5.0 lies in the transformation of the aforementioned values (human orientation, sustainability, and resilience) from being mere peripheral supplements to GDP growth to becoming the pivotal determinants of genuine regional and societal progress.

To provide context for the evolving operational landscape of contemporary organizations across diverse nations, we leveraged Global Competitiveness

Index 4.0 (GCI), which was developed by the World Economic Forum. Introduced in 2018, the GCI encompassed 141 economies that collectively represented 99% of the global GDP. This comprehensive index was comprised of a range of indicators that were meticulously organized into 12 distinct "pillars": Institutions, Infrastructure, ICT adoption, Macroeconomic stability, Health, Skills, Product market, Labor market, Financial system, Market size, Business dynamism, and Innovation capability.

An economy's performance on the comprehensive GCI, as well as its individual components, is conveyed through a "progress score" on a scale that ranges from 0 to 100. A score of 100 signifies the "frontier"—an optimal state where hindrances to productivity growth no longer persist. The GCI 4.0 framework empowers economies to track their progress across time, emphasizing that competitiveness is not a finite resource that is solely distributed among countries—it can be achieved universally (World Economic Forum, 2019).

The SDGs were endorsed by the United Nations in 2015 (Ghosh & Rajan, 2019); they served as a universal cry for addressing poverty, safeguarding the planet, and ensuring progress by 2030. Comprised of 17 objectives, the SDGs are interconnected, wherein the pursuit of one goal influences the outcomes of all of the others. This underscores the need for development to harmonize the sustainability triad: social, economic, and environmental aspects (UNDP, n.d.).

A critical consideration when evaluating the realized value of SDGs as compared to the components of the GCI is that, while the engagement of individual countries in environmental conservation endeavors is invaluable, matters of sustainability extend beyond national boundaries. These issues necessitate collective efforts from the global community, including the International System of Global Competitiveness Management and Implementation.

Materials and methods

For an intricate analysis, the GCI was utilized, focusing on the evaluation of four distinct pillars that were grouped into two thematic categories:

Human Capital:

- Health: assessed based on healthy life-expectancy years.
- Skills: evaluated using various criteria: current workforce (mean years of schooling), skills of the current workforce (extent of staff training, quality of vocational training, skillsets of graduates, digital skills among the active population, ease of finding skilled employees), future workforce (school life-expectancy years), skills of the future workforce (critical thinking in teaching, pupil-to-teacher ratio in primary education ratio).

Innovation Ecosystems:

- Business Dynamism: Evaluated through administrative requirements (cost of starting a business, time to start a business in days, insolvency recovery rate cents to the dollar, insolvency regulatory framework), entrepreneurial culture (attitudes toward entrepreneurial risk, willingness to delegate authority, growth of innovative companies, companies embracing disruptive ideas [Schwab, 2019]).
- Innovation Capability: Assessed based on interaction and diversity, diversity of the workforce, state of cluster development (international co-inventions per million citizens, multi-stakeholder collaboration), research and development (scientific publication score, patent applications per million citizens, R&D expenditures (%GDP), research institutions' prominence), and commercialization (buyer sophistication, trademark applications per million citizens).

Out of the 17 SDGs that were set for 2030, 12 variables were employed in the surveys. For the remaining 5 SDGs, comprehensive data was lacking across all 27 of the analyzed European Union (EU) countries (as depicted in Table 3.1). The data was sourced from Eurostat, which provides comprehensive annual summaries of performance for the SDGs of each EU member state (Eurostat, n.d.). A statistical analysis was executed using Pearson correlations, wherein the individual indexes of the four pillars were juxtaposed with the SDG 2030 indicators.

Results

The "Sustainable Development in the European Union" report (Eurostat, 2022) identified 17 key areas that contribute to establishing an increasingly robust foundation and rationale for developing sustainable economies within individual countries in the European Union. The study categorized these areas into three groups of variables, each reflecting the distinct dynamics of change over the past five years: moderate divergence, moderate progress, and significant advancement. Although the rates of change in individual SDGs reflect the increasing importance of specific variables, it fails to fully capture the diversity among countries in terms of implementing the principles of sustainable development. Based on 12 of the 17 SDGs that constitute the foundation of sustainable development, 4 dimensions can be discerned:

- Factor 1: defined by six SDGs—no poverty, decent work, and economic growth; sustainable cities and communities; quality education; peace, justice, and strong institutions; good health and well-being.

Table 3.1 Identification of sustainable development dimensions (factors) based on 12 out of 17 goals—factor loadings of original variables for the distinguished dimensions

Goals	*Factor 1*	*Factor 2*	*Factor 3*	*Factor 4*	*Signicant progress*
No poverty	**0.871**	−0.278	−0.122	0.117	x
Decent work and economic growth	**0.847**	0.178	0.402	0.11	x
Sustainable cities and communities	**0.763**	0.287	−0.246	0.319	
Quality education	**0.728**	0.466	−0.013	-0.107	
Peace, justice and strong institutions	**0.714**	0.467	0.204	0.163	x
Good health and well-being	**0.64**	0.279	−0.22	0.201	x
Industry, innovation and infrastructure	0.596	0.546	0.252	0.429	x
Zero Hunger	0.089	**0.769**	−0.074	−0.105	
Gender equality	0.137	**0.754**	0.179	0.343	
Responsible consumption and production	0.394	0.577	−0.404	−0.293	
Partnership for the goals	0.008	0.022	**0.936**	−0.167	
Affordable and clean energy	−0.239	0.013	0.182	**−0.884**	x

Source: Own elaboration.

- Factor 2: defined by two (out of four) SDGs—zero hunger; gender equality.
- Factor 3: Defined by 1 of the 12 distinguished SDGs—partnerships for goals.
- Factor 4: Defined by one SDG—affordable and clean energy (as presented in Table 3.1).

Collectively, these four identified components explain nearly 80% (79.33%) of the variance that represents the common variation.

All four dimensions of sustainable development can be described as soft factors. Factor 1 can be described as the basis for sustainable growth (34.2% of the common variance). This is due to the fact that this dimension is defined by two hard factors (namely, decent work and economic growth; no poverty) as well as three soft factors (peace, justice and strong institutions; quality education; sustainable cities and communities). However, this perspective on the first dimension (initially posited as a defining factor for the sustainable development of the scrutinized countries) is not confirmed by the correlation between this dimension and the second dimension concerning the gross domestic product per capita. In both dimensions, these correlations manifest as moderate relationships (respectively, for the first and second dimensions, the coefficients are *rij* = 0.480; *rij* = 0.459). If we exclude Ireland and Luxembourg due to their sizes of gross domestic product per capita and, thus, their deviations from the rest of the countries, the correlations increases accordingly (*rij* = 0.624; *rij* = 0.616). The relationships at this level can already be considered to be strong.

There is also a high correlation of per capita gross domestic product (GDP), with eight SDGs defining the first and second dimensions of sustainable development. In all eight cases, the correlation is positive and within a range of values from *rij* = 0.249 (no poverty) to *rij* = 0.763 (peace, justice, and strong institutions). The average correlation coefficient is *rij* = 0.526.

Factor 2 can be defined as preventing hunger with a view to achieving gender equality in relation to responsible consumption and production with the support of industry, innovation, and infrastructure (see Table 3.1). The Pearson correlation coefficients within the variables that make up this dimension are within <0.341; 0.646>.

Factor 3 is a partnership for the SDG, and Factor 4 is affordable and clean energy. It should be noted that the highlighted dimensions of sustainable development are the vehicles for the diversity of the countries that are concerned with these dimensions. This is due to the fact that, in the orthogonality of the highlighted dimensions, the correlation is at a level of zero.

It is worth emphasizing that the distinguished dimensions of sustainable development that were formed based on the objectives that defined this developmental framework encompass all six objectives that exhibit significant progress and dynamic development. The remaining objectives demonstrated moderate progress. Notably, SDGs within these recognized dimensions exhibited notably closer correlations as compared to those with other objectives. This observation was especially evident for the first dimension (Factor 1) (as shown in Table 3.2).

Socio-economic development finds its foundation in diverse pillars whose significance for development can vary over time. In the context of Economy 5.0, pivotal development is reliant on 4 specific pillars among the 12 that were pinpointed by the GCI. These pillars encompass health (Pillar 5), skills (Pillar 6), business dynamism (Pillar 11), and innovation capability (Pillar 12). Notably, these chosen pillars exhibit a positive and relatively robust correlation (as depicted in Table 3.3). This phenomenon is especially pronounced in the cases of three pillars (6, 11, and 12), wherein the correlation coefficients stand at no less than *rij* = 0.775. However, Pillar 5 (health) exhibits a comparatively looser association with these pillars—displaying correlation coefficients that range from *rij* = 0.350 to *rij* = 0.668. Upon contrasting the focal development pillars with the 12 analyzed SDGs (as illustrated in Table 3.3), 2 overarching conclusions can be derived.

Table 3.2 Pearson's linear correlation matrix among the Sustainable Development Goals (SDGs) within a system of the identified four dimensions

	No poverty	*Decent work and economic growth*	*Sustainable cities and communities*	*Quality education*	*Peace, justice and strong institutions*	*Good health and well-being*	*Industry, innovation and infrastructure*	*Zero Hunger*	*Gender equality*	*Responsible consumption and production*	*Partnership for the goals*	*Affordable and clean energy*
No poverty	1	**0.643**	**0.656**	**0.488**	**0.421**	**0.425**	0.391	–0.095	0.027	0.179	–0.152	–0.311
Decent work and economic growth	**0.643**	1	**0.608**	**0.689**	**0.745**	**0.494**	0.765	0.249	0.306	0.226	0.34	–0.254
Sustainable cities and communities	**0.656**	**0.608**	1	**0.563**	**0.725**	**0.608**	0.702	0.335	0.349	0.424	–0.27	–0.442
Quality education	**0.488**	**0.689**	**0.563**	1	**0.7**	**0.514**	0.579	0.483	0.401	0.497	-0.019	–0.156
Peace, justice and strong institutions	**0.421**	**0.745**	**0.725**	**0.7**	1	**0.531**	0.752	0.285	0.56	0.415	0.137	–0.234
Good health and well-being	**0.425**	**0.494**	**0.608**	**0.514**	**0.531**	1	0.549	0.171	0.321	0.47	–0.137	–0.343
Industry, innovation and infrastructure	0.391	0.765	0.702	0.579	0.752	0.549	1	**0.419**	**0.646**	0.351	0.175	–0.442
Zero Hunger	–0.095	0.249	0.335	0.483	0.285	0.171	**0.419**	1	0.341	0.344	-0.051	0.008

Gender equality	0.027	0.306	0.349	0.401	0.56	0.321	**0.646**	0.341	1	0.36	0.095	−0.199
Responsible consumption and production	0.179	0.226	0.424	0.497	0.415	0.47	0.351	0.344	0.36	1	−0.224	0.045
Partnership for the goals	−0.152	0.34	−0.27	−0.019	0.137	−0.137	0.175	−0.051	0.095	−0.224	1	0.268
Affordable and clean energy	−0.311	−0.254	−0.442	−0.156	−0.234	−0.343	−0.442	0.008	−0.199	0.045	0.268	1

Explanations:

1. The table illustrates discernible interdependencies among the objectives within the identified dimensions of sustainability, ranging from at least moderate levels of correlation.
2. No correlation coefficients are provided for the third and fourth dimensions, as these two objectives are delineated by singular objectives. Specifically, these dimensions pertain to “Partnership for the Goals” (factor 3) and “Affordable and Clean Energy” (factor 4).

Source: Own elaboration.

Table 3.3 Pearson's linear correlation matrix between the pillars of development and the goals of sustainable development

Pillars/goals	*5th Pillar: health*	*6th Pillar: skills*	*11th Pillar: business dynamism*	*12th Pillar: innovation capability*
5th Pillar health overall	1	0.35	0.471	0.668
6th Pillar: skills overall	0.35	1	0.864	0.775
11th Pillar: business dynamism overall	0.471	0.864	1	0.85
12th Pillar: innovation capability overall	0.668	0.775	0.85	1
No poverty	0.269	0.317	0.291	0.259
Decent work and economic growth	0.194	**0.775**	**0.711**	**0.572**
Sustainable cities and communities	**0.455**	**0.642**	**0.573**	**0.667**
Quality education	**0.526**	**0.708**	**0.709**	**0.596**
Peace, justice and strong institutions	**0.413**	**0.773**	**0.712**	**0.751**
Good health and well-being	**0.815**	**0.525**	**0.596**	**0.725**
Industry, innovation and infrastructure	0.303	**0.849**	**0.737**	**0.799**
Zero hunger	0.195	**0.523**	**0.612**	**0.472**
Gender equality	0.342	**0.455**	**0.543**	**0.688**
Responsible consumption and production	**0.67**	0.354	**0.434**	**0.6**
Partnership for the goals	**-0.401**	0.157	0.107	-0.061
Affordable and clean energy	-0.13	-0.396	-0.244	-0.345

Source: Own elaboration

The first rather apparent observation revolves around the differentiated strength of the correlation and, to a lesser degree, the direction of the correlation between the developmental pillars and the SDGs. Notably, a positive and directly proportional interdependence exists between the developmental pillars and the SDGs.

The second point pertains to the assertion that Pillar 5 (health) exhibits comparatively weaker interconnections with the 12 chosen SDGs as compared to the other pillars (6, 11, 12). This reduced correlation of Pillar 5 (health) with the SDGs can be attributed to the fact that life expectancy (a defining metric) is influenced by factors that extend beyond the purview of the analyzed objectives. These factors encompass lifestyle and habits, quality of healthcare systems, climatic conditions, and more.

To conclude, it is crucial to underscore that the four primary pillars that are identified as the foundation of Economy 5.0 are tightly interconnected with the designated SDGs as well as the four specific factors that were distilled from them (particularly, Factors 1 and 2).

Discussion

The groundbreaking Nature article by Rockström et al. (2009) highlighted ecological factors that have the potential to disrupt the Earth's ecosystem. Among these factors, three out of ten have already surpassed their presumed limits: climate change (due to greenhouse gas emissions), the nitrogen cycle (attributed to industrial agriculture), and biodiversity loss (stemming from multifaceted causes such as food production practices, energy-related by-products, rapid urbanization, industrial production, and waste management). The consequences of breaching these environmental thresholds are dire and extensive, encompassing rising sea levels, heightened instances of floods, hurricanes, heatwaves, and droughts, hastening biodiversity decline, and acidified seawater. These outcomes, in turn, will erode prosperity across extensive regions of the globe (WEF, 2019).

According to Rockström et al. (2009), the continuously expanding global population (projected to reach 9 billion by 2050—predominantly concentrated in Asia and Africa) has the potential to counteract endeavors that are aimed at diminishing per-capita resource consumption. This expansion could intensify the strain on factors within the planet's limits. The Global Footprint Network's estimation suggests that such a population would leave an ecological footprint that demands approximately 3.4 planets should it adopt the consumption standards of the average European today; this transcends environmental boundaries (World Economic Forum, 2019).

Throughout history, Europe has frequently assumed the role of a change leader. It was within this region that the inaugural industrial revolution was sparked, and it remains a hotbed for driving the forefront trends of the Fifth Industrial Revolution. In November 2018, the European Commission unveiled an extensive strategic vision that was aimed at curtailing greenhouse gas emissions. This vision not only illustrates how Europe can chart a course toward global climate neutrality but also lay the foundation for a carbon-neutral economy (Climate Neutrality by 2050, 2015, EU). Europe's prominence in sustainable development outcomes is vividly depicted in Table 3.4.

Highly competitive economies are better positioned to facilitate the challenging transition to a low-footprint economy, such as the move toward a low- or zero-carbon energy mix (which necessitates accelerated technological progress). Developed countries (including the majority of EU nations) are well-equipped to foster the emergence of new technologies across all sectors—particularly, breakthrough innovations in green technologies, human capital, and human-centric approaches. Moreover, these countries are, on average, more inclined to adopt environmentally friendlier energy sources (GCR, 2019, WEF).

Table 3.4 Regional performance and changes in regional performance [% change 2018–2019], by health, skills, business dynamism, and innovation capability [average score (0–100)]

	Regional performance				*Changes in regional performance*			
	Human capital		*Innovation ecosystems*		*Human capital*		*Innovation ecosystems*	
Region (alphabetical order)	Health	Skills	Business dynamism	Innovation capability	Health	Skills	Business dynamism	Innovation capability
East Asia and the Pacific	83.8	67.3	66.1	54	-0.6	0.6	0.6	2
Eurasia	71.3	66.1	61.9	35.5	-2.8	0.9	2.9	1.9
Europe and North America	89.1	74.6	68.3	58.1	-1.7	0.5	0	0
Latin America and the Caribbean	82.2	58.7	58.3	34.3	-0.6	2.2	2.8	1.8
Middle East and North Africa	80.8	62.9	58.2	41.3	1	2.2	2.1	4.3
South Asia	68.4	50.1	57.8	36.3	0	0.8	2.3	-0.1
Sub-Saharan Africa	50.8	44.3	51.8	29.4	5.8	2.1	1.4	3.6

Source: Own research-based elaboration.

Europe and North America have emerged as leaders in development across all of the four examined pillars (as shown in Table 3.4). Notably, they exhibit a distinct advantage in skills and innovation dynamism. Other regions also exhibit promising advancements, with Sub-Saharan Africa displaying progress in health, the Middle East and North America excelling in innovation capability, and Eurasia, Latin America, and the Caribbean demonstrating vigor in business dynamism. For lesser-developed countries and emerging economies, sustained economic growth remains pivotal for expanding education, health, nutrition, and overall well-being across their populations.

Striking a harmonious balance between technology integration and investments in human capital will prove to be pivotal in enhancing productivity throughout the upcoming decade. Across advanced and emerging economies, both technology adoption and innovation have taken center stage as priorities for governments and businesses alike. These endeavors serve as sources of value creation, productivity surge, and improved living standards (The Global Competitiveness Report 2019, WEF). The convergence of creativity, expertise, technology, and financial resources from all corners of society is imperative for realizing all of the SDGs—fostering their integration and upholding the equilibrium between the three primary dimensions of sustainability: social, economic, and environmental (all rooted in collaboration and peace).

References

Ahsan, M. M., & Siddique, Z. (2022). Industry 4.0 in Healthcare: A systematic review. *International Journal of Information Management Data Insights, 2*(1), 100079. https://doi.org/10.1016/j.jjimei.2022.100079.

Breque, M., De Nul, L., & Petridis, A. (2021). Euramet. https://msu.euramet.org/current_calls/documents/EC_Industry5.0.pdf

Ching, N. T., Ghobakhloo, M., Iranmanesh, M., Maroufkhani, P., & Asadi, S. (2022). Industry 4.0 applications for sustainable manufacturing: A systematic literature review and a roadmap to sustainable development. *Journal of Cleaner Production, 334*, 130133. https://doi.org/10.1016/j.jclepro.2021.130133.

Eurostat. (n.d.). *SDG country overview*. Eurostat. https://ec.europa.eu/eurostat/cache/infographs/sdg-country-overview/.

Eurostat. (2022). *Sustainable development in the European Union—Monitoring report on progress towards the sdgs in an EU context*. Sustainable development in the European Union—Monitoring report on progress towards the SDGs in an EU context—2023 edition—Products Flagship Publications—Eurostat. https://ec.europa.eu/eurostat/web/products-flagship-publications/w/ks-04-23-184.

Ghosh, S., & Rajan, J. (2019). The business case for SDGs: An analysis of inclusive business models in emerging economies. *International Journal of Sustainable Development and World Ecology*, 26(4), 344–353. https://doi.org/10.1080/13504509.2019.1591539

Huang, S., Wang, B., Li, X., Zheng, P., Mourtzis, D., & Wang, L. (2022). Industry 5.0 and Society 5.0—Comparison, complementation and co-evolution. *Journal of Manufacturing Systems, 64*, 424–428. https://doi.org/10.1016/j.jmsy.2022.07.010

Maddikunta, P. K. R., Pham, Q.-V., Prabadevi, B., Deepa, N., Dev, K., Gadekallu, T. R., et al. (2022). Industry 5.0: A survey on enabling technologies and potential applications. *Journal of Industrial Information Integration, 26*, 100257. https://doi.org/10.1016/j.jii.2021.100257

Majstorović, V. D., Velimirović, M., Glišić, M., Kostić, J., Đura, E., Rančić, M., et al. (2018). Cyber-physical manufacturing in context of Industry 4.0 model. *Lecture Notes in Mechanical Engineering*, 227–238. https://doi.org/10.1007/978-3-319-89563-5_17

Mourtzis, D., Angelopoulos, J., & Panopoulos, N. (2022). A literature review of the challenges and opportunities of the transition from Industry 4.0 to Society 5.0. *Energies, 15*(17), 6276. https://doi.org/10.3390/en15176276

Orso, V., Ziviani, R., Bacchiega, G., Bondani, G., Spagnolli, A., & Gamberini, L. (2022). Employee-centric innovation: Integrating participatory design and video-analysis to foster the transition to Industry 5.0. *Computers & Industrial Engineering, 173*, 108661. https://doi.org/10.1016/j.cie.2022.108661.

Rockström, J., Steffen, W., Noone, K., Persson, Å., Chapin, F. S., III, Lambin, E. F., Lenton, T. M., Scheffer, M., Folke, C., Schellnhuber, H. J., Nykvist, B., de Wit, C. A., Hughes, T., van der Leeuw, S., Rodhe, H., Sörlin, S., Snyder, P. K., Costanza, R., Svedin, U., … Foley, J. A. (2009). A safe operating space for humanity. *Nature, 461*(7263), 472–475. https://doi.org/10.1038/461472a

Schwab, K. (2019). *The global competitiveness reports 2019*. Geneva: World Economic Forum.

SDGS. (n.d.). *The 17 goals: Sustainable development*. United Nations. https://sdgs.un.org/goals

UNDP. (n.d.). *Sustainable development goals: United Nations Development Programme*. UNDP. https://www.undp.org/sustainable-development-goals

World Economic Forum. (2019). *The global competitiveness report 2019*. World Economic Forum. https://www3.weforum.org/docs/WEF_TheGlobalCompetitivenessReport2019.pdf

Xu, X., Lu, Y., Vogel-Heuser, B., & Wang, L. (2021). Industry 4.0 and Industry 5.0—Inception, conception and perception. *Journal of Manufacturing Systems, 61*, 530–535. https://doi.org/10.1016/j.jmsy.2021.10.006

4 Catalyzing business development

A case study

Agnieszka Faron, Barbara Karlikowska, and Wojciech Maciejewski

Entrepreneurial behavior in a turbulent environment arising from the COVID-19 crisis

Entrepreneurship is a distinctive trait of individuals who actively seek opportunities within the market. Through their innovative and audacious endeavors, they introduce products and services that cater to the market's needs. The unexpected and disruptive emergence of the Covid-19 pandemic brought about profound turbulence, exemplifying a scenario of drastic change. In such critical junctures, entrepreneurial mindsets assume a renewed significance, as entrepreneurs must swiftly respond with a heightened willingness to embrace risks.

Adapting to novel circumstances that pose threats to others and recognizing them as avenues for growth and enhanced competitive advantage demands courage and resolute action. Furthermore, the rapid spread of Covid-19 may signify an escalating frequency and magnitude of unfavorable events, ushering in a succession of "new normal" rather than an extended phase of a singular new norm (Shepherd, 2020). Thus, entrepreneurs should transform their crisis responses they undertake on a short-term basis into enduring strategies.

In some aspects of socio-economic life, the pandemic has triggered changes that will be permanent and will create a kind of new "normalcy."

Undoubtedly, one area of entrepreneurship that has experienced notably accelerated growth due to the pandemic is digitization. Across numerous sectors of the economy, operations have transitioned into the virtual realm, with companies having limited alternatives. Digitalization emerged as a vital means of survival and advancement (Trufin & Lucaci, 2022). It became imperative for companies to adopt digital strategies for their continued existence and growth. This necessity sparked new avenues for business development (Gavrila & Ancillo, 2021). Furthermore, the interplay between entrepreneurship and the digital economy is anticipated to persist beyond the post-Covid era (Belitski, 2021).

DOI: 10.4324/9781003502272-5

Until the outbreak of the pandemic, progress in digitization was gradual, slow, until the advent of Covid-19 accelerated the process and offered many opportunities for digital innovation (Modgil et al., 2022). As Grinin et al. (2022) argue, the covid-19 pandemic has become an accelerating factor in the start of the latest phase of the cyber revolution. However, a technological revolution always involves radical socio-political changes. Small and medium enterprises used digital technologies like mobile and collaborative technologies, telecommunication networks, big-data analytics or artificial intelligence, to cope with consequences of Covid-19 (Papadopoulos et al., 2020).

Changes were also evident in the work organization, where remote work has given even more opportunities, and the pandemic has stimulated innovation (Ratten, 2020). Managers have shifted their focus primarily toward overseeing virtual teams and adapting to new working conditions, emphasizing the importance of prioritizing human aspects, investing more effort into clarifying objectives, and displaying greater empathy. It turned out that the most effective approach entails servin the team and listening to them, rather than expecting to be served by them (Montenero & Cazorzi, 2022).

Enhanced collaboration and swift decision-making are valuable lessons acquired during this period, poised to assist companies in tackling forthcoming challenges (Onea, 2022). Despite the global economic downturn, numerous entrepreneurs have adeptly transformed the challenges stemming from Covid-19 into opportunities to conceive, develop, and launch their ventures. For small and medium-sized enterprises, which often excel in flexibility and close engagement with the environment, the crisis can present market openings by harnessing innovative and proactive approaches (Eggers, 2020).

In today's dynamic world, characterized by perpetual change, opportunities abound for entrepreneurs. As highlighted by Ratten (2020), the key pillars of entrepreneurship crucial for addressing the Covid-19 crisis include innovation, risk-taking, and active participation in the market. During times of crisis, it is common for locally based resources that rely on networking to surface; such resources may have been overlooked during calmer times (Muñoz et al., 2020).

Emergencies like COVID-19 amplify the inclination to embrace social innovations that might have provoked skepticism under different circumstances, such as integrating artificial intelligence and robotics instead of human labor. However, post-crisis, a comprehensive examination of the ethical dimensions of the solutions adopted will be imperative (Brem et al., 2021).

Challenges encountered by polish companies during the pandemic

Any abrupt crisis-induced change invariably harms millions of individuals, leading to job losses across small and large enterprises (Zahra, 2021).

Adverse trends have been discernible in each research domain within the broader socio-economic landscape since the onset of the Covid-19 pandemic (Ali et al., 2022). Ensuring adequate support from the environment and institutions is crucial during crisis scenarios (Liñán & Jaén, 2022).

Government responses to counter-cyclical fluctuations have involved the provision of subsidies. In the case of Poland, government sources indicate that approximately $72.5 billion was allocated, with around $41.5 billion directed toward enterprises (Serwis Rzeczypospolitej Polskiej, 2023). Public expectations aligned with these actions, as evidenced by Poland's unemployment rate rise by 0.6% in the pandemic's first year. Slightly worse unemployment figures were recorded in early 2021, with a 1.1% increase compared to the pandemic's outset. By the end of 2022, unemployment had reached 5.2% (Główny Urząd Statystyczny, 2023). Despite the optimistic unemployment statistics, it is essential to remember that expansionary monetary policies also carry the risk of high inflation. Many studies suggest that such aid forms can potentially lead to a long-term recession (Aizenman et al., 2022; Auerbach et al., 2022).

The pandemic era did not leave most Polish companies unaffected. Business proprietors had to alter their business approaches, with many revising their management strategies. According to the report by Helak, Czerniak, and Piznal (2021), five fundamental survival strategies dominated, each of which entrepreneurs implemented: "nihil novi" by 15%, "overwintering" by 14%, "pandemic is an opportunity" by 12%, "first and foremost, do not slow down" by 25%, and finally, "cut the business to the bone" by 26%. The remaining 8% did not fall into any specific category.

The strategy that stands out in the context of this analysis is the "pandemic is an opportunity" approach. Entrepreneurs within this category viewed the pandemic as a chance for growth and creating a competitive edge. They focused on effecting necessary changes while maintaining their planned investments, leading to a heightened advantage over their competitors.

What further distinguishes this group is their proactive stance in preserving employment by seeking and implementing aids, including salary increases for workers. They demonstrated the most negligible dependence on state assistance (41.1%) among all segmented groups. Additionally, they were the least frequent beneficiaries of deferred payment options (6.3%), co-financing for other expenditures (16.7%), and operational loans (20.4%). This indicates that their business situation remained relatively stable, enabling them to manage fixed operational costs without significant difficulties (Helak et al., 2021).

Methodology—case study

Zadeh (2022) analyzed the Covid-19 pandemic's influence on Small and Medium-sized Enterprises (SMEs), suggesting that these entities can transform the uncertainty stemming from the crisis into prospects for enhancing flexibility, fostering innovation, and acquiring new skills. However, the impact of labor disruptions has not been uniformly felt across all companies, making it intricate to definitively categorize the pandemic as an opportunity or a threat on a broad scale. In light of this, using case studies proves more advantageous than quantitative analysis, offering a more profound and contextually rich understanding. This study also aligns with such an approach, echoing the utilization of case studies to explore the intricate dynamics brought about by the pandemic on entrepreneurial endeavors.

Our comprehensive literature review served to identify shifts in the operational landscape of companies since the outbreak of the Covid-19 pandemic. This review served as the foundation for developing a set of 14 standardized open-ended questions for conducting interviews. These questions encompassed various facets, including human resources management, labor productivity, alterations in work structure, and an overarching overview of all operational aspects.

We have hypothesized that during the Covid-19 pandemic, the significance of entrepreneurial endeavors aimed at achieving competitive advantages within the examined companies escalated. This assertion will be scrutinized by examining the transformations experienced by each of the three companies under investigation.

The interviews we conducted involved representatives from diverse sectors, including Ecobike Ltd. (a company from the manufacturing industry), one logistics company, and a service provider in the hotel sector specializing in tourist and short-term accommodations that participated anonymously; the interviews included decision-makers ranging from board members to senior managers and owners. The data collection process spanned from November 2022 to January 2023, enabling a comprehensive assessment of the evolving dynamics within the companies during the post-pandemic period.

The case of a manufacturing company

Established in 2008, Ecobike Ltd. operates as an electric bicycle manufacturer, with its primary market being the European Union. The company also extends its product sales to the United Kingdom and Norway. In response to the Covid-19 pandemic, administrative staff were allowed to transition to remote work voluntarily. For manufacturing staff, stringent hygiene protocols and increased ventilation capacities were implemented. Before the pandemic, the company's communication and collaboration systems heavily relied on cloud computing and instant messaging, enabling a seamless transition to remote work for employees.

Despite the introduction of rigorous health measures, the company's work environment remained conducive, and no significant disruptions took place. Notably, the employees preferred working from the company headquarters, showcasing a lack of resistance to adhering to mandatory health guidelines. The disruption of supply chains necessitated a reorganization of the company's operations, leading to an initial reduction in production during the pandemic's onset. However, commendably, no workforce redundancies were incurred during this period.

Interview findings highlighted effective staff management and motivation, consistently performing tasks as expected. The pandemic's impact on productivity remained inconspicuous. Workers exhibited a strong sense of responsibility, rendering additional incentives unnecessary. Job descriptions were well-defined, and the motivation system remained consistent despite the work format (on-site or remote).

In cases of sick leaves, colleagues assumed the absent persons' duties based on their competencies. Given the industry's inherent seasonality, the pandemic did not noticeably alter productivity, with heightened workloads during spring and summer. The bicycle industry experienced growth during the pandemic due to increased health awareness and a greater inclination toward active leisure.

Remote work was not a novel concept for the company as employees often had the flexibility to conclude tasks at home after leaving the office early. This adaptable approach to work stemmed from a transparent distribution of responsibilities and collective team responsibility.

The company made noteworthy savings thanks to remote capabilities, particularly in customer relations and governmental interactions. Remote meetings effectively replaced stationary gatherings without compromising outcomes. The ability to exchange documentation with authorities remotely was particularly advantageous.

While the company explored remote conferencing, sales process innovations, and designing new bicycle models without requiring a physical presence, no other groundbreaking solutions were introduced. Existing IT systems sufficed during the pandemic, obviating the need for additional elements. The company remains primed for remote work in administration and is prepared to pivot as needed.

The case of a logistics company

The logistics company in this study opted to maintain anonymity but consented to participate; for disclosure, the company operates within the logistics and transport sector on a global scale. We conducted the interview with a senior manager at one of the company's branches situated in Poland. The employees of the company offer services with a global reach, which has inherently involved remote work. As the Covid-19 pandemic started, the company's employees transitioned to working from home.

This shift altered the work location but not the fundamental nature of their tasks.

When questioned, employees viewed this arrangement as temporary, anticipating a swift return to office-based work. Formal training did not occur; each employee received a designated portable computer with the necessary software. Their attitude to work fluctuated during the pandemic, primarily due to uncertainties regarding the ultimate work setup. As restrictions eased and the possibility of returning to the office emerged, most employees opted for a hybrid model, with remote work predominating. Significantly, the company noted improved work quality and productivity when employees worked from home.

During the interview, the employees underscored that the mode and format of work have minimal impact on their motivation. Nonetheless, effective communication, feedback on work results, guidance on actions, and illustration of the consequences of actions on work quality remained paramount. While the core principles of employee performance oversight remained unchanged, the communication approach shifted from synchronous to asynchronous. Generally, roles within the company required a high level of focus and direct communication during exceptional situations.

The incentive system is perpetually adjusted to cater to employee needs, often guided by their input on required modifications. An intriguing observation pertained to workforce turnover; the pandemic's impact on employment changes was minimal, and the new work structure generated additional job opportunities.

Throughout the pandemic, the logistics industry experienced higher-than-average growth in service provision. The company's adeptness at seamlessly adjusting its work organization without the need for substantial investments in new positions facilitated a rapid expansion of its workforce. The company had contemplated transitioning to remote work prior to the pandemic, given the nature of its services.

A notable outcome of the shift to remote work was reduced costs associated with media, office supplies, and coffee consumption. Due to the company's global reach and the substantial volume of services rendered, even prior to the pandemic, the company's commitment to maximizing operational automation remained steadfast, particularly in routine tasks. Many of the solutions implemented during the pandemic originated in measures adopted earlier. As such, it becomes challenging to discern whether the company introduced innovations exclusively in response to the pandemic.

The case of a service industry company

The "Południe" tourist resort (a name chosen for this publication at the owner's request to preserve anonymity) started operating in 2001.

This seasonal resort offers its services exclusively during the summer, from May to September. The company provides active leisure activities for families and organized groups. 2020 emerged as a pivotal period for shaping the company's new strategy and implementing operational modifications.

According to data from the Central Statistical Office (GUS), Poland registered 19.8 million hotel overnight stays from July to August 2020, marking a decrease of 6.9 million (25.8%) compared to the previous year (Emmerson Evaluation, 2021). Poland's hotel industry has been significantly affected by closures in the services sector. Its financial performance differed notably from the broader economic landscape. The Covid-19 outbreak led to the permanent closure of numerous service establishments. Revenues for the first to third quarters of 2020 dropped by over 40% compared to the same period in 2019. By the 4th quarter of 2020, the hotel industry's profitability rate reached –83.6%, with revenues decrease of 65% year-on-year (for companies employing over 49 people). The Chamber of Commerce of the Polish Hotel Industry reported a rise in closed hotels to 17% by March 2021, with 8 out of 10 open facilities experiencing occupancy levels well below the break-even point (2021). In this challenging economic context, the company chosen as an example had to navigate its way forward.

Given the nature of the hospitality, catering, and recreation sector, it was not possible to eliminate direct customer contact or transition to remote work, as many other industries did. One aspect that embraced remote work was the booking and accommodation management system. In contrast to previous years, communication through instant messaging replaced traditional "face-to-face" meetings. The need for additional training was minimized as the owner personally oversaw this aspect and had prior experience. Recruitment procedures for the center predominantly occurred online, utilizing virtual interviews. A critical aspect of prepping for the season involved training employees on adhering to safety protocols in the face of Covid-19-related high-risk conditions. The pandemic-induced employee stress stemming from direct customer interaction, especially at the beginning of the season, triggered adjustments to conform with the sanitary and epidemiological standards applicable to holiday centers. These adaptations ranged from modifying restaurant layouts to designating isolation rooms and establishing provisions for medical aid. Despite the challenging working conditions, the outcomes improved considerably, marked by heightened work efficiency and a meticulous approach, especially regarding self-protective measures such as face masks, gloves, and protective gear and equipment. Despite the considerable challenges faced during the summer of 2020, the collaborative endeavors of all stakeholders ensured that the season concluded without incurring any financial losses. Right after the summer campaign of 2020, strategic modifications were implemented to restructure the work organization and refine the particulars of the sector's activities.

The resort decided to transition the target customer base from families to youth and children groups, resulting in a rise in occupancy. Consequently, this change necessitated adjustments in accommodation arrangements to comply with health and safety regulations and the unique demands of group stays (such as adhering to the minimal space per individual as stipulated by the local Health Department, setting a maximum occupancy limit per room, and ensuring there is no mixing of different traveling groups in adjacent rooms).

Most of the resort's attractions were relocated outdoors to enhance safety for organizers and participants engaging in activities. Additionally, the resort undertook investments in building playgrounds and recreational facilities in open spaces to cater to the leisure time of guests, such as outdoor chess, a bowling alley, a climbing wall, inflatables, a "live football" playground, volleyball courts, badminton courts, and an outdoor gym. Tennis courts were designed to facilitate separate group activities, allowing multiple groups to engage simultaneously. Those waiting for their turn were designated to a specific waiting area. Stricter guidelines were implemented for using the swimming pool, emphasizing water hygiene and cleanliness.

The resort also invested in a retail point (a kiosk) where individuals could purchase essentials. In 2022, this kiosk was expanded and replaced with a pizzeria that offered a wide range of ice cream and selected products in response to customer demand. All these measures focused on minimizing the need for guests to leave the premises, thereby reducing potential contact with other individuals and reduce the spread of diseases. As a result, during the 2021 season, there were no issues with bed occupancy—all available beds were fully booked. The approach taken in the previous year was continued in the 2022 season. In the first season of summer 2021, only one individual contracted COVID, and fortunately, the disease did not spread. In the following year, 2022, there were no reported cases of illness, which underscores the effectiveness of the measures implemented.

The shift in customer preferences proved to be a fitting response to the desires of parents who aimed to ensure a safe and secure vacation for their children.

Conclusions and recommendations

The pandemic's inherent unpredictability has significantly disrupted SMEs. From the start, questions were raised about its potential impact on this sector, known for its susceptibility to emerging crises. Would the situation result in the zombification of small companies (Kuratko & Audretsch, 2022), or could it serve as a catalyst for transformation? Obtaining a definitive answer to this question still poses a challenge due to the diverse conditions under which companies operate.

Based on the interviews conducted, the authors suggest the following recommendations:

1. Entrepreneurship has shown its ability to succeed during challenging times. However, it is essential to remember that gaining a competitive advantage is ongoing, not solely dependent on sudden events. This mindset allows flexibility and adaptability in response to changes, regardless of industry, company size, or location.
2. Introducing new and innovative solutions should not be limited to times of turbulence; it should be a consistent practice. Implementing such solutions on a continual basis can help build an advantage, especially when facing unexpected changes.
3. Government support is crucial for fostering entrepreneurial activities. It includes providing targeted financial assistance and creating favorable laws and regulations that create a stable and encouraging environment for entrepreneurship in general.

Based on the case studies of companies across various sectors presented in this study, a general inference can be drawn that entrepreneurial endeavors have demonstrated resilience in turbulent environments. A shared trait among these companies was the early implementation of practical solutions, eliminating the need for additional training during the pandemic. It underscores the imperative for entrepreneurs and startups to integrate innovative measures as they become available consistently. Notably, the hospitality company underwent substantial adaptations due to governmental restrictions, yet its ability to pivot toward a different target demographic enabled survival and service expansion.

Moreover, a common thread among the studied companies was their agility and aptitude for adapting to new circumstances, often without extensive organizational upheavals. While confirming the hypothesis that the Covid-19 pandemic heightens the significance of entrepreneurial pursuits might be challenging, it is evident that consistent entrepreneurial engagement is pivotal. This approach precludes unwelcome surprises during unexpected shifts and enables swift adaptation in novel scenarios.

References

Aizenman, J., Jinjarak, Y., & Spiegel, M. M. (2022). Fiscal stimulus and commercial bank lending under Covid-19. *SSRN Electronic Journal*, 1–51. https://doi.org/10.2139/ssrn.4083026

Ali, M. J., Bhuiyan, A. B., Zulkifli, N., & Hassan, M. K. (2022). The COVID-19 pandemic: Conceptual framework for the global economic impacts and recovery. In M. K. Hassan, A. Muneeza, & A. M. Sarea (Eds.), *Towards a Post-Covid Global*

Financial System, 225–242. Emerald Publishing Limited. https://doi.org/10.1108/978-1-80071-625-420210012.

Auerbach, A., Gorodnichenko, Y., McCrory, P. B., & Murphy, D. (2022). Fiscal multipliers in the COVID19 recession. *Journal of International Money and Finance, 126*, 102669. https://doi.org/10.1016/j.jimonfin.2022.102669.

Belitski, M., Guenther, C., Kritikos, A. S., & Thurik, R. (2022). Economic effects of the COVID-19 pandemic on entrepreneurship and small businesses. *Small Business Economics, 58*(2), 593–609. https://doi.org/10.1007/s11187-021-00544-y.

Brem, A., Viardot, E., & Nylund, P. A. (2021). Implications of the coronavirus (COVID-19) outbreak for innovation: Which technologies will improve our lives? *Technological Forecasting and Social Change, 163*, 120451. https://doi.org/10.1016/j.techfore.2020.120451.

Eggers, F. (2020). Masters of disasters? Challenges and opportunities for SMEs in times of crisis. *Journal of Business Research, 116*, 199–208. https://doi.org/10.1016/j.jbusres.2020.05.025.

Emmerson Evaluation. (2021). Raport Rynek Hoteli Oraz condohoteli w Polsce 2021. https://www.emmerson-evaluation.pl/wp-content/uploads/2021/06/raport-rynek-hoteli-oraz-condohoteli-w-polsce-2021.pdf.

Gavrila, S. G., & Ancillo, A. L. (2021). COVID-19 as an entrepreneurship, innovation, digitization and digitalization accelerator: Spanish Internet domains registration analysis. *British Food Journal, 123*(10), 3358–3390.

Grinin, L., Grinin, A., & Korotayev, A. (2022). COVID-19 pandemic as a trigger for the acceleration of the cybernetic revolution, transition from e-government to e-state, and change in social relations. *Technological Forecasting and Social Change, 175*, 121348. https://doi.org/10.1016/j.techfore.2021.121348.

Helak, M., Czerniak, A., & Piznal, J. (2021). *Przedsiębiorca odporny: Jak przetrwał pandemię*. Warsaw: Polska Rada Biznesu. https://prb.pl/wp-content/uploads/2021/11/Przedsiebiorca-odporny.-Jak-przetrwal-pandemie.pdf

Kuratko, D. F., & Audretsch, D. B. (2022). The future of entrepreneurship: The few or the many? *Small Business Economics, 59*(1), 269–278. https://doi.org/10.1007/s11187-021-00534-0.

Liñán, F., & Jaén, I. (2022). The Covid-19 pandemic and entrepreneurship: Some reflections. *International Journal of Emerging Markets, 17*(5), 1165–1174. https://doi.org/10.1108/ijoem-05-2020-0491.

Modgil, S., Dwivedi, Y. K., Rana, N. P., Gupta, S., & Kamble, S. (2022). Has Covid-19 accelerated opportunities for digital entrepreneurship? An Indian perspective. *Technological Forecasting and Social Change, 175*, 121415. https://doi.org/10.1016/j.techfore.2021.121415.

Montenero, V., & Cazorzi, C. (2022). Virtual management during the Covid-19 era: Changes in leadership and management. *International Entrepreneurship Review, 8*(1), 77–94. https://doi.org/10.15678/ier.2022.0801.06.

Muñoz, P., Naudé, W., Williams, N., Williams, T., & Frías, R. (2020). Reorienting entrepreneurial support infrastructure to tackle a social crisis: A rapid response. *Journal of Business Venturing Insights, 14*, e00181. https://doi.org/10.1016/j.jbvi.2020.e00181.

Onea, I. A. (2022). Exploring the COVID-19 pandemic impact on innovation and entrepreneurship—Review and evidence from Global Innovation Index.

Proceedings of the International Conference on Business Excellence, 16(1), 527–544. https://doi.org/10.2478/picbe-2022-0051.

Papadopoulos, T., Baltas, K. N., & Balta, M. E. (2020). The use of digital technologies by small and medium enterprises during COVID-19: Implications for theory and practice. *International Journal of Information Management, 55*, 102192. https://doi.org/10.1016/j.ijinfomgt.2020.102192.

Ratten, V. (2020). Coronavirus (Covid-19) and entrepreneurship: Changing life and work landscape. *Journal of Small Business & Entrepreneurship, 32*(5), 503–516. https://doi.org/10.1080/08276331.2020.1790167.

Serwis Rzeczypospolitej Polskiej. (2023). *Tarcza Antykryzysowa*. Tarcza antykryzysowa. http://www.gov.pl/web/tarczaantykryzysowa.

Shepherd, D. A. (2020). COVID 19 and entrepreneurship: Time to pivot? *Journal of Management Studies, 57*(8), 1750–1753. https://doi.org/10.1111/joms.12633.

Trufin, E., & Lucaci, A. (2022). The impact of the Covid-19 pandemic on entrepreneurship. *The USV Annals of Economics and Public Administration, 22*(1 (35)), 18–25.

Zadeh, F. G. (2022). Entrepreneurship and SMEs under COVID-19 crisis: A literature review. *International Entrepreneurship Review, 8*(3), 23–35. https://doi.org/10.15678/ier.2022.0803.02.

Zahra, S. A. (2021). International entrepreneurship in the post Covid world. *Journal of World Business, 56*(1), 101143. https://doi.org/10.1016/j.jwb.2020.101143.

5 Intellectual capital

Measuring social capital in manufacturing companies

Elżbieta Jędrych, Dariusz Klimek, and Jacek Witkowski

Introduction

Social capital is an inventive interdisciplinary idea, serving as an overarching framework that unites various sociological, economic, and other theories, which could otherwise be excessively intricate and theoretical. From a research standpoint, this concept facilitates the integration of macro-societal structures with micro-level mechanisms, ultimately allowing us to transcend limitations that hinder our comprehension of social phenomena.

The concept of social capital brings fresh insight into social matters that were frequently sidelined by the prevailing rationalism and economic individualism paradigm. By regarding social elements as valuable "capital," this theory establishes a foundation for giving "communities" an equitable role in decision-making, alongside economic considerations.

Acknowledging the connections and ties between individuals as a kind of capital enriches comprehension of social challenges, leading to their integration into decision-making procedures often dominated by economic rationalism. Hence, the notion of social capital can reshape priorities and perspectives concerning various facets of human endeavors. It embodies a "third way," aiming to bridge the gap between the economy and the community.

The popularity of this concept is evidence of a gap (or even a vacuum) in science, indicating the need for decision-makers to take problems that are outside the scope of economics into account. It draws attention to the importance of culture, roots, and social support, as well as the consequences of mistrust, social isolation, etc. The notion of social capital also has the distinct advantage of being intuitively understood by most people regarding its meaning.

Although the underlying phenomena of social capital (including bonds, social cohesion, and solidarity) have been discussed by sociologists for a long time, the term "social capital" has appeared relatively recently. There is an ongoing debate about the first use of the term "social capital." Most authors agree that Hanifan first used the term in 1916; however, others have identified Jacobs (1961), Felkins (2002), Loury (1977), Lappe and

DOI: 10.4324/9781003502272-6

du Bois (1997), Leeder and Dominello (1999), and the Royal Commission on Canada's Economic Prospects (Schuller et al., 2000). Hanifan, a social reformer, used the term "social capital" in 1916; she referred to "goodwill, fellowship, mutual sympathy, and social intercourse in a group of individuals and families" (MacGillivray & Walker, 2000; Smith & Kulynych, 2002). Routledge and von Amsberg (2003) stated that Hanifan used the term "capital" to emphasize the importance of a social structure for individuals from a business and economic perspective. Smith and Kulynych (2002) stated that the first to use the term in a discussion on urban communities was J. Jacobs (1961). She said that "networks are cities" with indispensable social capital. The next to use the term was Loury (1977), which is cited extensively in the literature. Hofstede (2011) is another author who studied the concept, although he did not use the term "social capital"; however, he showed the importance of contemporary values such as individualism, equal opportunities, and "avoiding uncertainty" for generating what we call "social capital."

The social capital theory developed primarily in relation to society and local communities (a macroeconomic approach), gradually moving to the level of organization (a microeconomic approach). The theory of social capital is becoming increasingly important in the management sciences, becoming the key to explaining the various organizational and financial problems that arise from the relationships among one's employees.

Social capital is a portmanteau of two terms: "social" and "capital." Particularly controversial is the term "capital," which is most often used to describe a variety of material values (Falk & Kilpatrick, 1999; Hofferth et al., 1999; Inkeles, 2000). Generally defined, capital is those goods and resources that have some value for their owners and can be exchangeable for other goods; properly used, they multiply their value (that is, they bring a profit). The pure form of capital is money—an abstract symbol of value exchangeable for other goods and services. Over time, this basic concept of capital has been expanded and used in other areas of social life, including social capital, human capital, and cultural capital. Portes aptly described the location of social capital in relation to other forms of capital: "...while economic capital is in people's bank accounts and human capital is in their heads, social capital is part of the structure of their relationship" (Portes, 1998).

To sum up, social capital is similar to other forms of capital because it can be invested with the expectation of future profits (Adler & Kwon, 2002), it is suitable (Coleman, 1988), it is fungible (Wacquant, 1989), and it requires formation (Gant et al., 2002). Differences are due to the fact that it is rooted in social relationships, while other forms of capital may be in units (Gant et al., 2002; Glaeser et al., 2002; Robinson et al., 2002).

This review can be concluded by attempting to compile it, assuming that social capital in organizations is a functional whole of the values, norms, and networks that determine the relationships among people in order to achieve a synergistic effect of cooperation. The foundation of this whole is the trust that people engender in each other.

Dilemmas of measuring social capital

One of the biggest weaknesses of the concept of social capital is the lack of a consensus on how to measure it. According to many researchers, the measurement and assessment of social capital for individual, organizational, and social development are still in their infancy. At the same time, there is a consensus that social capital influences decisions that concern strategy and the development of enterprises, communities, and nations. The measurement of social capital allows measures to be taken to develop it at different levels and dimensions.

In research practice, the measurement of social capital is hampered by a number of difficulties due to the following groups of reasons:

First: the difficulty of measurement arises from the problems that are associated with the definition and content of the various components of social capital in different theoretical perspectives and within different scientific disciplines (sociology, economics, management, and political science). This prevents comparable measurement results. According to many researchers, "the basic difficulty with measurement is that we do not know what to measure (…)" (Serageldin, 1999). Daniere et al. (2002) considered that the existing measures of social capital were subject to criticism, as researchers defined terminology differently, and it was difficult to demonstrate concrete tangible evidence of social capital that would be suitable for quantitative analysis. Paxton (1999) noted the growing gap between the notion of social capital and its measurement. The popularity of this term seems to encourage the use of over-aggregated heterogeneous indices (Knack, 2002). Due to the abstract nature of social capital and its different definitions, the measurement results are often not comparable (Liu & Besser, 2003). Often, research has no justification for how its measures of social capital tie in with its theoretical definition (Paxton, 1999).

Stone (2001) concluded that there were insufficient tools for measuring empirical evidence and that this was an area where further studies were required (Australian Bureau of Statistics, 2002; Bullen & Onyx, 1998; Kawachi et al., 2000).

Second: there are problems in measuring the separation of the form of capital, its sources, and its consequences. Woolcock (1998) argued that social capital should be identified on the basis of its sources or circumstances (e.g., social ties and social networks) rather than its effects or outcomes. Laurence and Heath (2008) also argued that many measurement problems arise precisely from the lack of a proper clear distinction between the sources (or determinants) and the results (consequences). One example is trust, which is widely perceived as a component of social capital. Some authors equate trust with social capital (Fukuyama, 1997), and others view it as a source of social capital (Putnam, 1997) or as one form of social capital (Coleman, 1988). Still, others see trust as the effect of capital and understood as relational assets (Lin, 1999).

Third: there is also a lack of consensus in the literature on social capital indicators. Such a complex multidimensional concept of capital is understood to imply that, depending on the environmental and disciplinary contexts, alternative indicators must be used. Collier (2002) argued that social capital is difficult, if not impossible, to measure directly and that proxies are needed for empirical purposes. Social capital contains constructs that are inherently abstract and require subjective interpretation in their translations into operational tools (Grootaert & van Bastelaer, 2002; Narayan & Cassidy, 2001). Collier supported this view by stating that while it is difficult to measure social capital directly, it can be inferred from its effects. The choices of indicators for measuring social capital depend on the scope of the concept and the scope of the research being carried out (Collier, 2002). Social capital is such a complex concept that no single indicator can be applied (Baum & Ziersch, 2003).

When measuring the social capital of an organization, researchers most often take two research perspectives: the first is measuring the capital by its dimensions (structural, relational, cognitive), and the second is measuring it by the level of analysis (individual, group, community capital).

The measures of the structural dimension of social capital emphasize the pattern of the relationships between individuals and their networks. In contrast, the measures of the relational dimension emphasize the nature and quality of individual interactions. Measures of the cognitive dimension of social capital focus on common goals, standards, values, and reciprocity.

Test method

There are two types of social capital in business science and practice: intra-organizational capital (which represents the relationships among employees as well as among employees, managers, and business owners) and external social capital (which illustrates the social relationships among the employees of different organizations, groups of organizations, customers, etc.) (Leenders et al., 1999). This distinction is very important because it describes different not-necessarily-correlated relationships. The studies that are presented in this chapter focus on *intra-organizational social capital.*

This study aimed to determine the level of the social capital of selected enterprises (including relational, structural, and cognitive capital) and to identify the strengths and weaknesses of social capital.

To achieve the above objectives, the research process consisted of the following activities:

- development of a model for measuring social capital—including a set of indicators for measuring different dimensions of internal social capital;
- development of a psychometric tool for measuring attitudes, opinions, and evaluations of employees;
- carrying out studies in five manufacturing enterprises (from different sectors of the economy) aimed at measuring the level of social capital while taking the specificities of each enterprise into account.

The following research tools were used to carry out the research:

- A questionnaire interview that contained questions that were relevant to an assessment of the strategy, structure, organizational culture, financial situation, level of human resources management, etc., of each company ("Diagnosis of the state of the enterprise"). The survey was addressed to board members and middle managers; in total, 15 interviews were conducted with the managers and members of the management boards of the surveyed companies.
- A questionnaire for measuring the level of social capital ("Scale for social capital survey"). A total of 620 employees from the surveyed companies participated in the study, including administration employees, production workers, and managers.

Given the multidimensional and interdisciplinary nature of the concept of "social capital," the basic issue was to develop a model of social capital that defined the research content and formed the basis for constructing a research tool.

It is assumed that three dimensions can characterize the social capital of a company:

1 Structural dimension (**structural capital**). This dimension describes social capital from the point of view of the organizational perspective of a company (the type of organizational structure that favors the cooperation of employees in units and between units) as well as the type of communication system (access of employees to information, necessary knowledge, attitudes of managers toward activities that facilitate cooperation).
2 Relational dimension (**relational capital**). This dimension describes the quality of the contacts among employees (and their types) as well as the trust, credibility, and willingness of the employees to share knowledge and experience.

3 Cognitive dimension (**cognitive capital**). This dimension describes the coherence between the standards and values of a company and its employees, a common understanding of the company's problems, the use of a vocabulary everyone understands, etc.

The above-mentioned dimensions of social capital have been attributed to specific attributes and indicators; these are as follows:

1 For structural capital: trust (in co-workers, in other employees, and in managers), reciprocity (willingness to share knowledge, expectation of reciprocity in relationships, willingness to help others), and motivation to cooperate (positive energy to work, working with passion and energy, assessing the atmosphere of cooperation);
2 For relational capital: the structure of an enterprise (methods of organizing cooperation, communication within the company, assessment of cooperation with supervisors), the state of the relationships in the enterprise (knowledge of the competencies of others, type of contacts in the organizational unit, type of contacts with employees from outside the organizational unit), and the status of the employee (appreciation of the employee, impact on the environment);
3 For cognitive capital: values and standards (consistency of standards and principles of employee and enterprise, assessment of standards and values of enterprise, clearly defined forms of acceptable behavior in an organization), proactivity (voluntary activity for the benefit of the company), and a common language (understood communication, common terminology).

Results and conclusions

Conclusion 1: The diagnosis of intra-organizational social capital levels revealed a diverse social landscape among the surveyed companies. Two distinct groups of companies emerge:

- companies with high levels (very high and high) of total social capital, as well as relational, structural, and cognitive capital. In these companies, their teams embody significant strength and value.
- companies with low levels (very low and low) of total social capital, as well as relational, structural, and cognitive capital. Within these companies, over half of their staff exhibit low levels of social capital. While this group holds potential, it remains largely untapped thus far.

The study also revealed that within the examined companies, the level of relational capital was notably higher compared to other forms of capital,

Table 5.1 Social capital of surveyed companies, N = 620 (%)

Surveyed companies	*Total social capital*		*Relational capital*		*Structural capital*		*Cognitive capital*	
	High capital	*Low capital*	*High capital*	*Low capital*	*High capital*	*Low capital*	*High capital*	*Low capital*
Case study 1	75.0	25.0	78.3	21.7	70.9	29.1	75.7	24.3
Case study 2	68.7	31.3	73.1	26.9	65.7	34.3	67.1	32.9
Case study 3	66.4	33.6	72.3	27.7	61.6	38.8	65.4	34.6
Case study 4	44.3	55.7	48.0	52.0	41.7	58.3	43.3	56.7
Case study 5	34.4	65.6	38.1	61.9	31.6	68.4	33.3	66.7

Source: Own study

Table 5.2 Social capital of groups of workers surveyed, N = 620 (%)

Case study	*Managers*		*Administration*		*Production work*	
	High	*Low*	*High*	*Low*	*High*	*Low*
1	83.2	26.8	69.6	30.4	78.7	34.3
2	75.0	25.0	72.1	27.9	66.6	33.4
3	76.0	24.0	78.4.	21.6	68.7	31.3
4	49.3	50.7	48.6	51.4	40.6	59.4
5	39.3.	60.7	38.6.	61.4	30.6	69.4

Source: Own study

such as trust, employee connections, and reciprocity in external relationships (Table 5.1).

Conclusion 2: The analysis of the findings revealed variations in the degrees of social capital across distinct worker groups, including managers, administrators, and production workers, among others. Among the surveyed companies, managers generally exhibited the highest levels of social capital. An exception to this trend was noted in Case Study 3, where the administrative employees demonstrated the highest social capital levels. Conversely, the group of production workers displayed the lowest levels of social capital. Given the crucial role of this group, especially in companies with a production-oriented profile, targeted strategic and operational interventions are necessary to enhance their social capital (Table 5.2).

Conclusion 3: An in-depth analysis of both general and specific indicators enabled the identification of strengths and weaknesses within the realms of relational, cognitive, and structural capital across the surveyed companies. This analysis, in turn, facilitated the development of customized strategies to fortify the targeted capital dimensions.

Here are the distinctive features characterizing the social capital within the five surveyed companies:

Case Study 1

This particular company showcased an exceptionally high degree of social capital among its employees, standing out as the highest among the five companies under examination. A staggering 75% of the respondents within this company displayed remarkably elevated levels of social capital. This aspect reflects the company's tangible investment in its workforce, cultivating profound trust and loyalty among employees. Notably, this group encompassed individuals occupying diverse positions and representing various organizational units within the company.

The highest level of social capital could be found in the group of managers and production workers, while lower amounts could be found among the administrative staff.

An analysis of the levels of relational, structural, and cognitive capital indicated that the greatest strength of the capital lay in the relational capital of the employees (high levels of trust, good contact among the employees, willingness to share knowledge, etc.) and their cognitive capital. The managers held the highest level of relational capital, while the lowest level could be found in administrative employees (ten percentage points less than in the group of managers).

Case Study 2

This company featured a high social capital of its employees—68.7% of the respondents held very high and high levels of social capital. This was an extremely valuable resource for the company (employees who exhibited a high level of trustworthiness and could be relied upon for their loyalty). This group comprised employees at different positions and from various organizational units within the company.

The highest level of social capital occurred in the group of managers and administrative staff; however, these levels were much lower among the productive employees.

An examination of the levels of relational, structural, and cognitive capital indicated that the most robust aspects of the capital resided in employees' relational capital (characterized by high levels of trust, effective inter-employee communication, willingness to share knowledge, etc.) and their cognitive capital. The lowest levels were associated with their structural capital. Among managers, the highest relational capital levels were evident, while the lowest could be found among administrative employees. At the same time, the company also had a relatively sizeable group of employees with low and very low social capital. This group was a potential reservoire of social capital for the company.

In general, the most pronounced social capital deficit occurred within the production worker group, where 33.4% held low and very low capital. This posed a concerning situation for a professional group vital to the company's operation.

Case Study 3

This company was characterized by the high social capital of its employees—66.4% held high and very high levels of social capital. This part of the crew is the real potential of the company, which owners and management can rely on for work, commitment, and loyalty. In this group, there were employees in different positions and from different organizational units. The highest level of social capital could be found among administrative employees (including specialists from various fields).

An analysis of the levels of relational, structural, and cognitive capital indicated that the greatest strength of the capital lied in the relational capital of the employees (high levels of trust, good contact among the employees, tendencies to share knowledge, etc.). Among the various employee categories, administrative staff exhibited the highest levels of relational capital, while production employees displayed the lowest levels.

Even though a relatively high level of social capital was present, there were still segments of workers characterized by low and very low levels of both general and specific forms of capital across different dimensions. These segments hold the potential to serve as a reservoir for capital accumulation, thus warranting the implementation of social capital-enhancing strategies. In sum, the most substantial deficit in the capital (across all its dimensions) was observed within the production worker category—a group of employees of paramount importance.

Case Study 4

The extent of social capital within this examined company prompted us to categorize it among those with low capital levels. A significant

55.7% of the workforce displayed low to very low levels of social capital, with the lowest level identified within the production worker segment, comprising nearly 60% of the respondents. This highlights the need for the company to recognize the significance of this vital employee group in its strategic and operational endeavors. Addressing this group is paramount, given its involvement in numerous organizational challenges, such as elevated turnover rates and a high frequency of accidents.

Simultaneously, it can be asserted that the "company's capital" predominantly resided with employees in administrative and managerial roles, despite their social capital levels being notably lower than those observed in the previously examined firms.

An evaluation of distinct forms of social capital revealed diminished levels of structural capital across all employee categories. This raised concerns pertaining to the organizational framework of collaboration, communication dynamics among employees, and their interactive behaviors.

Case Study 5

This company exhibited extremely low levels of social capital, ranking as the least socially capitalized among the group of surveyed production companies. A significant 65.6% of the workforce demonstrated low to very low capital levels. Subpar capital levels were evident across all employee segments, with the most deficient levels recorded within the productive worker category, where a substantial 70% held low to very low capital levels.

Merely around 40% of the workforce constituted the essential core and capital of the company. The company could rely on the active participation of approximately 40% of its managerial and administrative staff, whereas the engagement of production employees was only around 30%.

An examination of the various forms of social capital revealed diminished levels across all dimensions. However, the lowest levels were observed within the realm of structural capital, which encompassed the organization of cooperation, employee communication patterns, and the weakened state of interpersonal relationships. Consequently, significant issues were identified concerning the overall organizational structure of the company and the configuration of its internal network of relationships.

Conclusion 4. The analyses of the levels of social capital and the characteristics of the examined enterprises allowed us to draw overarching conclusions regarding the correlation between levels of social capital and the specificity (profile) of each company. And so, all of the surveyed companies with high levels of social capital were large entities (production/service companies boasting extensive logistics, trade, and marketing departments) characterized by sound financial health and adopting modern technologies that implemented aggressive innovation strategies. Divergence occurred in their approaches to employee management—from internal service provision (Case Study 1) to business partnership (Case Study 2) to administrative level (a low level; encompassing basic payroll services—Case Study 3). As reported by management boards, Case Studies 1 and 2 encountered minimal social issues; in Case Study 3, however, conflicts among employees and elevated turnover rates among production workers occurred.

The examined companies with diminished levels of social capital belonged to the manufacturing sector, excluding any service-related activities which were instead undertaken by other entities within the parent group. These surveyed companies were of medium size, boasting favorable financial standings and advanced technological capabilities while pursuing assertive, strategic approaches. Notably, there were disparities in their approaches to employee management: Case Study 4 operated as an internal client service provider, while Case Study 5 focused on providing basic payroll services. As per their respective management boards, both companies grappled with challenges involving significant turnover rates among productionworkers, absenteeism, accidents, and internal conflicts between employees and management.

Conclusion 5: Examining the attitudes of managers and owners of the surveyed companies regarding the conducted research revealed a nuanced landscape. On the one hand, business proprietors and board members showcased comprehension of the significance of social capital, acknowledging its profound influence on company operations and overall value. Nevertheless, it is important to note that these acknowledgments often remained mere declarations, as observable actions to manage social capital within the companies were largely absent.

In contrast, middle and lower-level managers exhibited indifference or reluctance, displaying limited interest in recognizing any correlation between social capital and company performance.

Conversely, all surveyed enterprises demonstrated a collective willingness to sustain research efforts. This entails assessing the monetary value of social capital, introducing specific operational measures designed to augment social capital, and another study to measure the level of social capital in subsequent years.

Recommendations

Advancing the measurement of social capital

There exists a widespread consensus that while measuring social capital might be challenging, it remains imperative. This is because it facilitates the formulation of decisions pertaining to strategies aimed at its enhancement. Managers necessitate appropriate tools to ascertain not only the composition but also the extent of this capital. In this regard, the current chapter introduces a novel approach to gauging social capital, enabling the quantification of its levels (high, medium, and low). Furthermore, this approach identifies specific areas within enterprises or professional groups where social capital levels exhibit such variations. By systematically evaluating social capital, it becomes feasible to design investments that effectively mold and cultivate it.

Toward reporting on social capital

The importance of reporting social capital within businesses is growing worldwide. Such reporting confirms how well social goals are being achieved at different levels of management. This reporting can indirectly boost overall social capital levels. Unlike formal financial statements, social capital reports exhibit a diverse range owing to their qualitative and quantitative research methodologies. In addition to numerical data, these reports frequently incorporate visuals such as drawings and diagrams, which not only depict the current state of social capital but also capture the dynamics of its transformations. These narratives often constitute "a story" detailing a company's undertakings. Such a story can be tailored for different audiences, serving purposes such as management reports, stakeholder engagement, etc.

References

Adler, P. S., & Kwon, S. (2002). Prospects for a new concept. *Academy of Management Review*, *27*(1), 17–14.

Baum, F. E., & Ziersch, A. M. (2003). Social capital. *Journal of Epidemiology Community Health*, *57*, 320–23.

Bullen, P., & Onyx, J. (1998). Measuring social capital in five communities in NSW. Center for Australian Community Organizations and Management (CACOM) CACOM Working Paper Series No. 41.

Coleman, J. S. (1988). Social capital in the creation of human capital. *American Journal of Sociology*, *94*, 121–24.

Collier, P. (2002). Social capital and poverty: A microeconomic perspective (in French). In T. Van Bastelaer (Ed.), *The role of social capital in development*. Melbourne: Cambridge University Press.

Daniere, A., Takahashi, L. M., & NaRanong, A. (2002). Social capital and environmental management: Culture, perceptions and action among slum dwellers in Bangkok. In S. Ramaswamy (Ed.), *Social capital and economic development: Well-being in developing countries.* Cheltenham: Edward Eglar.

Falk, I., & Kilpatrick, S. (1999). *What is social capital? The study of interaction in a rural community.* Launceston: Center for Research and Leaning in Regional Australia.

Felkins, P. K. (2002). *Linked communities and social capital. Creating and celebrating community in organizational life.* New Jersey: Hampton Press Inc.

Fukuyama, F. (1997). *Social capital and the modem capital economy. Creating a high trust work place.* New York: Stern Business School.

Gant, J., Ichniowski, C., & Shaw, K. (2002). Social capital and organizational change in high-involvement and traditional work organizations. *Journal of Economics and Management, 11,* 289–328.

Glaeser, E. L., Laibson, D., & Sacerdote, B. (2002). An economic approach to social capital. *The Economic Journal, 112*(483), F437–F458. https://doi.org/10.1111/1468-0297.00078.

Grootaert, Ch., & van Bastelaer, T. (2002). *The role of social capital in development: An empirical assessment.* Cambridge: Cambridge University Press.

Hanifan, L. J. (1916). The rural school community center. *Annals of the American Academy of Political and Social Sciences, 67,* 130–38.

Hofferth, S. L., Boisjoly, J., & Duncan, G. (1999). The development of social capital. *Rationality and Society, 11* (1), 79–110. https://doi.org/10.1177/104346399011001004.

Hofstede, G. (2011). *Cultures and organizations.* Warsaw: THE EUP.

Inkeles, A. (2000). Measuring social capital and its consequences. *Policy Sciences, 33,* 245--268.

Jacobs, J. (1961). *The death and life of Great American Cities.* New York: Vintage Books.

Kawachi, I., Berkman, L., & others. (2000). Social cohesion, social capital, and health. *Social Epidemiology, 174*(7), 174–190.

Knack, S. (2002). Social capital and the quality of government: Evidence from the states. *American Journal of Political Science, 46*(4), 772–785.

Lappe, F. M., & du Bois, P. M. (1997). Building social capital without looking backward. *National Civic Review, 86*(2):119–128.

Laurence, J., & Heath, A. (2008). *Predictors of community cohesion: Multilevel modeling of the 2005 Citizenship Survey.* London: Department for Communities and Local Government.

Leeder, S., & Dominello, A. (1999). Social capital and its relevance to health and family policy. *Australian and New Zealand Journal of Public Health, 23*(4), 424–9.

Leenders, R. Th. A. J., Gaabay S. M., & Fiegenbaum A. (1999). https://www.researchgate.net.

Lin, N. (1999). Social networks and entertainment status. Annual Review of Sociology, 25, 467–487.

Liu, A. Q., & Besser, T. (2003). Social capital and participation in community improvement activities by elderly residents in small towns and rural communities. *Rural Sociology, 68*(3): 343–365.

Loury, G. (1977). A dynamic theory of radical income differences. In *Women, minorities and employment discrimination* (pp. 153–186). Lexington, MA: Lexington Books.

MacGillivray, A., & Walker, P. (2000). Local social capital: Making it work on the ground. In *Critical perspectives*. Oxford: Oxford University Press.

Narayan, D., & Cassidy, M. F. (2001). A dimensional approach to measuring social capital: Development and validation of a social capital inventory. *Current Sociology, 49*(2), 59–102.

Paxton, P. (1999). Is social capital declining in the United States? A multiple indicator assessment. *The American Journal of Sociology, 105*(1), 88–127.

Portes, A. (1998). Social capital: Its origins and applications in modern sociology. *American Review of Sociology, 24*, 1–24.

Putnam, R. (1997). *Democracy in action*. Warsaw: Znak.

Robinson, L. J., Schmid, A. A., & Siles, M. E. (2002). Is social capital really capital? *Review of Social Economy, 60* (1):1–21.

Routledge, B. R., & Amsberg von, J. (2003). Social capital and growth. *Journal of Monetary Economics, 50* (1), 167–193.

Saskatchewan, A. (2005). Social capital as a factor of labor efficiency. *Labor and Social Security, 1* (4), 39–52.

Schuller, T., Baron, S., & Field, J. (2000). Social capital: A review and critique (in French). In T. Schuller (Ed.), *Critical perspectives* (pp. 1–38). Oxford: Oxford University Press.

Serageldin, (1999). *A multifaceted perspective*. Washington, DC: World Bank.

Smith, S. S., & Kulynych, J. (2002). It may be social, but why is it capital? The social construction of social capital and the politics of language. *Politics & Society, 30* (1):149–186.

Stone, L. (2001). *Family, sex and marriage in England 1500–1800*. London: Penguin.

Wacquant, L. J. D. (1989). Towards a reflexive sociology: A workshop with Pierre Bourdieu. *Sociological Theory, 7*(1), 26.

Woolcock, M. (1998). Social capital and economic development. Toward a theoretical synthesis and policy framework. *Theory and Society, 27*(2), 151–208.

6 Future-proof skillset for Industry 5.0

Justyna Berniak-Woźny, Marlena Plebańska, and Monika Sak-Skowron

Introduction

The Fourth Industrial Revolution and its associated megatrends, such as Industry 4.0, Industry 5.0, Economy 4.0, Smart factories, Society 5.0, Sustainable production and consumption (SPC) have brought about significant transformations in human labor dynamics and the requirement for employee competencies (Saniuk et al., 2022). This revolution signifies a change in the approach to industry development, combining new technologies with sustainable social and environmental development, but also the unprecedented pace of these changes causing, inter alia, the convergence of Industry 4.0 and Industry 5.0.

Industry 4.0

The concept of Industry 4.0 originated in Germany between 2011 and 2015, and its vision, both historically and currently, revolves around utilizing new digital technologies in production. Characteristic elements of Industry 4.0 are Big Data and Analytics, Simulations and digital twins, Autonomous robots, Horizontal and Vertical System Integration, Internet of Things (IoT), Machine Learning, Artificial Intelligence, and Cybersecurity. These concepts facilitate communication between intelligent machines, management of production lines by said machines, data-driven decision-making, and resolving production problems with minimal human involvement. These Smart Factories allow for flexible and fast production, dynamic reconfiguration, and optimization of production depending on changes in the business model and consumer behavior. In turn, this leads to increased efficiency, higher quality, and lower costs. Therefore, robotization and automation are progressing at an unprecedented pace. According to the World Robotics report, 517,385 new industrial robots were installed in factories around the world in 2021 alone, reflecting an increase of 31% year-on-year and exceeding pre-2018 pandemic records of robot installations (Salvadorinho & Teixeira, 2023).

DOI: 10.4324/9781003502272-7

Industry 4.0, however, represents a significant threat to employees through diminished task autonomy. The growing use of sensors, analytics, and artificial intelligence will reduce human workers—reducing factory operators to roles scarcely distinguishable from machines and, over time, their elimination by subsequent generations of robots (Turner et al., 2022). That is why the European Union (EU) promotes the idea of Industry 5.0—a vision of connected, innovative production that reinstates the human/employee at the center of business processes and decision-making (Sivarethinamohan et al., 2021).

Industry 5.0

To further advance digital transformation while mitigating the risks associated with Industry 4.0, the European Union proposed the Industry 5.0 concept. This framework "provides a vision of industry that aims beyond efficiency and productivity as the sole goals, and reinforces the role and the contribution of industry to society" and "It places the wellbeing of the worker at the center of the production process and uses new technologies to provide prosperity beyond jobs and growth while respecting the production limits of the planet." (Breque et al., 2021). However, it should be noted that this concept is not replacing Industry 4.0 but is parallel and complementary. Moreover, according to the European Commission (EC), Industry 5.0 aims to take into account the constraints of the planet and respect its natural resources, which is not adequately addressed in Industry 4.0, which focuses on creating cyber-physical systems, not on sustainable development (Salvadorinho & Teixeira, 2023). The EU approach assumes that Industry 5.0 is based on three pillars—sustainability, human-centricity, and resilience.

Industry 5.0 is not limited to "industry" but encompasses every sector and every organization. According to Doyle Kent and Kopacek (2021), Industry 5.0 consolidates the agile, data-driven digital tools of Industry 4.0 and synchronizes them with highly trained humans working with collaborative technology resulting in innovative, personalized, customized, high-value, environmentally optimized, high quality products. In Industry 5.0, humans are regaining the central role with assisted collaborative robots ("cobots") that not only meet customer expectations but also make the work of human workers more advanced and devoid of routine. Industry 5.0 is also understood as a human-machine concept in which employees will play a significant role in the labor market and a thriving production process. The best attributes of humans and machines will be combined, enabling faster digitization of processes through seamless integration of human and machine tasks. In this scenario, robots will not take control of enterprises, which was so feared in the era of Industry 4.0. In Industry 5.0, robots become equal partners, eliminating routine and dangerous tasks and providing the knowledge necessary to make effective decisions in an uncertain and rapidly changing environment.

The Forrester research group takes an additional step. It proposes that manufacturers adopt the "automation triangle," combining the automation capabilities of hardware and software with employees' adaptability, creativity, and resilience. This proposition assumes that repetitive tasks are handled by hardware automation, and software automation performs repetitive data processing and analytics functions. People are free to supervise automation and address issues like sustainability. This approach offers employees many benefits. Releasing human workers from managing current production activities significantly reduces uncertainty and stress, giving them more space for creative activities and increasing autonomy in the workplace. For employers, the benefit is a more motivated, engaged, creative, and innovative workforce. In this context, industry 5.0 means industrial operations focused on employees supported by new breakthrough technologies that promote the synergistic integration of man and machine while improving working conditions, employment, and productivity. Future workplace concepts of Industry 4.0 and 5.0 are redefining work and the workplace. Their main attributes are Mass Customization, Cultural Collaboration, Customer Centric, Cyber-Physical Systems, and Green Computing (Pathak et al., 2019). These features are achieved through, among others: innovative circular products, technical assistance for employees, intelligent automation, open and sustainable innovation, integration with renewable sources, and enhanced supply chain flexibility (Ghobakhloo et al., 2022;).

A hallmark of Industry 5.0 is the cooperation of people and robots, which will determine the nature of the future workplace (Nagy et al., 2022). As noted by Sivarethinamohan et al. (2021), in Industry 5.0, human work, on the one hand, is supported by intelligent devices and machines. On the other hand, people must interact and exchange information with intelligent machines (human-machine cooperation). According to Accenture research, as many as 85% of 500 manufacturing company directors declared that the joint work of employees and robots on production lines had already become standard in 2020 (Grabowska et al., 2022). Imagining a more radical change in contemporary work and its nature is challenging.

A new generation of robots called "collaborative robots" or "cobots" will foster collaboration between humans and the next generation of robots. Cobots are made to operate in tandem with human counterparts and, more importantly, to help humans execute routine tasks (Destouet et al., 2023). Concurrently, employees dedicated to cooperation with robots called "robo-cooperators" or "cobots" will be trained (Doyle Kent & Kopacek, 2021). This emergent category of factory workers is still in its development phase, and our understanding remains limited. Further insights can be gleaned from literature about the operator 5.0 presented as an intelligent and qualified operator who uses his creativity, ingenuity, and innovation, with the support of new technologies and data analyzed by them in the process of making decisions and developing new, innovative and practical solutions to ensure long-term production activities (Kalateh et al., 2022).

Furthermore, robots will extend their influence beyond structured environments such as manufacturing plants and enter people's daily lives, such as hospitals, offices, homes, hotels, etc., as service robots. These robots will emerge in human-inhabited environments where they will coexist alongside humans (Singh et al., 2023). Future work in almost all industries will be based on big data from Internet of Things (IoT) devices. Only the cooperation of machine and human intelligence, i.e., hybrid intelligence, can transform and translate such extensive data sets into actionable insights for business processes. It is noteworthy that hybrid intelligence combines human and machine intelligence, augmenting human intellect instead of replacing it. Hybrid Intelligence capitalizes on human expertise and purposefulness in decision-making and actions, incorporating ethical, legal, and social values. Currently, AI outperforms humans in many pattern recognition and machine learning tasks. Still, it lacks general knowledge of the world, common sense, and human abilities such as Collaboration, Adaptability, Accountability, and Explainability (CARE).

Industry 5.0 will engender the creation of new jobs in smart systems, artificial intelligence and robotics, programming, maintenance, training, planning, repurposing, and inventing the next generation of manufacturing robots (Grabowska et al., 2022). Additionally, the research underscores that 39%–58% of global work activities in operationally intensive sectors like manufacturing, transportation, or retail can be automated. Automation will significantly shift the skill set for tomorrow's jobs (Ellingrud et al., 2020). While manual labor requirements are anticipated to diminish by 30%, the demand for cognitive or technological skills is projected to rise by 30%–50% (Beier et al., 2022). There are also new qualifications and professions, such as Chief Robotics Officer (CRO), device teacher, solution mentor, process controller, robot assistant, machine programmer, mobile robot manager, cyber-physical systems analyst, collaborative operator, device connector, artificial intelligence, and virtual operator (Grabowska et al., 2022).

Such transformation in work and workplace dynamics impel organizations to rapidly change and adapt, particularly with regard to the evolving qualifications and competencies of employees. (Brauner & Ziefle, 2022). Consequently, organizational commitment, collaboration training, organizational culture, talent management, and the introduction of independent projects are essential factors in developing the future workplace (Roth et al., 2022; Sivarethinamohan et al., 2021). However, redefining work and the workplace requires a redefinition of work culture, which is the most critical determinant of a successful digital transformation. Implementing new tools and automating business processes hinges upon a workforce willing and capable of leveraging these tools and methods. Digital organizational culture allows for the development, rapid innovation, and adaptation to the environment and customer needs, as well as maintenance flexibility and preparation of the organization for the challenges of the future (Ghobakhloo et al., 2022; Sivarethinamohan et al., 2021).

Methods

This chapter presents a systematic literature review on skills for work in Industry 5.0. The search was conducted in March 2023 using the Scopus database to find related publications employing the keywords "Industry 5.0" AND "skill*." Authors searched for records with this phrase in the title, abstract, or keywords. The results of these searches contributed to selecting 54 documents that matched the query. Subsequently, authors screened the titles and abstracts, which limited the database to 26 records. As access to the full content of the articles is necessary to conduct the thematic analysis, the base was narrowed to 21 records.

Thematic analysis is a popular qualitative data analysis method that involves reading a dataset and identifying, analyzing, and interpreting defined patterns. The researchers carefully analyzed the eligible publications to find common themes—repeated ideas or ways of addressing the research problem. This method allowed for the analysis of selected 21 articles in terms of proposed skill sets that meet the work and work environment needs in Industry 5.0.

Results

Industry 4.0 and Industry 5.0 parallelly forecast a future where employees must transition from technological to socio-technological production and computer systems. This evolution assumes the cooperation of man and machine, and thus, continue to acquire, update, and retrain their knowledge, skills, and qualifications to ensure ongoing employability (Shanahan & Organ, 2022). The study's findings underscore the significance of skills and competencies corresponding to Industry 4.0 and 5.0 demands. While research is gaining more interest, few authors define a set of skills in accordance with the requirements of Industry 5.0. The analysis of the available research results covered by this chapter shows that these competencies should be defined in three distinct groups: technical, soft, and green.

Technical skills

The European Union argues that digitization provides industry with unprecedented opportunities through digital technologies like artificial intelligence (AI) or robotics that enable radical innovation in the workplace. The optimization of human-machine interaction allows for leveraging the additional value that employees contribute to shop floor production. Digital transformation requires technical skills, as Industry 5.0 is based on advanced digital technologies, automation, and robotization. Carayannis and Morawska-Jancelewicz (2022) emphasize the lack of technical skills is a significant barrier for 36% of manufacturers to maximize their investment in smart factories. Moreover, 57% of industry leaders acknowledge lacking the AI expertise for implementing autonomous and intelligent solutions. Therefore, future work requires such competencies as (Agarwal & Chauhan, 2022; Broo et al., 2022; Carayannis & Morawska-Jancelewicz, 2022; Salvadorinho & Teixeira, 2023):

- deep knowledge of and use of new technologies such as artificial intelligence, machine learning, nanotechnology, robotization, the Internet of Things, augmented reality, and digitalization.
- deep understanding of modern programming or software engineering techniques.
- digital skill, or leveraging existing and emerging technologies for practical business outcomes.
- data science skills.
- connectivity skills.
- cybersecurity manufacturing skills.

These skills can and should be acquired via learning contexts such as mobile technologies, tablets, and smartphone applications (Rojko et al., 2020).

Soft skills

The authors of the analyzed literature concur that the current education system develops inappropriate competencies and that a fundamental change is necessary to facilitate the development of cognitive and non-cognitive skills, commonly referred to as "soft skills." This includes the "4Cs of the 21st Century," which are Critical thinking, Creativity, Collaboration, and Communication (Broo et al., 2022).

As Kalateh et al. (2022) note, Industry 5.0 ushers in an era of socio-technical improvements in which human and collaborative robots (cobots) collaboratively enhance organizational efficiency. In addition to technical proficiencies, this entails the need to develop social, managerial, and interdisciplinary competencies, in particular (Agarwal & Chauhan, 2022; Carayannis & Morawska-Jancelewicz, 2022; Kolade & Owoseni, 2022; Salvadorinho & Teixeira, 2023):

- cognitive and metacognitive skills—critical thinking, creative thinking, self-regulation, adaptation, and open thinking.

- social skills—empathy, cooperation, teamwork, communication and intercultural communication, skills, networking, integration,
- managerial skills—decision-making, problem-solving, conflict resolution, risk management, crisis management, change management, process, and project management, combining engineering and organizational knowledge, planning and organizing.
- analytical thinking skills.
- openness to lifelong learning, striving for continuous improvement, and openness to working with robots.
- entrepreneurship, self-management, initiative, and flexibility.
- leadership and strategic vision.

Green skills

As sustainable development is one of the pillars of Industry 5.0, green skills emerge as a natural facet of future skills. Nonetheless, despite the acknowledgment of the authors on the need for green skills, their broader definition is rarely presented and infrequently included in the curricula. The European Center for the Development of Vocational Training defines green skills as knowledge, skills, values, and attitudes needed to live, develop and foster a sustainable and resource-efficient society (CEDEFOP, 2012). This encompasses the proficiencies required to adapt products, services, and processes to climate change and related environmental requirements and regulations. The European Union has further introduced "GreenComp," a reference framework for sustainability competencies that provides a common foundation for learners and offers guidance for educators, promoting a consensual definition of what sustainability entails as a competence. GreenComp consists of 12 competencies organized into four areas (Bianchi et al., 2022):

- Embodying sustainability values (valuing sustainability, supporting fairness, promoting nature).
- Embracing complexity in sustainability (systems thinking, critical thinking, problem framing).
- Envisioning sustainable futures (futures literacy, adaptability, exploratory thinking)
- Acting for sustainability (political agency, collective action, individual initiative).

Green skills hold significance across diverse industries, sectors, and at all levels of management. Karin Kimbrough, Chief Economist at LinkedIn, highlights that there is no longer a separate green sector today because green jobs are increasingly found in various industries—from renewable energy through finance to transport and the fashion and automotive industries.

In accordance with LinkedIn's Global Green Skills Report 2022, the most desirable green skills are managing the sustainable development of organizations, environmental remediation, occupational health and safety advisory (OSHA), managing climate ecosystems, ecosystems management, environmental auditing, pollution mitigation and waste prevention, sustainable procurement, energy generation, and management.

It should be noted, however, that although green skills transcend industry boundaries, their specific attributes are intrinsically linked to the industry and its impact on the natural environment and the utilization of natural resources.

Conclusions and recommendations

Industry 4.0, introducing digitization, automation, and robotization of entire sectors, has enabled an unprecedented increase in efficiency and productivity. Although it is based on man's innovativeness, it is for a man that it carries a considerable threat related to the loss of jobs and the progressive marginalization of his human roles in the workplace. To address this threat, Industry 5.0 emerges. Industry 5.0 leverages opportunities in digitization and automation, concurrently restoring people to their central and decision-making role and simultaneously placing the digitization process in the context of sustainable social and environmental development meeting the climate and social crisis (Neumann et al., 2022). However, to meet the challenges of Industry 5.0 and prepare staff equipped with the competencies defined in this chapter, it is necessary to revolutionize the education, training, and development systems, specifically:

1 The public and non-public education systems, from primary schools to universities, must rapidly modernize education curricula, adapting them to a greater extent to changing technologies and the needs of the labor market by including digital and green competencies in them.
2 Universities must move away from silo programs focused on one narrow set of competencies and include all three competencies—technical, soft, and green—in their study programs.
3 The importance of lifelong learning should be raised, which is conducive to developing employees' creativity and innovation and the result of talents.
4 Labor market institutions must prepare a system for transferring the workforce from old to new jobs and shorten the adaptation period by preparing an upskilling and reskilling system to acquire industry 5.0 skills.
5 Employers must join the process of employee transformation by improving skills and adapting to new technologies by developing and implementing modern training and development programs.

References

Agarwal, N., & Chauhan, S. (2022). Amplifying employability skills to create co-working space for human and cobots in the E-commerce industry. *Procedia Computer Science, 214*, 1040–1048.

Beier, G., Matthess, M., Shuttleworth, L., Guan, T., de Oliveira Pereira Grudzień, D. I., Xue, B., & Chen, L. (2022). Implications of Industry 4.0 on industrial employment: A comparative survey from Brazilian, Chinese, and German practitioners. *Technology in Society, 70*(2022), 102028, https://doi.org/10.1016/j.techsoc.2022.102028.

Bianchi, G., Pisiotis, U., Cabrera Giraldez, M. (2022). GreenComp—The European sustainability competence framework. In M. Bacigalupo, & Y. Punie(Eds.), *EUR 30955 EN*. Luxembourg: Publications Office of the European Union. ISBN 978–92-76–46485-3, https://doi.org/10.2760/13286, JRC128040.

Brauner, P., & Ziefle, M. (2022). Beyond playful learning—Serious games for the human-centric digital transformation of production and a design process model. *Technology in Society, 71*, 102140.

Breque, M., De Nul, L., & Petridis, A. (2022). *Industry 5.0: Towards a sustainable, human-centric and resilient European industry*. Luxembourg: European Commission, Directorate-General for Research and Innovation.

Broo, D. G., Kaynak, O., & Sait, S. M. (2022). Rethinking engineering education at the age of industry 5.0. *Journal of Industrial Information Integration, 25*, 100311, https://doi.org/10.1016/j.jii.2021.100311.

Carayannis, E. G., & Morawska-Jancelewicz, J. (2022). The futures of Europe: Society 5.0 and Industry 5.0 as driving forces of future universities. *Journal of the Knowledge Economy, 13*(4), 1–27.

CEDEFOP. (2012). *Green skills and environmental awareness in vocational education and training*. Luxembourg: European Centre for the Development of Vocational Training.

Destouet, C., Tlahig, H., Bettayeb, B., & Mazari, B. (2023). Flexible job shop scheduling problem under Industry 5.0: A survey on human reintegration, environmental consideration and resilience improvement. *Journal of Manufacturing Systems, 67*, 155–173.

Doyle Kent, M., & Kopacek, P. (2021). Do we need synchronization of the human and robotics to make industry 5.0 a success story? In *Lecture notes in mechanical engineering* (pp. 302–311). https://doi.org/10.1007/978-3-030-62784-3_25.

Ellingrud, K., Gupta, R. & Salguero, J. (2020). *Building the vital skills for the future of work in operations*. McKinsey &Company. Retrieved from https://www.mckinsey.com/business-functions/operations/our-insights/building-the-vital-skills-for-the-future-of-work-in-operations.

Ghobakhloo, M., Iranmanesh, M., Mubarak, M. F., Mubarik, M., Rejeb, A., & Nilashi, M. (2022). Identifying industry 5.0 contributions to sustainable development: A strategy roadmap for delivering sustainability values. *Sustainable Production and Consumption, 33*, 716–737.

Grabowska, S., Saniuk, S., & Gajdzik, B. (2022). Industry 5.0: Improving humanization and sustainability of Industry 4.0. *Scientometrics, 127*(6), 3117–3144. https://doi.org/10.1007/s11192-022-04370-1.

Kalateh, S., Estrada-Jimenez, L. A., Pulikottil, T., Hojjati, S. N., & Barata, J. (2022, October). The human role in human-centric industry. In *IECON 2022—48th annual conference of the IEEE industrial electronics society* (pp. 1–6). Brussels: IEEE. https://doi.org/10.1109/iecon49645.2022.9968440

Kolade, O., & Owoseni, A. (2022). Employment 5.0: The work of the future and the future of work. *Technology in Society, 71*, 102086. https://doi.org/10.1016/j.techsoc.2022.102086.

Nagy, L., Ruppert, T., Löcklin, A., & Abonyi, J. (2022). Hypergraph-based analysis and design of intelligent collaborative manufacturing space. *Journal of Manufacturing Systems, 65*, 88–103. https://doi.org/10.1016/j.jmsy.2022.08.001.

Neumann, E. M., Vogel-Heuser, B., Haben, F., Krüger, M., & Wieringa, T. (2022). Introduction of an assistance system to support domain experts in programming low-code to leverage Industry 5.0. *IEEE Robotics and Automation Letters, 7*(4), 10422–10429. https://doi.org/10.1109/lra.2022.3193728.

Pathak, P., Pal, P. R., Shrivastava, M., & Ora, P. (2019). Fifth revolution: Applied AI & human intelligence with cyber physical systems. *International Journal of Engineering and Advanced Technology, 8*(3), 23–27.

Rojko, K., Erman, N., & Jelovac, D. (2020). Impacts of the transformation to Industry 4.0 in the manufacturing sector: The case of the US. *Organizacija, 53*(4), 287–305.

Roth, E., Moencks, M., Beitinger, G., Freigang, A., & Bohné, T. (2022, December). Microlearning in human-centric production systems. In *2022 IEEE international conference on industrial engineering and engineering management (IEEM)* (pp. 37–41). Kuala Lumpur: IEEE. https://doi.org/10.1109/ieem55944.2022.9989589

Salvadorinho, J., & Teixeira, L. (2023). Happy and engaged workforce in Industry 4.0: A new concept of digital tool for hr based on theoretical and practical trends. *Sustainability, 15*(3), 2781.

Saniuk, S., Grabowska, S., & Grebski, W. (2022). Knowledge and skills development in the context of the fourth industrial revolution technologies: Interviews of experts from Pennsylvania state of the USA. *Energies, 15*(7), 2677. https://doi.org/10.3390/en15072677.

Shanahan, B. W., & Organ, J. (2022). Harnessing the benefits of micro credentials for Industry 4.0 and 5.0: Skills training and lifelong learning. *IFAC-Papers OnLine, 55*(39), 82–87. https://doi.org/10.1016/j.ifacol.2022.12.015.

Singh, K. J., Kapoor, D. S., Abouhawwash, M., Al-Amri, J. F., Mahajan, S., & Pandit, A. K. (2023). Behavior of delivery robot in human-robot collaborative spaces during navigation. *Intelligent Automation & Soft Computing, 35*(1), 795–810. https://doi.org/10.32604/iasc.2023.025177

Sivarethinamohan, R., Kavitha, D., Koshy, E. R., & Toms, B. (2021). Reimagining future of future by redesigning talent strategy in the age of distraction and disruption. *International Journal of Systematic Innovation, 6*(4), 33–45.

Turner, C., Okorie, O., & Oyekan, J. (2022). XAI sustainable human in the loop maintenance. *IFAC-PapersOnLine, 55*(19), 67–72. https://doi.org/10.1016/j.ifacol.2022.09.185.

7 Exploring workforce skills in Industry 5.0 amid cultural diversity

Agnieszka Knap-Stefaniuk

Introduction

The exploration of employees' skills in changing circumstances is analyzed by many researchers in various contexts (including Acemoglu & Restrepo, 2018; Adel, 2022; Demir et al., 2019; Ernst et al., 2019; Frey & Osborne, 2017; Kolade & Owoseni, 2022; Peters, 2019; Pereira et al., 2020). This topic is significant, particularly in transitioning from Era 4.0 to Era 5.0. According to the author of this chapter, the skills of employees in the perspective of changes related to the 5.0 era are significant in a multicultural working environment. In these settings, managers and employees from different cultures, having different experiences, values, working styles, attitudes, and behaviors, work together in multicultural teams to achieve organizational goals.

Numerous authors (e.g., Elim & Zhai, 2020; Fukuyama, 2018; Grabowska et al., 2022; Grundke et al., 2018; Javaid & Haleem, 2020; Nahavandi, 2019; Pathak et al., 2019) indicate that by the beginning of Industry 5.0, a new business model for modern organizations (with automation systems for humans, robots, and algorithms) will emerge. Inconsequentially, the way in which companies perform various activities and tasks and the skills required of employees to perform professional activities will change. Therefore, the researchers point to the need to study the skills of workers that will be needed in the Industrial Age 5.0 (İşcan, 2021; Paschek et al., 2019). The objective of this chapter is to present the employee skills identified as particularly important in Industry 5.0 and desired by employers in the forthcoming years. This focus is especially underscored by the opinions of managers from different European countries who manage multicultural teams.

The concept of completed interviews is based on the classification of skills discussed in the World Economic Forum Report (Future of Jobs Report, 2020). Combining this classification of skills with the interview results, the author identifies four skill groups that will play a key role in

DOI: 10.4324/9781003502272-8

the future. These are: problem-solving, working with people, technology use and development, and self-management. According to the managers interviewed, intercultural communication, cultural intelligence, and effective networking in multicultural teams will also be important in the forthcoming 5.0 Era.

The following research issue was created in relation to the chapter's goal: What abilities do managers and staff members of multicultural teams see as being especially crucial in the 5.0 era?

Literature analysis and interviews have shown the importance of different skills for workers in the context of the changing and demanding Industry 5.0, especially regarding cultural diversity.

Literature review

Industry 5.0 and skill requirements for workers

Theorists and practitioners are still discussing the effective implementation and use of solutions within Industry 4.0. Concurrently, a new trend of the fifth industrial revolution is already discernible, extending beyond the mere production of goods and services for profit. According to the researchers, Industry 5.0 introduces a new perspective on the industry and necessitates a paradigm shift in mindset and behavior (Broo et al., 2021; Xu et al., 2021).

The concept of Industry 5.0 was first introduced by Michael Rada in the 2015 article "Industry 5.0: From Virtual to Physical" (Yücebalkan, 2020). Since 2017, Industry 5.0 and related changes have been increasingly written about in the literature (Demir & Cicibaş, 2017; Nahavandi, 2019; Paschek et al., 2019; Skobelev & Borovik, 2017; Vaidya et al., 2018). Central to Industry 5.0 is the emphasis on human reintegration into the production process. In this revolution, man and machine collaborate to improve the quality and efficiency of production. Human interaction and artificial intelligence hold paramount significance within Industry 5.0. According to researchers, the Fifth Industrial Revolution is also more environmentally friendly as companies develop renewable energy systems and eliminate waste (Breque et al., 2021; Demir et al., 2019).

Industry 5.0 can be defined as a green and digital technological transformation aimed at fostering sustainable industry practices. It is a greener and more human-oriented version of Industry 4.0. Industry 5.0 is the synergy of humans and robots in the manufacturing process that can be achieved by placing human involvement at the center of an integrated system established by Industry 4.0.

Industry 5.0's key objectives are to provide personalized production and service delivery in human-robot collaboration, supported by algorithms, with a view to building a sustainable economy (Demir et al., 2019).

Table 7.1 **Top ten in-demand skills of 2025, divided into four categories**

Solving problem	*Working with people*	*Technology use and development*	*Self-management*
Analytical thinking and innovation	Leadership and social influence	Technology use, monitoring and control	Active learning and learning strategies
Complex problem-solving		Technology design and programming	Resilience, stress tolerance and flexibility
Critical thinking and analysis			
Creativity, originality and initiative			
Reasoning, problem-solving and ideation			

Source: Own study based on: The Future of Jobs Report (2020).

In line with the European Commission's perspective, the social objective of Industry 5.0, which goes beyond creating jobs and prosperity, is also to focus attention on the fact that production respects the Earth's constraints and prioritizes the well-being of employees within the production process (European Commission, 2021).

In the 5.0 era, automation is forecast to accelerate, and new industrial areas and jobs will emerge. By 2025, it is predicted that 85 million jobs traditionally performed by humans will be automated (Future of Jobs Report, 2020). New jobs, the so-called professions of the future, will require employees to acquire and develop new skills.

Above all, in the era of Industry 5.0, the complexity of cyber-physical systems is anticipated to rise. Employees are expected to engage in more strategic decision-making to solve more intricate challenges. Workers will be managing increasingly complex processes in collaboration with robots, necessitating increasing creativity. Therefore, the development of skills necessary for effective governance and cooperation in the framework of Era 5.0 becomes imperative (Güğerçin & Güğerçin, 2021). The basis for in-depth analysis can be the guidelines developed in the report of The World Economic Forum (Future of Jobs Report, 2020), which presents, among other things, the ten most desirable skills anticipated in 2025. These skills are divided into four categories: problem-solving, working with people, technology use and development, and self-management (Table 7.1).

Table 7.1 provides an overview of the building blocks within the four categories. Category one – problem-solving is very significant. In Industry

5.0, employees will solve more involved problems, necessitating analytical and critical thinking, innovative creativity, and creative exploration in search of new and original solutions.

The second category—working with people, is equally essential, underscoring leadership and social influence. While working with robots and algorithms, employees must also effectively collaborate and communicate with internal and external stakeholders. Leadership roles will focus on building effective teams, team collaboration, employee motivation, and community relations. The third category, technology use and development, is required in the industrial age of 5.0, where work environments require mastering advanced technological skills. Category four: self-management, includes proficiencies tied to active learning, flexibility, resistance, and tolerance to stress. These skills will be essential for finding a new way of working and working efficiently in the evolving dynamics of the forthcoming years (Güğerçin & Güğerçin, 2021).

It should be emphasized that Era 5.0 challenges employees regarding their skills requirements and enterprises and Human resources (HR) departments in strategic human resource development management. Developing the potential of human resources will require time and financial investment dedicated to improving all HR management functions, including recruitment and selection, training initiatives, performance evaluation, disciplinary protocols, and methods of rewarding staff.

Employees' cultural diversity: an essential element of contemporary work environments

Employee diversity refers to the simultaneous presence of people emerging from different sociocultural contexts within a single enterprise (Chmielecki & Sułkowski, 2017). Cultural diversity among employees is prevalent in many contemporary organizations today. While it can be viewed as an opportunity for the development of individuals, teams, and organizations, the functioning of multicultural teams and the cultural diversity of employees can be perceived as a reason for mutual resentment and conflict and present challenges in team communication.

Cultural diversity plays a vital role in organizations operating in an international context (Reddy, 2011). Therefore, managers working in multinational companies need to deal effectively with the complexity of management in the context of cultural diversity (Grosse, 2012), especially in the context of changes related to the age of 5.0.

Effective management of multicultural teams requires awareness of the potential benefits of cultural diversity among all employees. These benefits include the ability to act flexibly in an international environment, the ability to adapt quickly to changing conditions in the intercultural environment, and the building of a competitive advantage for the company based on the knowledge and experience of employees who come from different cultures (Knap-Stefaniuk & Burkiewicz, 2019, p. 65). The cultural diversity of organizations makes it easier to adapt to varying market situations, as members of multicultural teams from diverse cultures can approach the problem from different perspectives. In addition, members of such teams learn from each other how to be flexible and how to react quickly to changes, and, what is particularly important, diversity develops creativity and innovation (Chmielecki & Sułkowski, 2017, p.41). It should be stressed that effective management of cultural diversity improves communication between employees from diverse cultures, effectively resolves conflicts, and increases mutual sensitivity to the problems of other multicultural team members.

In multicultural teams, employees can share knowledge and experience, develop their skills, and analyze ideas and solutions that are helpful in achieving the goals of organizations and teams. Cultural diversity, therefore, affects productivity and quality of work (including Chaturvedi, 2022; Cherian et al., 2020; Shrestha & Parajuli, 2021). However, diversity can also give rise to challenges within the functioning of multicultural teams, related, among others, to communication, mutual comprehension, potential ambiguity, complexity, and confusion in diverse situations (Chmielecki & Sułkowski, 2017). Other problems in multicultural groups include a lack of trust, conflict, or misunderstanding, which arise precisely from cultural differences. Unfortunately, these phenomena can adversely affect the attitudes and behavior of employees, their motivation, and the quality of their tasks, disintegrate work and achieve team goals, and often destroy relationships and cooperation, which may be particularly important in the context of challenges with the 5.0 era.

Managing multicultural teams is undoubtedly exposed to more barriers than in a culturally undifferentiated environment. Barriers hinder practical cooperation and create misunderstandings. Among the most frequently identified barriers are biases and stereotypes (Glinkowska, 2016). Intercultural conflicts and problems around intercultural communication undoubtedly have a detrimental effect on both employees and managers. As Rahman underscores, continuous conflicts create a hostile and unhealthy working environment, leading to poor efficiency (Rahman, 2019).

Therefore, modern managers should develop the ability to integrate diversity within cultures and, at the same time, be open to cultural diversity (Herciu, 2014).

Managers must communicate effectively in a multicultural working environment and possess the ability to connect with employees from diverse cultures. They must continuously develop themselves, including an understanding of diverse cultures. They should be characterized primarily by their ability to respect organizational cultural diversity (Glinkowska, 2016).

In multicultural teams, workers originate from disparate cultures. This poses a number of challenges for managers, especially in the face of changes in the 5.0 Era. It is, therefore, worth emphasizing that a lack of understanding of intercultural problems affects every aspect of the organization's functioning (Rahman, 2019). Therefore, managing problems and misunderstandings in multicultural teams should be essential for modern managers. It influences the perception of the strength of the team and the manager who controls it, as well as the effective implementation of the objectives (Pauliene et al., 2019).

Methodology

Sample and data collection

In 2022, the author conducted 12 in-depth interviews among Polish, Spanish, Italian, and Czech managers (3 interviews with managers of each nationality). All the interviews were held in direct meetings (with Spanish, Italian, and Czech managers during research trips abroad). The criteria for selecting managers for interviews were their experience: working in an international company, a minimum of three years as a manager, and managing a team in which employees come from at least three different countries or cultures.

The interviews were qualitative, lasting from 60 to 75 minutes. They were carried out based on an interview scenario developed earlier. It should be emphasized that qualitative studies are characterized by subjectivity but also by a flexible methodological structure, and a small sample in these studies is collected intentionally (Juszczyk, 2013). Interviewees were recruited using targeted selection, which consists of a deliberate choice for testing units that meet specific criteria (Nowak, 2007). The author used one of the non-random sampling methods, i.e., snowball sampling.

Polish managers were interviewed in English and Spanish, and Italian and Czech managers in English. At the beginning of each interview, the managers received information about the research's method and technique, the interview's purpose, and important formal issues, such as the anonymity of the study's results. Interviews were not recorded, and the author took notes during interviews. The research material collected has been subjected to qualitative analysis and, where possible, due to the design of the scenario (research tool), also to quantitative analysis. Table 7.2 presents the characteristics of the respondents.

Table 7.2 Characteristics of survey respondents (managers)

Criterion	*Poland*	*Spain*	*Italy*	*Czech republic*
Age	42–49	38–46	39–44	40–45
Women	2	1	1	1
Main	1	2	2	2
Work experience on a managerial position	6 TO 14	7 TO 12	6 TO 10	8 TO 13
Number of different nationalities	At least 3 nationalities (3 nationalities)	At least 3 nationalities (5 nationalities)	At least 3 nationalities 4 nationalities	At least 3 nationalities (3 nationalities)

Source: Own study based on the interviews with the Polish, the Spanish, the Italian, and the Czech managers (2022)

Data analysis and results

In 2022, detailed interviews with individuals were conducted among Polish, Spanish, Italian, and Czech managers to achieve the following goals:

- Obtain information from managers about their understanding of Industry 5.0/Era 5.0.
- Identify employees' skills (following the World Economic Forum 2020 classifications) that managers believe are particularly important in Industry 5.0.
- Identify the areas of multicultural team management where the skills of employees in Industry 5.0 will be crucial for the effective functioning of the teams and the effectiveness of their achievement of the organization's objectives.
- Getting information from managers on the challenges of developing employees' skills necessary for efficient and effective functioning in organizations (in multicultural teams) in Industrial Age 5.0.

In this chapter, only partial results of the interviews are presented due to the publication volume. Table 7.3 shows the manager's responses to identify the employees' skills, essential in Industry 5.0 (Objective 2 of the study).

As shown in Table 7.3, the most indications (3 responses, managers of all nationalities) were given skills such as complex problem-solving, leadership and social influence, technology use, monitoring and control, technology design, programming, resilience, stress tolerance, and flexibility.

Table 7.3 Managers' responses to the ten most in-demand skills of 2025

Top ten in-demand skills of 2025	*Polish managers*	*Spanish managers*	*Italian managers*	*Czech managers*
Analytical thinking and innovation	2	2	2	3
Complex problem-solving	3	3	3	3
Critical thinking and analysis	3	3	2	3
Creativity, originality and initiative	3	3	2	3
Reasoning, problem-solving, and ideation	3	3	2	3
Leadership and social influence	3	3	3	3
Technology use, monitoring and control	3	3	3	3
Technology design and programming	3	3	3	3
Active learning and learning strategies	3	3	2	3
Resilience, stress tolerance and flexibility	3	3	3	3

Source: Own research based on interviews with managers from Poland, Spain, Italy, and the Czech Republic (2022).

Discussion

For now, a limited number of studies have addressed the relationship between Industry 5.0 and workers' skills (Breque et al., 2021; Paschek et al., 2019). However, the growing interest of researchers in this issue is linked to the impact of workers' skills on the organization's different areas of operation and its relationship with its environment. Nevertheless, researchers point out a growing need to analyze and study the skills needed in the 5.0 era (İşcan, 2021; Paschek et al., 2019).

Qualitative research (individual in-depth interviews) conducted by the author in 2022 has enabled the achievement of the intended objectives (in the case of this publication, it is about Objective 2 of the study). The results of interviews conducted with Polish, Spanish, Italian, and Czech managers provided the answer to the research question formulated in the introduction. From the perspective of industrial challenges, managers from four European countries have identified complex problem-solving, leadership and social influence, technology use, monitoring and control, technology design, programming, resilience, stress tolerance, and flexibility as the most critical skills of employees.

Particular skills useful in culturally diverse workplaces in Industry 5.0 indicated by managers who took part in the interviews also include intercultural communication (all managers), cultural intelligence (all managers), and practical relationship building in multicultural teams (all managers).

Research limitations and recommendations for future research

The only limitation of this research is the number of managers participating in the interviews. This research can be expanded to encompass more managers to achieve an even more in-depth analysis. This limitation could be addressed by gathering primary data from a more extensive and diverse group of managers from different European countries focusing on managing multicultural teams.

Additional avenues for research should include the acquisition of information on the issues being analyzed from employees of different nationalities and the development of employee skills issues around manager skills necessary for managing multicultural teams in Industry 5.0.

Conclusions

Industry 5.0 requires a shift in companies' approaches toward their employees. Emerging business models in the forthcoming years will necessitate an analysis in the context of the 5.0 challenges of the new skills of the workforce necessary for rapid and efficient operation. The upcoming transition will require significant changes in staff skills, organizational frameworks, manager attitudes, and management practices, especially in multicultural teams. To keep pace with the technological revolution, employers and HR departments should devise fresh strategies for human resources management, especially in employee training and skills development.

The need for diverse cultures to coexist within a single organization, a single team, means that it is also becoming crucial to build relationships between employees and between managers and employees based on values such as understanding, respect, and acceptance. Proficiencies in intercultural communication, cultural intelligence, and building practical cooperation in multicultural teams will be fundamental.

Employee skills are pivotal in shaping relationships in a culturally diverse working environment. Particularly in Industry 5.0, employees' skills will be crucial to building efficient and effective operations of culturally diverse teams, advancing the organization's international objectives, and enhancing its competitiveness in the global market.

References

Acemoglu, D., & Restrepo, P. (2018). Low-skill and high-skill automation. *Journal of Human Capital, 12*(2), 204–232. https://doi.org/10.1086/697242

Adel, A. (2022). Future of industry 5.0 in society: Human-centric solutions, challenges and prospective research areas. *Journal of Cloud Computing, 11*(1), 40. https://doi.org/10.1186/s13677-022-00314-5.

Breque, M., De Nul, L., & Petridis, A. (2021). *Industry 5.0. Towards a sustainable, human-centric and resilient European industry.* Luxembourg: Publications Office of the European Union. https://doi.org/10.2777/308407.

Broo, D. G., Kaynak, O., & Sait, S. M. (2021). Rethinking engineering education at the age of Industry 5.0. *Journal of Industrial Information Integration, 25*, 100311. https://doi.org/10.1016/j.jii.2021.100311

Chaturvedi, K. (2022). Impact of cross-cultural diversity on organizational productivity. *International Journal of Research in Engineering, Science and Management, 5*(2), 70–73. https://www.ijresm.com. ISSN (Online): 2581–5792.

Cherian, J., Gaikar Vilas, B., & Paul Raj, P. (2020). The role of cultural diversity and how they impact work team performance. *International Journal of Mechanical Engineering and Technology, 11*(9), 11–22. https://doi.org/10.34218/IJMET.11.9.2020.002.

Chmielecki, M., & Sułkowski, Ł. (2017). Methods of intercultural management. In L. Sułkowski, & G. Ignatowski (Eds.), *Communication and intercultural management. Contemporary legal and organizational challenges* (pp. 37–53). Warsaw: Difin SA,

Demir, K. A., & Cicibas, H. (2017). Industry 5.0 and a critique of Industry 4.0. In *4th international management information systems conference in Istanbul* (pp. 1–11), Peter Lang GmbH, Internationaler Verlag der Wissenschaften, Turkey.

Demir, K. A., Döven, G., & Sezen, B. (2019). Industry 5.0 and human-robot co-working. *Procedia Computer Science, 158*, 688–695. https://doi.org/10.1016/j.procs.2019.09.104.

Elim, H. I., & Zhai, G. (2020). Control system of multitasking interactions between society 5.0 and industry 5.0: A conceptual introduction & its applications. *Journal of Physics: Conference Series, 1463*(1), 012035. DOI 10.1088/1742–6596/1463/1/012035.

Ernst, E., Merola, R., & Samaan, D. (2019). Economics of artificial intelligence: Implications for the Future of Work. *IZA Journal of Labor Policy, 9*(1). https://doi.org/10.2478/izajolp-2019-0004.

European Commission. (2021). Industry 5.0: Human-centric, sustainable and resilient. *Publications Office.* https://data.europa.eu/doi/10.2777/073781.

Frey, C. B., & Osborne, M. A. (2017). The future of employment: How susceptible are jobs computerization. *Technology Forecasting and Social Change, 114*, 254–280. https://doi.org/10.1016/j.techfore.2016.08.019.

Fukuyama, M. (2018). Society 5.0: Aiming for a new human-centered society. *Japan Spotlight, 27*(5), 47–50.

Future of Jobs Report. (2020). *World economic forum.* Retrieved from: https://www.weforum.org/reports/the-future-of-jobs-report-2020.

Glinkowska, B. (2016). Managing teams in the multicultural organizations. *Journal of Intercultural Management, 8*(2), 55–69. https://doi.org/10.1515/joim-2016–0009.

Grabowska, S., Saniuk, S., & Gajdzik, B. (2022). Industry 5.0: Improving humanization and sustainability of Industry 4.0. *Scientometrics, 127*(6), 3117–3144. https://doi.org/10.1007/s11192-022-04370-1.

Grosse, Ch. U. (2012). Intercultural management cases for the business language class. *Innovation and Tradition, 17*, 81–90. http://docs.lib.purdue.edu/gbl/vol17/iss1/7.

Grundke, R., Marcolin, L., The Linh Bao Nguyen, & Squicciarini, M. (2018). Which skills for the digital era?: Returns to skills analysis. *OECD Science, Technology and Industry Working Papers, 9*, 1–37. Paris: OECD Publishing. https://doi.org/10.1787/9a9479b5en.

Güğerçin, S., & Güğerçin, U. (2021). How employees survive in the Industry 5.0 Era: In-demand skills of the near future. *International Journal of Disciplines Economics & Administrative Sciences Studies, 7*(31), 524–533. https://doi.org/10.26728/ideas.452.

Herciu, M. (2014). A synergistic approach of cross-cultural management and leadership style. *Journal of International Studies, 7*(2), 106–115. https://doi.org/10.14254/2071-8330.2014/7-2/9.

İşcan, E. (2021). An old problem in the new Era: Effects of artificial intelligence to unemployment on the way to Industry 5.0. *Journal of Yaşar University, 16*(61), 77–94. https://doi.org/10.19168/jyasar.781167.

Javaid, M., & Haleem, A. (2020). Critical components of Industry 5.0 towards a successful adoption in the field of manufacturing. *Journal of Industrial Integration and Management, 5*(3), 327–348. https://doi.org/10.1142/s2424862220500141.

Juszczyk, S. (2013). *Badania jakościowe w naukach społecznych szkice metodologiczne*. Katowice, Poland: Wydawnictwo Uniwersytetu Śląskiego.

Knap-Stefaniuk, A., & Burkiewicz, Ł. (2019). Contemporary managers in intercultural management. *Przedsiębiorczość i Zarządzanie, 20*(6), 63–75.

Kolade, O., & Owoseni, A. (2022). Employment 5.0: The work of the future and the future of work. *Technology in Society, 71*, 102086. https://doi.org/10.1016/j.techsoc.2022.102086.

Nahavandi, S. (2019). Industry 5.0-A human-centric solution. *Sustainability, 11*(16), 4371. https://doi.org/10.3390/su11164371.

Nowak, S. (2007). *Metodologia badań społecznych* [*Methodology of social sciences*]. Warsaw: PWN.

Paschek, D., Mocan, A., & Draghici, A. (2019). Industry 5. 0–The expected impact of next industrial revolution. In *Management knowledge learning international conference*, Piran, Slovenia: ToKnowPress, 125–132.

Pathak, P., Pal, P. R., Shrivastava, M., & Ora, P. (2019). Fifth revolution: Applied AI & human intelligence with cyber physical systems. *International Journal of Engineering and Advanced Technology, 8*(3), 23–27.

Pauliene, R., Diskiene, D., & Matuzevičiūtė, E. (2019). Complex approach on multicultural teams management & leadership. *Journal of Educational and Social Research, 9*(2), 8–16. https://doi.org/10.2478/jesr-2019-0008.

Peters, M. A. (2019). Beyond technological unemployment: The future of work. *Educational Philosophy and Theory, 52*(5), 485–491. https://doi.org/10.1080/00131857.2019.1608625.

Pereira, A. G., Lima, T. M., & Santos, F. C. (2020). Industry 4.0 and society 5.0: Opportunities and threats. *International Journal of Recent Technology, 8*(5), 3305–3308. https://doi.org/10.35940/ijrte.D8764.018520.

Rahman, A. (2019). Leadership for multicultural teams: The challenges in managing cross-cultural conflicts. *Journal of Economics, Business and Management*, *7*(1), 41–44. https://doi.org/10.18178/joebm.2019.7.1.578.

Reddy, A. (2011). Cultural dimensions & impact on performance management. *International Journal of Multidisciplinary Research*, *1*(6), 300–311.

Shrestha, P., & Parajuli, D. (2021). Impact of workforce diversity on employee performance. *International Journal of Management*, *12*(2), 86–95. https://doi.org/10.34218/IJM.12.2.2021.009

Skobelev, P. O., & Borovik, S. Y. (2017). On the way from Industry 4.0 to Industry 5.0. *International Scientific Journal Industry 4.0*, *2*(6), 307–311.

Vaidya, S., Ambad, P., & Bhosle, S. (2018). Industry 4.0- A glimpse. *Procedia Manufacturing*, *20*, 233–238. https://doi.org/10.1016/j.promfg.2018.02.034.

Xu, X., Lu, Y., Vogel-Heuser, B., & Wang, L. (2021). Industry 4.0 and Industry 5.0—Inception, conception and perception. *Journal of Manufacturing Systems*, *61*, 530–535. https://doi.org/10.1016/j.jmsy.2021.10.006

Yücebalkan, Ö. Ü. B. (2020). Endüstri 4.0'dan Endüstri 5.0'a geçiş sürecine genel bakış. *Pearson Journal of Social Sciences & Humanities*, *5*(9), 241–250. http://dx.doi.org/10.46872/pj.181.

8 Leadership skills development

A study of leading MBA program

Arif Erkol, Jan Fazlagić, and Agnieszka Rzepka

Introduction

Leadership skills are among those competencies that might not seamlessly integrate into a rigid academic framework. Achieving success as a scholar doesn't necessarily hinge on excelling at leadership skills. Consequently, universities may encounter challenges in furnishing students with high-quality leadership education solely relying on their own faculty resources. Tushman et al. (2007) emphasize that business schools are increasingly becoming detached from practical application, and that their research often lacks real-world applicability. In a changing educational landscape, policymakers and state governments are increasingly urging educational institutions to showcase clear strategies, prudent resource utilization, and successful student education outcomes (Green, 2012).

The primary objective of this chapter is to assess the current landscape of leadership education by examining the curricula of MBA programs. The findings of this research can be particularly insightful for business leaders interested in executive education. When seeking to understand the latest trends and advancements in the field, it is advisable to turn to industry leaders. Considering the prestige and high expectations, coupled with substantial tuition fees, of top-tier MBA programs, the curriculum content of these programs can serve as a valuable indicator of the skills, including leadership skills, most sought after by both employers and candidates today.

This chapter commences by focusing on the significance of MBA education and outlining its benefits, as well as the reasons driving its value for candidates and graduates. Subsequently, we present the outcomes of our examination of curricula from leading MBA programs. In our analysis, we explore the role of leadership within these programs (whether dedicated leadership courses are included), delve into the core content elements when available, and highlight any unique and distinctive features. The chapter concludes with a comprehensive discussion.

DOI: 10.4324/9781003502272-9

The value of MBA education

The initiation of MBA programs traces back to Harvard University in Cambridge, MA, which established its MBA program at the Harvard University Graduate School of Administration in 1908. Historically, the MBA education landscape was dominated by U.S. universities, where the first MBA courses were launched. Among the top ten 2021 global MBA programs listed in The QS Global MBA Rankings 2021, six belong to the U.S., one to the UK, and two to France (Linda, 2021). Vassilev (2019) observes the emergence of reputable Asian B-schools that are increasingly competitive with their Western counterparts. Leadership education programs have long been an integral part of higher education offerings in prominent business and economics universities worldwide. The executive education movement originated in universities to provide advanced management training to experienced, mature, and highly motivated individuals (Crotty and Soule, 1997).

The value of MBA education is assessable through both quantitative and qualitative measures. A prominent financial indicator is the salaries of MBA graduates. Postgrad.com (2021) reports that MBA graduates earn salaries twice as high as those with "ordinary" university degrees. Papanatos (2021) suggests that the investment in an MBA course can be recouped within four years post-graduation. Many of the analyzed business schools provide compelling data to encourage enrollment. For instance, Wharton MBA graduates had a median annual base salary of $150,000 in 2019, consistently the highest among all MBA programs. Additionally, those with an MBA degree can expect to earn 28% more than counterparts without an advanced degree (Wharton, 2021). Qualitative indicators of MBA education value include enhanced career progression and improved management performance (Lewis, 1992; Mihail and Elefterie, 2006). Kirkpatrick (2020) highlights that MBA graduates (class of 2020) experience an average starting salary $20,000 higher than those with an undergraduate business degree.

Several sources, including the websites of leading business schools (Postgrad.com, 2021; Papanatos, 2021; Wharton, 2021; DeGraca, 2021), provide compelling reasons for pursuing an MBA course:

- personal freedom: An MBA equips graduates with knowledge and practices essential for managing their own businesses and attaining independence.
- better career opportunities: MBA courses encompass a wide range of topics such as finance, human resources management, marketing, communication, and more. These courses offer elective options to align personal interests with learning opportunities, and the acquired skills can be applied across various industries (DeGraca, 2021).

- networking: Collaborating with motivated, goal-oriented peers provides opportunities for forging friendships and initiating new business ventures. MBA graduates may become ideal business partners.
- flexibility: Many MBA programs offer online or part-time options, allowing students to combine professional commitments with university education.
- personal development: Most studied MBA curricula incorporate unique learning components uncommon in regular BA and MA programs. Many of the business schools, though not all, go to great lengths to distinguish their learning experiences from traditional university education, often involving experiential learning and study visits. Abundant social interactions make MBA courses distinct and enriching for personal growth.
- credibility: An MBA diploma, especially from a reputable institution, is a source of pride for graduates and a signal to potential employers. Spence's "Job Market Signaling" theory (1973) suggests that employers are willing to pay higher wages for more skilled workers. A university degree like an MBA diploma reduces information asymmetry between the graduate and the employer. The increased credibility's value extends globally, offering international career opportunities. For some, obtaining an MBA from a prestigious program enables employment abroad that might not be feasible with a less renowned university's MA degree. An MBA can serve as a distinctive factor when applying for high-level positions, especially when faced with numerous candidates.
- development of Specific Skills: MBA programs can help graduates overcome personal weaknesses and barriers hindering them from realizing their aspirations. Such programs contribute to narrowing skill gaps among graduates. For instance, numerous MBA courses emphasize honing communication skills, training students to become persuasive and impactful speakers, masters of language, proficient in delivering effective and exceptional presentations, among other attributes. Increased confidence is identified as a significant non-financial benefit of earning an MBA degree (DeGraca, 2021). Skills like strategic thinking, enhanced creativity, self-discipline, and improved time management are cultivated during MBA programs (DeGraca, 2021).

The absence of "leadership skills" in the aforementioned list could imply that leadership is perceived as an instrumental skill for attaining other objectives, particularly career advancement. Nevertheless, a study conducted by Grzęda and Miller (2009) among MBA students unveiled that leadership ranked among the top three most crucial reasons for pursuing an MBA degree:

1. "Will broaden my perspective of business"
2. "Will provide me with new ways of thinking about the world"
3. "Will enable me to be a more effective leader"

Recognizing the significant value, high expectations, and global popularity of MBA programs, we specifically focused our attention on the development of leadership skills within these programs. One of the foremost challenges in executive education is to effectively balance academic rigor and real-world relevance, as highlighted by Van de Ven and Johnson (2006). It is worth noting that all the business schools we examined implement distinct recruitment procedures to carefully select their candidates. As aptly noted by Lockhart (2013), mere participation by executives in educational programs does not inherently equate to the creation of executive education.

Research methodology

Our primary research question was: "What is the role of leadership skills and competencies in the MBA programs offered by top business schools?" To select the MBA programs for our study, we utilized two rankings:

1 2022 Best Business Schools by U.S. News, and
2 Top 10 MBA Programs in the World 2021 (https://www.topmba.com/mba-rankings/full-time-mba-rankings-global/top-10-mba-programs-world-2021).

In addition, we expanded our sample to incorporate two other institutions: the Oxford Executive Leadership Programme and the Cambridge Advanced Leadership Programme, considering the distinguished reputation of these two universities. Our sample includes the global top five in the specialization category of leadership, as outlined by QS Global 200 Business Schools. This list comprises only five schools, in contrast to other specializations. The schools included are as follows (Dhoul, 2021):

1 Harvard Business School
2 Wharton Business School
3 INSEAD
4 London Business School
5 Stanford GSB

Six of the best MBA programs in the US also hold positions within the World Top Ten rankings, with Stanford securing the top spot in both lists. Our analysis covered the top 36 programs in the US Ranking, where some of them were tied for the same positions. In total, our sample encompassed 42 business schools. For a few programs, leadership education information was not available. We consider the absence of such information as noteworthy, illustrating that not all prominent MBA programs are inclined to share their leadership course content.

In our study, we aimed to address the following specific research questions concerning the leadership component in the examined MBA courses:

1 Is there at least one leadership course in the curriculum? We examined the existence and quantity of leadership courses offered within the curriculum. It's noteworthy that a few MBA programs did not include such a course in their core course list.
2 What are the main themes and topics conveyed in the course descriptions? We assessed the extent of elaboration and the succinct descriptions of the courses within the curriculum.
3 What sets the course(s) apart in terms of uniqueness or originality? Does it distinguish itself from other MBA courses in the realm of leadership education? We examined specific features and original keywords that are absent or scarcely present in other courses' descriptions (e.g., "wisdom," "leadership capital," etc.). Conversely, some of the non-original/standard keywords would include phrases like "developing a vision of the future" and "motivating people." The presence of non-original keywords doesn't necessarily denote a lower course quality, but in this study, we were particularly focused on innovation and fresh perspectives in leadership education. Additionally, we believe that the inclusion of innovative content signifies an inventive approach to curriculum development by the school's management team.

Table 8.1 presents our findings.

Discussion

Based on the information presented in Table 8.1, the following observations can be made:

1 Seven out of forty-two business schools do not offer specific leadership courses within their MBA programs, or at least such courses are not visible on their websites. The absence of a dedicated "leadership" course does not necessarily mean that leadership skills are not developed; it may signify a lower priority given to them.
2 Several schools have introduced specialized programs within their MBA courses, such as the Leadership Laboratory at Stanford, Off-Campus Leadership Seminar at HEC Paris, Global Leadership Assessment for Managers (GLAM) at London Business School, The Transformational Leadership Program at IE Business School, Leadership Development Programme at INSEAD, and The Johnson Outdoor Experience at Cornell University.

Table 8.1 A review of the content of core courses in MBA programs of the leading MBS business schools

Business school	*Is "Leadership" included as a separate/distinct course?*	*Main themes related to leadership skills (some of them are direct quotes)*	*Distinctive features*
Stanford University	Yes	Strategic Leadership—setting an organization's strategic direction, aligning structure to implement strategy, and leading individuals within the firm Leadership Labs—"Why would someone follow me?"—students receive feedback about their approach to leadership Rather than offer a single model of leadership, this course entails a set of experiences from which students derive their own model of leadership. Managing Groups and Teams	Leadership Laboratory—the course is experiential
University of Pennsylvania (Wharton)	Yes	Leadership: Foundations of Teamwork and Leadership—developing future personal leadership style and capabilities. Management Communication: Speaking and Writing	Teamwork and Leadership Simulation
University of Chicago (Booth)	Yes	Leadership Exploration and Development—exploring oneself as a leader and building strategies for lifelong learning and growth. Leadership Capital	experiential course Wisdom as a learning goal Establishing a point of view on the leadership themes that matter most to each student

(*Continued*)

Table 8.1 (Continued)

Business school	*Is "Leadership" included as a separate/distinct course?*	*Main themes related to leadership skills (some of them are direct quotes)*	*Distinctive features*
Northwestern University (Kellogg)	Yes	Leadership in Organizations—the course provides students with the social science tools needed to solve organizational problems and influence the actions of individuals, groups and organizations. It prepares managers to understand how to best organize and motivate the human capital of the firm, manage social networks and alliances, and execute strategic change. This is accomplished through knowledge of competitive decision making, reward system design, team building, strategic negotiation, political dynamics, corporate culture and strategic organizational design.	Manage social networks and alliances
Harvard University	Yes	Leadership and Organizational Behavior (LEAD)—the course consists of three modules: (1) teams, individuals, and networks; (2) how managers become effective leaders; (3) a model for strategic career management	Human side of enterprise Establishing productive relationships successful leaders in action
HEC Paris	Yes'	Enabling you to step back, assess and transform your leadership style' The Science of People in Organizations Predicting the behavior of individuals, groups and organizations	Innovative approach such as „The Science of People in Organizations Off-Campus Leadership Seminar The annual two day seminar, which brings together participants from all five EMBA tracks, is specifically designed to help improve your team-leadership skills through a series of increasingly difficult tasks supervised by leadership experts The Off-Campus Leadership Seminar's physical and mental challenges

London Business School	Yes	Decision Making Strategies for Leaders	Global Leadership Assessment for Managers (GLAM)
IE Business School	Yes	The program focuses on your needs, taking you on a path of personal growth to develop your desired skills a deep understanding of oneself, before addressing the individual team member, the broader team and ultimately the organization as a whole. TLP begins with a pre-program assessment of your leadership style and finishes with a personalized six-month action plan that you create in order to hold yourself accountable and increase your success. Students are assigned a Leadership transformational leadership skills to thrive in the VUCA world. Leading High Performing Teams Authentic Communication Assessment & Development Creating a Leader Vision Leading through Emotions Agile Thinking	The Transformational Leadership Program (TLP) designed to transform experienced managers into business leaders who can design, drive and manage change by expanding their mindsets and skills. Compared with many other programs the leadership program is extremely elaborate and rich with innovative topics
INSEAD	Yes	Observing, understanding and leading behavior in organizations Leadership Communication Foundations a personal "tool-kit" of techniques for effective communication	Understanding "communication intelligence" for leaders Leadership Development Programme (LDP) is a unique feature of the INSEAD EMBA
Massachusetts Institute of Technology (Sloan)	Yes	The only course with "leadership" in it is Communication for Leaders. Students focus on the writing and speaking skills necessary for a career in management in this course. Leadership and Personal Effectiveness Coaching acts as a lab component to Communication for Leaders	Strong focus on communication skills of leaders Emphasis is on both individual and team communication

(*Continued*)

Table 8.1 (Continued)

Business school	*Is "Leadership" included as a separate/distinct course?*	*Main themes related to leadership skills (some of them are direct quotes)*	*Distinctive features*
Columbia University	Yes	Lead: People, Teams, Organizations—the course is designed to get students to the next level in their careers.	Emphasis is on the practical classroom experiments "The assumption is that their careers have peaked at the point where their technical expertise and IQ can take them; their future success requires getting the ordinary people around them to do extraordinary things"
University of California—Berkeley (Haas)	Yes	Leading people—motivating and influencing people Leadership Communication—the fundamentals of public speaking in today's business environment	No relevant information available
Yale University	Yes	The Executive—this course consists of series of interdisciplinary cases structured to describe challenges faced by leaders of organizations Workforce—the purpose of the course is to enhance the student's capability as a manager and leader to take actions that align employees' actions with organizational goals and objectives Power and Politics—diagnosing the true distribution of power in organizations, implementing skills that build cooperative networks, influencing others, and expand one's sources of power	Leadership is explained from the three perspectives the executive workforce and power and politics. Strong emphasis on case study method

Dartmouth College (Tuck)	Yes, partly	The most relevant to leadership is the course on strategy. This course offers the "essential" tool-kit of the executive involved in the strategy process—the key ideas, concepts, and tools that are necessary to properly exercise strategic leadership. The course is divided into two parts. The first focuses on the strategy problem at the business unit level. The second part of the course focuses on the challenge of managing multiple business units.	The "essential" tool-kit of the executive
New York University (Stern)	Yes	Business Ethics/Law—the course tackles professional responsibility and encourages students to think critically about the broader context and consequences of the decisions they make as managers Leading Through Change—the course delves into the histories and emerging theories of business and the definitions and practices engaged in "diversity," "equity," "inclusion Leadership in Organizations Leadership—the course focuses on the design of organizations and on how managers can make organizations more effective by maximizing the performance of their members	Emphasis on the ethical side of leadership Diversity and inclusion as business assets
Duke University (Fuqua)	Yes	The program includes two courses on Leadership Communication and additionally, Leadership, Ethics & Organizations	Three courses with the word "leadership," strong emphasis on communication
University of Michigan—Ann Arbor (Ross)	Yes	Leading People and Organizations—the course prepares students to lead high-performing, successful groups and organizations and seeks an understanding of human behavior to enhance management practice	Influencing others without relying on formal power and authority How to build and utilize one's social capital

(Continued)

Table 8.1 (Continued)

Business school	*Is "Leadership" included as a separate/distinct course?*	*Main themes related to leadership skills (some of them are direct quotes)*	*Distinctive features*
University of Virginia (Darden)	Yes	Management Communication—this course gives students the guidance and hands-on experience that will allow them to communicate effectively as managers and leaders Leading Organizations—this course helps students cultivate mind-sets, use tools to influence behavior in organizations and build skills in understanding their strengths and weaknesses as leaders	Adopting adopt a global mind-set
Cornell University (Johnson)	Yes	Orientation Retreat—the Johnson Outdoor Experience (J.O.E.) is an orientation retreat in the beautiful Finger Lakes region. This includes team-building challenges Leadership Skills Program—supplemental half-day and whole-day workshops throughout the academic year in order to enhance and accelerate your leadership development. Leadership Expeditions—designed to give students the opportunity to go through the Johnson leadership learning cycle of instruction, experience, and review multiple times in an intensive, condensed time frame. Expeditions include trips to Patagonia, the Adirondacks, and the United States Marine Corps Base Quantico.	The Johnson Outdoor Experience (J.O.E.) Leadership Expeditions

Carnegie Mellon University (Tepper)	Yes	Incoming students begin their leadership education by completing an assessment. Afterwards, students meet one-to-one with a leadership coach for detailed feedback and tips for enhancing their leadership skills. Tepper MBA students have myriad touchpoints with the Accelerate Leadership Center throughout their time in the program. Each encounter with Accelerate is designed to enhance leadership skills, adding more tools to a students' toolkit, and preparing them for their internships and the working world Deploy Through Practice—specific behavioral opportunities, ranging from internships and jobs to student club leadership roles and team-based initiatives give our students ample opportunities to develop their leadership skills Students who wish to fully immerse themselves in their leadership development join the Leadership Development Certification program	Very extensive leadership program with ongoing support from a special organizational unit Dual focus on strategic analytics and leadership development Accelerate Leadership Center
University of Southern California (Marshall)	Yes	Communication for Management—this course is designed to start one's development as a true leader Foundations of Your Professional Value—this course is designed to help students put into place the foundational knowledge Organizational Behavior and Leadership— leading, managing, and working collaboratively with others	Three courses on leadership skills Application of clinical research in leadership Foundations of Your Professional Value

(*Continued*)

Table 8.1 (Continued)

Business school	*Is "Leadership" included as a separate/distinct course?*	*Main themes related to leadership skills (some of them are direct quotes)*	*Distinctive features*
University of California—Los Angeles (Anderson)	Yes	Leadership Foundations—the course includes Self-evaluation of leadership strengths and weaknesses • Individual problem-solving and decision-making • Goal-setting and goal-achievement skills • Peer coaching and teamwork • Individual career development • Executive communication and negotiation skills	Students learn to recognize cognitive biases in themselves and in others and gain skills to re-calibrate group dynamics in order to achieve better results. These skills are taught experientially through participatory simulations and post hoc analyses
University of Texas—Austin (McCombs)	Yes	There are three courses linked to leadership (no description is provided): Leading People and Organizations Creating and Managing Human Capital Managing Corporate Diversification and Renewal	No information available
University of North Carolina—Chapel Hill (Kenan-Flagler)	Yes	Ethical Leadership—the course addresses ethical and moral aspects of leadership using cases, exercises, simulations, and readings. Additionally, students will assess and articulate their personal value system, and learn to think critically about numerous psychological, organizational, and cultural processes that complicate ethical decision-making. Leading and Managing—the course covers core concepts and theories from psychology and organizational science, which form the knowledge base for leadership and management skills	Ethical Leadership Assessing and articulating their personal value system

Georgetown University (McDonough)	Yes	There are three courses linked to leadership (no description is provided): Ethical Leadership Leadership Communications Leading Teams for Performance and Impact	No information available
University of Washington (Foster)	Yes	"Leadership, communication, presentation skills, networking, and teamwork [...] are incorporated throughout the entire UW MBA Program": 1st year: Assessment, Career Coaching And Practice 2nd Year: Mentoring And Polishing, Packaging Accomplishments Core study teams are carefully selected to ensure a strong and diverse set of skills, experiences, and perspectives: Required Leadership Development course—offers an opportunity to develop teamwork skills Collaboration and Conflict Seminar—provides tools to promote success in teams and resolve issues that may arise Leadership Fellows—second-year MBA students mentor first-year study teams to help them improve communication and working relationships Case Competitions—develops team presentation, analysis and collaboration skills during required case competitions	Career coaches will give you feedback on mock interviews Strong emphasis on evaluation in a variety of professional skill areas ongoing training in leadership communication guidance from a second-year MBA to help members reach optimal teamwork performance The ethic of interactive learning, teamwork, and peer support forms the foundation for every aspect of the Foster MBA experience Core study teams

(*Continued*)

Table 8.1 (Continued)

Business school	*Is "Leadership" included as a separate/distinct course?*	*Main themes related to leadership skills (some of them are direct quotes)*	*Distinctive features*
Indiana University (Kelley)	Yes	There is one course: Leadership Development. Additionally, students working in Core Teams complete class projects, build the functional skills in the First-Year Academy and work in Student Clubs expand their network and skills.	Me, Inc. Explore yourself—your strengths, your weaknesses, what you add to your team and organization—so you can better lead others Building the functional skills in the First-Year Academy
Vanderbilt University (Owen)	Yes	There is two courses: Leading Teams and Organizations and Management Communication. No additional information is provided	No information available
Rice University (Jones)	Yes	There is one course: Leadership 1st year. No additional information is provided	No information available
Emory University (Goizueta)	No information available	–	–
University of Florida (Warrington)	No information available	–	–
Georgia Institute of Technology (Scheller)	Yes	There are three courses linked to leadership: Leading People and Organizations—the course provides a focused understanding the inputs and processes in predicting individual and group behavior within organizations Business Communications—this course provides future leaders and managers with the communication skills that enable them to sell themselves and their ideas.	The course descriptions indicate good quality content, including both bot theoretical and the practical, but lacking any distinctive features

		Leadership Development Workshop—this course is designed to integrate the student's work experience into their development as a leader. It will enable students to prepare themselves to become leaders of organizations, to exercise leadership, and to embark on paths of personal leadership development.	
University of Minnesota—Twin Cities (Carlson)	No information available	–	–
Arizona State University (W.P. Carey)		There is only one course: Leadership & Teamwork—the course prepares students to become more comfortable and skilled at dealing with ambiguous situations by building skills in design thinking, improvisation, super-flexibility, sense-making, rapid execution.	Leading transformative change Experiential learning activities to experiment and recalibrate in real time, building immediate applied confidence and finesse
Brigham Young University (Marriott)	Yes	There is only one course: "Leadership." No additional information is provided.	No information available
University of Texas- Dallas	No information available	–	–
Pennsylvania State University—University Park (Smeal)	No	"Our graduates carry the honor code and its responsibilities with them into the business world. Other leadership elements include intensive communications training, a focus on teamwork, and a structured 360-degree survey program, which helps you objectively identify strengths and opportunities for growth and sets the stage for individualized leadership coaching?	Very unstructured information on the leadership skills development

(*Continued*)

Table 8.1 (Continued)

Business school	*Is "Leadership" included as a separate/distinct course?*	*Main themes related to leadership skills (some of them are direct quotes)*	*Distinctive features*
University of Rochester (Simon)	No information available	–	–
University of Notre Dame (Mendoza)	No information available	–	–
Washington University in St. Louis (Olin)		According to the university's website: „The EMBA program provides one of the most academically comprehensive curricula in the country.Courses and residencies focus on leadership development.Timely updates—such as the Business of Policy: DC Immersion, offered in partnership with public-policy think tank the Brookings Institution; courses on analytics and data-driven decisions; a team-based consulting project." The course includes 3 leadership-related modules: Module 1: Values-Based/Data-Driven Leadership—GO! Week Module 2: The Power of Purpose—Mid Program Module 3: Your Leadership Development Journey—Capstone	Data-Driven Leadership The involvement of the public tank the Brookings Institution Lessons in Leadership and Character from the Top examines these situations by bringing in notable leaders

Oxford Executive Leadership Programme	Yes	Module 1: Effective leadership: Leading for high performance Reflect on the relationship between effective leadership and performance in organizations. Module 2: The job of the leader: Envisioning and engaging Module 3: The job of the leader: Choosing and connecting Learn about decision-making and connection as two core activities of leaders. Module 4: Leading with power and influence Module 5: Leading teams for effective performance Module 6: Strategies and models for leading change Module 7: Mastering complexity and plurality Explore strategies to manage the complexity inherent in leadership. Module 8: Reflect on your purpose as a leader Establish alignment between your personal purpose and the purpose of your organization	Well-structured program broken down onto 8 parts Reflection on one's purpose as a leader
Cambridge Advanced Leadership Programme	Yes	Three major themes span the program, weaving discussion and debate into a coherent fabric on which participants can chart their next moves. Making sense of turbulent times Building organizational and personal capabilities Leading into the future The Cambridge ALP will encourage students to examine their personal management style.	Innovative, holistic approach, clearly distinct from the offered of US business schools

Source: Own elaboration

3 Business ethics is present in a few programs, with New York University (Stern) having the most comprehensive approach in its curriculum.
4 Despite the growing importance of Industry 4.0 and Artificial Intelligence, only one school offers a module specifically focused on "Data-Driven Leadership."
5 Some schools follow traditional approaches in organizing leadership skills within their curriculum, such as "Leading Teams and Organizations" and "Management Communication" at Vanderbilt University (Owen) or "Leading People and Organizations," "Creating and Managing Human Capital," and "Managing Corporate Diversification and Renewal" at the University of Texas—Austin (McCombs). Others break away from academic tradition with unique course names like "The Executive," "Workforce," and "Power and Politics" at Yale University or "Foundations of Your Professional Value" at the University of Southern California (Marshall).
6 Many programs emphasize experiential learning, exemplified by Columbia University, Cornell University, and Stanford University's Leadership Labs.
7 The term "Communication" is a commonly used keyword present in 18 programs.
8 "Change" is a less common keyword, appearing in only 4 programs.
9 Some schools introduce unique words and concepts in their course descriptions, such as "wisdom" and "leadership capital" at the University of Chicago.
10 Surprisingly, "diversity and inclusion," despite their relevance, are present in the curriculum of only one program: New York University.
11 Developing specialized programs like the ones at the Accelerate Leadership Center (Carnegie Mellon University) or the Orientation Retreat—the Johnson Outdoor Experience (Cornell University) provides a distinctive competitive advantage in marketing MBA programs.
12 Personalization of educational offerings is evident in most programs through elective courses. Additionally, several MBA programs emphasize evaluating leadership skills and potential at the program's outset, as seen at the University of Washington and IE Business School.
13 According to Lockhart (2013), the quality of business schools' education involves a compromise between the needs of the research community and the business community. The majority of the analyzed courses have managed to strike this balance. The fact that a few business schools do not provide comprehensive insights into their curricula indicates that they too are not solely inward-focused.
14 The example of the Cambridge Advanced Leadership Programme demonstrates that there is not a single approach (as promoted by many US schools) for developing engaging and intriguing course content.

Some candidates may be drawn to Cambridge's holistic approach toward global issues.

15 The main focus of curriculum development teams in these business schools seems to be on introducing innovative methods for leadership skills development. In terms of academic content, the curricula remain relatively conservative, avoiding "buzzwords" or management fads.

Executive education programs, along with the business schools that have been their primary drivers, have directed their focus toward understanding not only the dynamics of business but also the dynamics of executives themselves (Moulton and Fickel, 1993). According to Lockhart (2013), a successful executive program comprises three interrelated attributes:

- A strong affiliation with an academic discipline.
- A notable national (and possibly international) standing, either for the discipline or for a prominent member of the university staff in that field.
- An established external client or client group to anchor the program, or a well-defined strategic plan for acquiring such clients.

All of the analyzed programs fulfill the above criteria. They have maintained a strong connection with academic disciplines, possess esteemed reputations, and are supported by robust client bases.

Conclusions

In this chapter, we have presented a comprehensive review of the primary benefits of participating in MBA programs. The extensive list of advantages and financial incentives offered to MBA graduates suggests that this segment of adult education will remain an integral component of higher education institutions' offerings. In our study, we analyzed the content of 42 MBA programs to identify courses designed to cultivate leadership skills. The majority of the analyzed schools indeed offered such courses within their curricula. Based on our analysis, we have drawn a set of conclusions. These conclusions hold relevance for various stakeholder groups:

1 Prospective candidates seeking the most suitable MBA program.
2 University leadership aiming to align with the latest trends in executive education.
3 Business school faculty, who should strive for both research excellence and practical impact (Tushman et al., 2007).
4 Scholars in the field of leadership.
5 Business leaders with an interest in executive education.

As previously mentioned, our research highlights that the focus in leadership education is shifting toward more innovative methods of skill development, rather than solely enhancing academic knowledge in the realm of leadership. Furthermore, our study uncovers that leadership themes are not universally incorporated across all the analyzed programs.

References

USNews. (2023, February 11). *2022 Best Business Schools*. U.S. News & World Report LP. https://www.usnews.com/best-graduate-schools/top-business-schools/mba-rankings.

Crotty, P. T., & Soule, A. J. (1997). Executive education: Yesterday and today, with a look at tomorrow. *Journal of Management Development, 16*(1), 4–21. https://doi.org/10.1108/02621719710155445.

DeGraca, M. (2021, February 11). *16 benefits of an MBA*. Berkeley MBA Blog. https://blogs.haas.berkeley.edu/the-berkeley-mba/16-benefits-of-an-mba.

Dhoul, T. (2021, March 22). *Top business schools for leadership development*. TopMBA.com. https://www.topmba.com/mba-programs/top-business-schools-leadership-development.

Green, M. F. (2012). *Measuring and assessing internationalization*. Association of International Educators, Washington.

Kirkpatrick, L. (2020). *Is an MBA degree really worth it?* https://hbr.org/2020/12/is-an-mba-degree-really-worth-it (Accessed 25.8.21).

Lewis, J. (1992). Student expectations on the Open Business School's MBA. *Management Development Review, 5*(2). https://doi.org/10.1108/eum0000000000671.

Linda, M. (2021). *Top 10 MBA programs in the world 2021*. https://www.topmba.com/mba-rankings/full-time-mba-rankings-global/top-10-mba-programs-world-2021 (Accessed: 25.8.21)

Lockhart, J. C. (2013). *Executive education: Can it be too good?* DigitalCommons@Kennesaw State University. https://digitalcommons.kennesaw.edu/jee/vol12/iss1/5/?utm_source=digitalcommons.kennesaw.edu%2Fjee%2Fvol12%2Fiss1%2F5&utm_medium=PDF&utm_campaign=PDFCoverPages.

Mihail, D. M., & Antigoni Elefterie, K. (2006). Perceived effects of an MBA degree on employability and career advancement: The case of Greece. *Career Development International, 11*(4), 352–361. https://doi.org/10.1108/13620430610672559.

Moulton, H. W., & Fickel, A. A. (1993). *Executive development: Preparing for the 21st century*. New York: Oxford University Press.

Papanatos, P. (2021). *Six reasons to get an MBA degree*. Benedictine University. https://online.ben.edu/programs/mba/resources/six-reasons-to-pursue-an-mba-degree.

Postgrad.com. (2021). *Top 10 Reasons to Do an MBA*. https://www.postgrad.com/business-schools/mba-program/reasons-to-study-an-mba/ Accessed 25.08.21.

Spence, M. (1973). Job market signaling. *The Quarterly Journal of Economics, 87*(3), 355. https://doi.org/10.2307/1882010.

Tushman, M. L., O'Reilly, C., Fenollosa, A., Kleinbaum, A. M., & McGrath, D. (2007). RelevanceandRigor: Executive education as a lever in shaping practice and research. *Academy of Management Learning & Education, 6*(3), 345–362. https://doi.org/10.5465/amle.2007.26361625.

Van De Ven, A. H., & Johnson, P. E. (2006). Knowledge for theory and practice. *Academy of Management Review, 31*(4), 802–821. https://doi.org/10.5465/amr.2006.22527385.

Vassilev, V. (2019, November 27). *The global MBA market today.* Access MBA. https://www.accessmba.com/articles/view/the-global-mba-market-today.

Wharton. (2021). *Should I get an MBA?* MBA Program. https://mba.wharton.upenn.edu/why-get-an-mba.

9 Exploring soft factors

Job crafting and the dynamics of diverse workforce teams

Grażyna Bartkowiak and Agnieszka Krugiełka

Introduction

Assuming that the currently emerging trends in organizational development lead to the concept of Economy 5.0, particularly the experience economy (Glinka & Kostera, 2016), the significance of intra-organizational collaboration gains particular importance. This collaboration translates into productivity, individual agency, satisfaction, and a high quality of life for all market participants (which is widely acknowledged in integrated theory).

At the core of this study lies the assumption that, for professional development within an organization, an individual should feel like a significant entity capable of shaping their work environment in accordance with their preferences, interests, and competencies. Therefore, the focus of this chapter is on the subject of job crafting and the importance of agency in work as a factor that influences the functioning of diverse workforce teams.

This study explores how job crafting manifests within different project teams of Polish academic teachers operating in both on-site and virtual environments. It seeks to understand the operational dynamics of diverse project teams and determine if there is a noticeable correlation between the extent of job crafting and the evaluation of team performance.

The study utilizes the Job Crafting Questionnaire (JCQ) developed by Slemp and Vella-Brodrick, the adapted Job Shaping Questionnaire by Kasprzak et al., and Patrick Lencioni's Syndrome Evaluation Questionnaire. A total of 137 participants from project teams of Polish academic teachers and international employees in the IT industry, operating within on-site and virtual teams, took part in the study. Despite the fact that the issue of job crafting has been the subject of numerous studies, there is a lack of research on the relationship between the ability to shape work and the effectiveness of employee teams. Therefore, it can be expected that the research procedure discussed further will "shed new light" on the functioning of diverse employee teams. Therefore, the research discussed below will shed new light on the functioning of diverse workforce teams.

DOI: 10.4324/9781003502272-10

Exploring diverse perspectives on the concept of job crafting

Over the past few decades, an increasingly prevalent idea in the humanities and social sciences has been advocating that individuals, to foster their own growth, should perceive themselves as the architects of their life choices and actions. They should view the world around them as a canvas for their capabilities and regard their planned and achieved objectives as the outcomes of their intentions.

This acknowledgment of the prerequisites for self-development stems from an individualized perspective on people as employees and members of specific organizations. This perspective emphasizes the pivotal role of the values they generate, forming the foundation for understanding their role in the world. This subjective outlook also involves motivating individuals to enhance their awareness not just of their place in the world but also to encourage self-reflection, which entails recognizing their values, goals, and preferences, identifying their interests, and striving to find their niche within the world—whether it be in a community, culture, or workplace that meets their needs. An individual aware of their capabilities has a higher likelihood of experiencing a sense of agency in their life and is capable of developing themselves in a way that, through their creativity, contributes not only to the advancement of the organization they belong to but even to the progress of civilization (Obuchowski, 2002).

In contrast to the presented subjective approach, the objective perspective assumes that the values acknowledged in the world should be traced back to social institutions, including the organizations to which individuals belong. The conduct and demeanor of an individual within an organization are favorably appraised when they align with the immediate needs of the organization. However, this approach primarily benefits the organization in the short run. It limits the potential for personal development, transforming individuals into passive entities who merely assess themselves through the lens of criteria established by others representing the organization. Consequently, their capacity to innovate dwindles, hindering their ability to become creators of change. Depriving oneself of the capacity to detach from external evaluations is a process that can ultimately result in learned helplessness, eroding the initiative for innovative action. This trajectory contributes to the conventional Tayloristic categorization of individuals linked to the organization into decision-makers and implementers (to avoid the word "robots").

The coexistence of both approaches gives rise to several challenges. One of these challenges revolves around the discrepancies between the emerging subjective paradigm, with values and goals shaped by individuals, and the established expectations for behavior within organizational structures. This misalignment persists despite employees having their own expectations that may not always align with the standardized procedures within organizations.

On the other hand, an extensive body of literature indicates that the dominance of a subjective behavioral pattern becomes a prerequisite for effective human functioning within societies, economies, and the concurrently labeled post-industrial culture. The requirements of this cultural work model and organizational functioning are based on the assumption that higher employee productivity, enhanced product and service quality, and, importantly, greater job satisfaction and well-being depend not only on the rapid adoption of new technologies, their rationalization during implementation, swift modifications, shifts, and replacement with new technologies but also on the creative potential and personal initiative of employees at all levels of the organizational structure. In summary, individualism replacing collectivism emerges as the desired pattern of life aspirations for members of various organizations and employees.

One manifestation of individualism is the customization of performed work, with its external form being the behaviors of "job crafting," which have been considered in the literature for just two decades. This term was introduced into practice and theory by two researchers, Wrześniewski and Dutton (2001). It is defined as a way of shaping work by the employee and involves actions aimed at adapting it to one's own preferences, motivations, and passions. In the subject literature, job crafting refers to the physical and cognitive modification of activities and tasks during the employee's work, giving it a personal dimension. At that point, the work performed becomes proactive and individualized. It results from an internally adopted, non-imposed strategy (bottom-up strategy), leading to changes in task structure, relationships, and the perception of work (Berg et al., 2010, p. 179).

This concept is understood as a process in which employees adjust and modify their work in three ways: (1) altering the scope and nature of tasks in relation to formal requirements, (2) modifying their interpersonal relationships at work (including their scope and nature, such as maintaining email contacts beyond purely formal interactions), and (3) making cognitive changes by altering their perception of work-related goals and life goals, recognizing specific tasks as tedious but important due to the nature of the job.

Job crafting is not an episodic behavior; rather, it constitutes a certain process that often involves systematic and repetitive actions. Modifications can simultaneously affect all three mentioned forms of behavior, but their intensity may vary (Bartkowiak & Krugiełka, 2018; Krugiełka, 2019). Specific changes in the task domain (structural form) do not always entail specific changes in the area of interpersonal relationships or the perception of performed work. This model will be utilized for the empirical research discussed in the methodological section of the chapter.

Other authors emphasize that the mentioned task modification stems from employees' ingenuity and leads them to pursue goals aligned with their own preferences, motivational drive, and passion (Tims et al., 2012, p. 173). From an employee's perspective, job crafting not only involves modifying professional tasks but also, as a result, enhances stress resilience and increases job satisfaction (Berg et al., 2008). Zhang and Parker (2019) highlighted that job crafting involves conscious action related to job characteristics, excluding external reinforcements (such as compensation). A characteristic of this model is its focus on job resources and demands. On the other hand, the concept presented by Bindl et al. (2019) emphasizes promotive and preventative forms of shaping tasks, relationships, thinking about work, and necessary skills. In their opinion, the concept includes two distinct forms of shaping tasks, relationships, work mindset, and skills: promotion-focused and prevention-focused (Bindl et al., 2019, p. 608). Kooij et al. (2017) view the main idea of job crafting as individuals striving to fit their job by aligning them with their preferences, motivations, and passions. According to Kasprzak et al. (2017, pp. 460–461), job crafting behaviors occur in three stages. The first stage involves motivation to change one's work. The second stage typically entails the employee recognizing the possibilities available to them due to the nature of the job. In the third stage, the employee applies job crafting to their work. In their view, job crafting is a derivative of individual disposition and situational factors. Individual dispositions refer to the specifics of cognitive processes, flexible thinking, and proactivity. Situational factors are linked to job characteristics and the specific organization (such as task structuring, procedural rigidity or flexibility, and levels of autonomy). Thus, job crafting (as illustrated in Table 9.1) represents the outcome of striving to maintain a balance between employee characteristics and predispositions, along with the possibilities associated with work organization and tasks to be completed within that organization.

In summary of the aforementioned concepts, it becomes evident that there is a variation in the understanding of job crafting and its constituent elements. Consequently, these theoretical frameworks can be categorized based on whether they center around the thinking-action perspective or the increasing-avoiding perspective. Some authors even encompass both viewpoints (Hu et al., 2020).

One of the more noticeable distinctions involves the inclusion (or omission) of negative actions involving avoidance, reduction, or withdrawal from certain work aspects. Additionally, the underlying motives behind job crafting are portrayed differently. Various researchers identify different driving forces, such as the need to lower job demands, enhance personal resources (Tims et al., 2012), or align employees with their work (Kooij et al., 2017, 2020; Wrześniewski et al., 2013). However, all these actions serve a common goal, which is to improve working conditions and the quality of employees' lives.

Table 9.1 Selected definitions of job crafting

Authors	*Definition*	*Components*
Wrześniewski and Dutton (2001)	"physical and cognitive changes that individuals make within the task or relational boundaries of their work" (Wrześniewski & Dutton, 2001, p. 179) and "actions taken by employees to shape and redefine their work" (Wrześniewski & Dutton, 2001, p. 180)	Task crafting, relational crafting, cognitive crafting
Tims et al. (2012)	"Changes that employees can introduce to align their job demands and job resources with their own abilities and needs" (Tims & Bakker, 2012, p. 174)	Increasing structural resources, increasing social resources, increasing challenging demands, decreasing hindering demands.
Zhang and Parker (2019)	Volitional, conscious, and intentional changes in inherent job characteristics (not in its external aspects like salary and not during leisure time) undertaken by employees engaged in jobs with specific tasks (not self-employed) with the aim of improving their own work, taking place within an area accepted by supervisors and colleagues (not requiring additional permission), with a lasting (or semi-permanent but not temporary) effect (Zhang & Parker, 2019, p. 128).	Behavioral crafting increasing resources; behavioral crafting increasing demands; cognitive crafting increasing resources; cognitive crafting increasing demands; behavioral avoidance in the category of resources; behavioral avoidance in the category of demands; cognitive avoidance in the category of resources; cognitive avoidance in the category of demands.
Bindl et al. (2019)	Actions undertaken by employees to shape and redefine their work (Wrześniewski & Dutton, p. 180; Bindl et al., 2019, p. 605)	Two distinct forms of crafting tasks, relationships, work mindset, and skills: promotion-focused and prevention-focused (Bindl et al., 2019, p. 608)
Kooij et al. (2017)	"Changes initiated by an individual within the boundaries of their job tasks aimed at enhancing alignment with the job by adapting it to their own preferences, motivations, and passions" (Kooij et al., 2020, p. 1)	Shaping work to align it with the employee's strengths, interests, and personal development

Source: Own study based on Kapica and Baka (2022, pp. 431–433).

Team and models of its effectiveness

Currently, employee teams have become essential for the effective execution of tasks and projects. A team is defined as a group in which individuals share a common goal, and the tasks and skills of each member complement the others' (Adair, 2001, p. 131). Employee teams have become commonplace in today's organizations, building high-engagement environments, aiding organizational evolution and its products in highly competitive settings by leveraging employee competencies, recruiting talents, and engaging employees at all levels.

The effectiveness of a team is defined by the outcome achieved through collaborative efforts (Salas et al., 2008). Striving to maintain and enhance team effectiveness is a current challenge for managers, especially in a changing operational environment that also affects employees.

In the contemporary business world, digital transformations have undergone significant and impactful changes over the past few decades, contributing to the development of the concept of virtual teams, where geographically dispersed team members work toward a common goal. However, as the literature suggests, virtual teams often experience more process-related losses than their face-to-face counterparts (e.g., Karunathilaka, 2022).

The models showcased in Table 9.2 exhibit variations in terms of the identified component elements that contribute to team effectiveness. These elements include focused action, trust, individual member capabilities, overall team competencies, leader alignment, and the absence of dysfunctions. Additionally, a distinguishing factor is the interrelationship among these model components and their influence on team effectiveness, along with the management of these relationships linked to group structure, interpersonal dynamics, bond types, product or service nature, team members' competencies, and their motivation to undertake tasks demanding collaborative effort.

When evaluating the attributes of an effective team, as outlined by Katzenbach and Smith (2015), the following prerequisites must be met:

- Pursuit of a challenging goal that engrosses the entire team;
- Establishing of a mutually agreed-upon modus operandi for all members, encompassing meeting protocols, discussions, and schedules;
- Fusion of complementary specialized and interpersonal skills.
- A team size that remains within a limit of 25 individuals;
- Individual commitment from each member to fulfill specific team tasks and assume shared responsibilities, embodying a "one for all, all for one" ethos;
- Responsibility that is founded on collaborative contribution and active involvement in the tasks and cultivating action-driven engagement rather than a mere sense of duty.

Table 9.2 Summary of employee team definitions in relation to their efficacy

Name	*Components*	*Description of the relationship in the model and the impact on the efficiency of the team*
Rubin, Plovick, Fry (1978)	GRPI (goals, roles, processes, relationships)	The GRPI model constructs Maslow's pyramid of needs, but its analysis begins from the top, where each letter in the name, an acronym for Goals, Roles, Processes, and Interpersonal Relations, signifies a crucial aspect. This model emphasizes starting with the team's goals, which evolve through decision-making processes, task establishment, and conflict resolution, resulting in the development of beneficial interdisciplinary relations.
Katzenbach and Smith model (1993)	Focusing on the fundamentals of the team	The Katzenbach model addresses individuals' resistance to transcending their roles and responsibilities, emphasizing taking responsibility for others. Successful teams achieve goals and maintain mutual responsibility, prioritizing teamwork, personal development, and achieved results. Key guiding principles include appropriate skill sets among team members, a high level of responsibility, and member engagement.
Lombardo and Eichinger T7 (1995)	Recognizing and managing essential team elements	The T7 model recognizes five essential elements for effective teams: competent team members, team relationships, problem-solving, leadership, and organizational environment. Optimizing team efficiency involves enhancing each component. For instance, teams should comprise competent individuals possessing traits like openness, supportiveness, action orientation, and a positive personal style. Improving the team's effectiveness entails aligning behaviors with other components, such as fostering relationships, accommodating leadership preferences, and promoting trust and commitment through organizational processes.
LaFasto and Larson (2001)	The dynamics of teamwork and cooperation	This model emphasizes understanding and managing five essential elements or conditions: team members, team relationships, problem-solving, team leadership, and organizational environment. Enhancing each component's effectiveness, such as ensuring the right people with traits like openness, support, action orientation, and positive personal style, contributes to overall team success. Aligning behaviors with other components fosters improved effectiveness, facilitating team success through relationship management, leadership alignment, and organizational support.

(*Continued*)

Table 9.2 (Continued)

Name	*Components*	*Description of the relationship in the model and the impact on the efficiency of the team*
Hackman Model (2002b)	Enabling effective teamwork within a supportive organizational context	In the Hackman model, team effectiveness is predicated on its reality, clear direction, purpose, and a structure enabling action. Effective teams operate within a supportive organizational context with coaching masters facilitating teamwork. Performance indicators include exceeding customer expectations, continual team improvement, and meeting members' learning needs. Clear task delegation and stable membership foster effective teamwork, ensuring task clarity, decision-making authority, and membership stability.
Lencioni model (2012)	Understanding team dysfunction	The Lencioni model identifies five dysfunctions: lack of trust, fear of conflict, lack of commitment, avoidance of responsibility, and inattention to results. Addressing each dysfunction involves understanding its type and level. The model highlights building trust as foundational, leading to desired outcomes. A pyramid metaphor illustrates trust as the base, upon which other dysfunctions are addressed, culminating in achieving results at the pinnacle.

Source: Own study based on Pyszka (2015, p. 48).

Contemporary research on team effectiveness underscores the array of factors shaping their performance. Qualitative investigations conducted within interdisciplinary undergraduate teams underscore the pivotal role of partnership in achieving predetermined team objectives. Effective undergraduate teams transitioned from the pre-cooperative stage to the partnership stage across all other scrutinized dimensions, underscoring the significance of fulfilling initial prerequisites and collectively navigating the team's developmental dynamics to reach elevated levels of partnership in terms of accrued benefits (Kilty & Burrows, 2022). The analysis of the interviews revealed that collaborative learning contributed to higher levels of team collaboration and resonated with the value of this learning approach advocated by other scholars (Magen-Nagar & Shonfeld, 2018). Additionally, team members frequently highlighted in interviews the importance of communication and the heightened uncertainty stemming from its absence during project execution (More et al., 2020; Paletz et al., 2017).

Other research findings related to team effectiveness have emerged from studies conducted among both Turkish and Polish team members, with women serving as leaders (Akkaya & Bagieńska, 2022). These studies have highlighted that interpersonal trust plays a crucial mediating role between the effectiveness of women's leadership and the overall effectiveness of the team. Moreover, these investigations have shed light on how increasing trust in managers contributes to the emergence of team effectiveness and the adoption of agile leadership practices over time.

Research conducted among Chinese participants has explored the factors that contribute to the resilience of project teams when facing various distractions and challenges in turbulent environments (Moore et al., 2020). These studies have highlighted the significant roles of cognitive and social proximity, congruence in cultural values, and knowledge sharing within diverse team configurations (independent and mediating variables). These factors have been identified as crucial in enhancing team resilience and successful task execution, even in challenging circumstances.

Beata Krawczyk-Bryłka (2016) and Ganga Sajeewani Karunathilaka (2022) have conducted noteworthy research regarding virtual teams, shedding light on the substitution of direct interactions with technology-mediated communication as a crucial aspect of functioning within an information society. Notably, Karunathilaka's study explored individual differences impacting employees' adaptation to virtual teams, including age, gender, language proficiency, and IT skills. The study involved 175 private sector employees in Sri Lanka, situated across various global locations during the COVID-19 pandemic. The findings underscored that individual language and technological competencies play a significant role in employees' ability to adapt to virtual teams and effectively communicate within such contexts.

In the context of studying virtual teams, Bennet (2022) emphasizes the utilization of augmented reality, simulation modeling concentrating on processes, and text exploration and analysis as tools for evaluating the efficiency of employee teams within virtual and digital domains. Real-time event analysis and data-driven operational management using artificial intelligence technologies (Adams, 2022; Hollensen et al., 2023; Yeh et al., 2022) are enhancing the virtual workspaces of team members within the 3D economy.

The methodological section of this chapter focuses on Lencioni's model, which warrants a more comprehensive discussion. Lencioni's model highlights the existence and necessity of understanding and overcoming five dysfunctions (Lencioni, 2012, p. 217). The first dysfunction pertains to **a lack of trust within the team**. As conceptualized by the author, trust involves the ability to accurately anticipate the behavior of another team member based on past experiences. The inability to trust leads to **a fear of conflict** and subsequent dysfunction. In such a scenario, open communication and spontaneous discussions about ideas are lacking, and the team confines itself to cautious remarks. The lack of conflict begets **a lack of commitment among team members**, manifested by a lack of motivation to act and the expression of feigned agreement. Due to a lack of commitment, team members cultivate an atmosphere of **evading responsibility**. They hesitate to provide feedback to their peers, an issue that, according to Lencioni, affects team productivity. The inability to enforce individual accountability results in a **disregard for outcomes**. Team members prioritize their personal needs over the collective goals of the team. According to the author, a single dysfunction can contribute to a decline in team effectiveness (Lencioni, 2012, p. 211).

Research methodology

In designing the study, it was hypothesized that teams vary based on the nature of the tasks that demand diverse skill sets, the necessity for interpersonal trust, cultural factors influencing leadership alignment, embraced values, and whether these teams function on-site or in a virtual setting.

Research questions

This study aimed to investigate the following questions:

1 How does job crafting become evident within distinct project teams of Polish academic teachers operating in both on-site and virtual environments?
2 What are the operational dynamics of diverse project teams?
3 Is there a discernible correlation between the extent of job crafting and the evaluation of team performance?

Research tools

The assessment of job crafting was conducted using the Australian Job Crafting Questionnaire, developed by Galvin Slamp and Diana Vella-Brodrik (2013). This questionnaire is built upon the job crafting framework introduced by Wrześniewski and Dutton (2001), encompassing three distinct dimensions of job crafting behaviors: the structural aspect, the interpersonal relationships aspect, and the perception aspect. Despite validation studies being conducted on a relatively modest sample size (N = 180), the instrument showcases robust reliability measures. Cronbach's alpha coefficients for the subscales related to the structural aspect of job crafting, interpersonal relationships aspect, and perception aspect stand at 0.87, 0.83, and 0.89, respectively, with the overall scale exhibiting an alpha of 0.91 (Slamp & Vella-Brodrik, 2013).

The Team Assessment Questionnaire, devised by the author of the model (Lencioni, 2016, pp. 213–216), consists of 15 statements that provide insights into team dynamics. These statements correspond to the presence of distinct categories of five dysfunctions: absence of trust (statements 4,

6, 12), apprehension of conflict (statements 1, 7, 10), lack of commitment (statements 3, 8, 13), avoidance of accountability (statements 2, 11, 14), and disregard for outcomes (statements 5, 9, 15). Respondents are tasked with attributing 1–3 points to each statement. A higher total score (with a maximum of 45 points) denotes a more effective team.

This questionnaire was subjected to reliability testing by the authors of this study, employing Cronbach's alpha coefficient on a sample of 94 managerial professionals from small and medium-sized enterprises. The reliability of the individual subscales ranged between 0.74 and 0.77.

Research sample

The participants for this study were purposefully selected. The study encompassed individuals with higher education who were members of four distinct teams: Polish academic teachers (32), Academic teachers from other countries (32), participants in on-site teams composed of employees from service and commercial enterprises (37), and IT professionals constituting virtual teams (35). The initial two groups comprised academic teachers, while the subsequent two groups consisted of individuals in IT roles. In the case of IT professionals, involvement in the study was associated with activities conducted within postgraduate studies. Participation in the study was voluntary and preceded by the obtaining of informed consent. At any point, study participants could withdraw from completing the questionnaires.

As indicated by the data provided in Table 9.3, the average age of the participants in the study did not exceed 44 years, while the work experience ranged around 12 years.

Research findings

Job crafting and team performance—descriptive statistics

The collected data indicated that among all the analyzed variables, the aspect of shaping one's perception of work received the highest ratings within the participating teams (see Table 9.4). This aspect, alongside the sense of purpose in carrying out the work, pertains to the willingness to embrace

Table 9.3 Respondent characteristics

	N	*Minimum*	*Maximum*	*Average*	*Standard deviation*
Age	137	25	65	43.8978	9.85429
Work experience	137	1	35	11.8832	7.78863

Source: Own elaboration.

Table 9.4 Descriptive statistics pertaining to job crafting

	N	*Min*	*Max*	*Average*	*Standard deviation*
Evaluation of team Performance	137	15	54	29.4818	7.90021
Shaping task	137	10	29	18.9416	4.63802
Shaping work perspective	137	8	30	20.0146	4.88091
Shaping work relationships	137	9	30	19.6569	4.69424

Source: Own elaboration

Table 9.5 Overview of team performance, individual job crafting elements, and final outcomes

Team		*Evaluation of team performance*	*Shaping Tasks*	*Shaping attitude toward work*	*Shaping work relationships*	*Job crafting*
Polish academic teachers	M	32.5625	20.1875	22.9375	20.5313	64.0312
	SD	5.94023	3.93034	3.82637	2.72366	9.71691
Academic teachers from other countries	M	31.375	18.5313	19.1875	18.625	56.0625
	SD	9.40744	4.73139	5.25748	4.91049	12.99116
On-site team	M	27.8947	17.8947	18.5	19.1316	54.7368
	SD	7.81817	5.21323	4.86438	5.8641	14.43847
Virtual Team	M	26.6571	19.3143	19.7429	20.3714	58.5714
	SD	6.85112	4.35736	4.43477	4.40645	11.19949
Total	M	29.4818	18.9416	20.0146	19.6569	58.1971
	SD	7.90021	4.63802	4.88091	4.69424	12.66993

Source: Own elaboration.

challenges and demands associated with the specific tasks undertaken (Berg et al., 2010, p. 179).

As indicated in Table 9.5, and according to Lencioni's framework, the most effectively functioning teams are those composed of Polish academic teachers, followed by international academic teachers and those working abroad. Virtual teams received the lowest ratings. Similarly, within the Polish academic teacher teams, the highest values for individual job crafting elements and the overall test result can be observed, with "shaping work perspective" scoring the highest compared to other job crafting elements. This signifies a strong aspiration to uphold subjectivity in the work of this group, manifested through physical and cognitive adjustments to activities and tasks performed during work, imbuing it with a personalized dimension

(Bartkowiak, 2021, p. 5; Kapica & Baka, 2021, p. 425). This approach results in a more proactive nature of the work and individualization and stems from internally adopted strategies. The relatively higher score in shaping perception within Polish academic teacher teams, followed by virtual teams, might be attributed to a profound sense of purpose in their work.

The numbers above show that the Polish academic teacher teams performed the best, followed by international academic teachers and those working abroad. Virtual teams, on the other hand, had the worst results. Among Polish academic teacher teams, there's a strong trend toward customizing their work, with "shaping the perspective on work" being the most prominent feature compared to other elements of job crafting. This underscores a pronounced inclination to uphold personal agency among this specific group. It encompasses cognitive and physical adaptations of tasks undertaken in the course of their work, which adds a distinct personalized dimension (Bartkowiak, 2021, p. 5; Kapica & Baka, 2021, p. 425). Consequently, this approach renders the work more proactive, personalized for each person, and one that stems from an internal strategy. The relatively elevated score observed in shaping perception among Polish academic teachers and virtual teams may be rooted in a profound sense of meaning connected to their job.

The comparison of individual job crafting elements between and within groups (found in Tables 9.6 and9.7) also highlights "shaping attitude toward work" as a distinguishing factor among the groups.

On the other hand, conducting multiple comparisons among each group and the other groups demonstrates the uniqueness of Polish academic

Table 9.6 Team-specific job crafting components

		Sum of squares	*df*	*Medium square*	*F*	*Relevance*
Shaping Tasks	Between groups	101.567	3	33.856	1.595	0.194
	Within groups	2823.966	133	21.233		
	Total	2925.533	136			
Shaping attitude toward work	Between groups	385.035	3	128.345	5.979	0.001
	Within Groups	2854.936	133	21.466		
	Total	3239.971	136			
Shaping relationships at work	Between groups	86.894	3	28.965	1.324	269
	Within groups	2909.982	133	21.88		
	Total	2996.876	136			

Source: Own elaboration.

Table 9.7 Comparative analysis of attitude formation toward work among academic teachers in different teams with Bonferroni test

Dependent variable	*(I) Team*	*(J) Team*	*Average gap (I–J)*	*Standard error*	*Relevance*
Shaping attitude toward work	Polish academic teachers	Foreign academic teachers	3.75000*	1.15828	0.009
		On-site	4.43750*	1.11162	0.001
		Virtual	3.19464*	1.13318	0.033
	Foreign academic teachers	Polish academic teachers	-3.75000*	1.15828	0.009
		On-site	0.6875	1.11162	1
		Virtual	-55536	1.13318	1
	On-site team	Polish academic teachers	-4.43750*	1.11162	0.001
		Foreign academic teachers	-0.6875	1.11162	1
		Virtual Team	-1.24286	1.08545	1
	Virtual team	Polish academic teachers	-3.19464*	1.13318	0.033
		Foreign academic teachers	0.55536	1.13318	1
		On-site	1.24286	1.08545	1

Source: Own elaboration.

teacher teams, particularly regarding their level of job crafting and how they perceive their jobs. In this context, the attitude toward work and how work is viewed among Polish academic teachers stand out significantly compared to the other teams. This distinction, similar to the one described earlier, could be attributed to a stronger sense of purpose in their work. This sense of purpose likely stems from the esteem given to teachers in the Polish context, their ability to overcome the obstacles that the job presents, and their intellectual interests, expressed through specific academic endeavors.

The difference in how academic teacher teams and IT department staff perceive their work could be attributed to academic teachers' greater commitment and involvement in their tasks. Their engagement is further fueled by the opportunity to pursue research efforts, which can serve as an additional source of job fulfillment.

Team and its performance evaluation

Team performance assessment and its type

Statistical analysis revealed variations in the evaluation of the performance of each team participating in the study. As seen in Table 9.8, research indicates

Table 9.8 Evaluation of team performance: analysis of variance (ANOVA)

Evaluation of team					
	Sum of squares	*df*	*Average square*	*F*	*Relevance*
Among groups	793.365	3	264.455	4.571	0.004
Inside Groups	7694.84	133	57.856		
Total	8488.204	136			

Source: Own elaboration.

Table 9.9 Comparative analysis of performance differences among academic teacher teams (Bonferroni test)

(I) Team	*(J) Team*	*Average difference (I–J)*	*Standard error*	*Relevance*
Polish academic teachers	Academic teachers from other countries	1.1875	1.90158	1
	One-site	4.66776	1.82497	0.07
	Virtual team	5.90536*	1.86038	0.011
Academic teachers from other countries	Polish academics	-1.1875	1.90158	1
	One-site	3.48026	1.82497	0.352
	Virtual	4.71786	1.86038	0.074
On-site	Polish academic teachers	-4.66776	1.82497	0.07
	Academic teachers from other countries	-3.48026	1.82497	0.352
	Virtual team	1.23759	1.78201	1
Virtual	Polish academic teachers	-5.90536*	1.86038	0.011
	Academic teachers from other countries	-4.71786	1.86038	0.074
	one-site	-1.23759	1.78201	1

Source: Own elaboration.

a significant difference among groups regarding how their staff assesses team functioning.

As shown in Table 9.8, studies have shown that there is a statistically significant discrepancy between groups in terms of the evaluation of the functioning of the teams by their staff.

Through the statistical analysis presented in Table 9.9, it has been demonstrated that the most notable and statistically significant differences in assessing team performance emerged for teams of Polish academic teachers and virtual teams. These differences could be attributed to the distinctive communication dynamics within virtual teams, where communication

Table 9.10 Correlation analysis: relationships between individual job crafting elements, total test results, and team functioning

		Team Assessment
Shaping Tasks	Pearson correlation	.439**
	Relevance (bilateral)	0
Shaping attitude toward work	Pearson correlation	.291**
	Relevance (bilateral)	0.001
Shaping relationships at work	Pearson correlation	.324**
	Relevance (bilateral)	0
Job Crafting	Pearson correlation	.381**
	Relevance (bilateral)	0

Source: Own elaboration.

is primarily confined to email and digital messaging platforms, lacking the opportunity for direct nonverbal interaction or immediate feedback (Krugiełka, 2019). Moreover, the information gathered within virtual teams might undergo greater modification driven by projection mechanisms as compared to teams that engage in direct communication.

Level of job crafting and team performance evaluation

The research findings revealed a clear linear connection between the individual job crafting elements (and the total test result) and the functioning of the team, as illustrated in Table 9.10.

Regarding task crafting opportunities and the overall test score, the correlation was moderate, while in other cases, it was weak but still statistically significant. These results imply that greater possibilities for structurally tailoring tasks within teams result in enhanced team efficiency.

Team performance evaluation and job crafting: linear regression

What the study also highlighted was that task crafting, considered a structural aspect of job crafting, distinctly influences team performance in a statistically significant manner. This underscores that the opportunity to tailor tasks to one's skills and interests within the framework of project work holds substantial influence, ultimately shaping the team's effective functioning.

Discussion of the results

As highlighted in the earlier sections of this study, human beings need to feel a sense of control over their lives to participate in society actively, find fulfillment in their professional and personal endeavors, and foster personal growth. This sense of control translates into a feeling of agency and effectiveness (Bartkowiak, 2021) when tackling tasks. It encompasses a sense of purpose in carrying out these tasks, deriving satisfaction from social interactions by building and maintaining relationships with others, and possessing the ability to collaborate and cooperate with them (Bandura, 1997). Moreover, individuals must effectively manage challenges and the inherent difficulties associated with employment (Rana et al., 2021). In today's world, teamwork and employee collaboration are critical for successfully completing tasks and projects.

The results obtained from the research have highlighted statistically significant differences in the extent of job crafting between Polish academic teachers and other groups, particularly in changing their views of employment. Similarly, comparable variations were also identified between the on-site IT team and the group of Polish academic teachers. This validates the job crafting concept, particularly its element of shaping the perception of work (as envisioned by its creators). This concept refers to cognitive adjustments that allow for a shift in how work goals are perceived, or the acceptance of tasks that may appear mundane but are important within the job context. Moreover, this shift in the perception of work facilitates a view of it as a challenge, thereby becoming a source of satisfaction (Berg, 2007; Wrześniewski & Dutton, 2001).

The divergence in how work is perceived between academic teacher teams and IT department employees could be attributed to the distinctive personalities and cognitive competencies of academic teachers. Due to the nature of their work, they must go beyond standard procedures and algorithms in favor of heuristic thinking, which is cognitively challenging (Dale, 2015).

The results also showed that the representatives' assessments of the teams' performance varied greatly. Teams of Polish academic teachers and virtual teams, the latter characterized by a limited form of communication, were found to have the most pronounced differences (Gunasekare, 2018; Karunathilaka, 2022).

In the realm of teamwork, it would be difficult to disregard the essential role of knowledge sharing. This practice is particularly impactful when fostered through open communication, shared values, and social closeness, all of which facilitate more effective feedback loops. Consequently, the observed disparities in team performance evaluations based on team types might find their origins in these dynamics.

Furthermore, the research findings also shed light on a correlation between job crafting and the assessment of team performance levels.

This correlation extends to individual components of job crafting (such as shaping tasks, nurturing relationships, and perceiving work) as well as the overall extent of job crafting. This reaffirms the significance of consciously aligning work with employees' competencies, catering to their subjective preferences, especially when functioning within a team (Lencioni, 2016).

Simultaneously, it was revealed that the structural component of job crafting within teams could serve as an effective predictor of their performance assessment. This correlation appears to hold particular significance during the stages of team creation and development.

From a cognitive perspective, the study seems novel, and the practical implications of the findings are encouraging. They highlight the need for the management to take the following actions:

- ensuring an adequate level of autonomy in work, providing employees across various team types with a degree of independence concerning their tasks,
- carefully choosing members of virtual teams based on shared values and social closeness,
- arranging the workstations of on-site teams in accordance with the principles of proxemic communication to promote developing relationships more easily,
- fostering the opportunity for informal interactions that are linked to personalized tacit knowledge,
- creating optimal circumstances and environments for exchanging information, both within virtual and on-site teams.

Like most studies of this nature, the study described in this chapter is not immune to limitations. These include the deliberate selection of participants and the relatively modest size of the research sample. Therefore, it is prudent to conceptualize future investigations with a more expansive research sample. Moreover, when interpreting their findings, the analytical approach should involve juxtaposing distinct categories of team dysfunctions with the specific elements of the job crafting framework.

References

Adair J. (2001). *Business Anatomy. Build a team.* Warsaw: EMKA Studio.

Adams, D. (2022). Virtual retail in the metaverse: Customer behavior analytics, extended reality technologies, and immersive visualization systems. *Linguistic and Philosophical Investigations, 21*(0), 73. https://doi.org/10.22381/lpi2120225.

Akkaya, B., & Bagieńska, A. (2022). The role of agile women leadership in achieving team effectiveness through interpersonal trust for business agility. *Sustainability, 14*(7), 4070. https://doi.org/10.3390/su14074070.

Bandura, A. (1997), *Self-Efficacy: The exercise of control.* New York: Freeman.

Bartkowiak, G. (2021). *Job crafting: Kształtowanie podmiotowości pracy-perspektywa pedagogiki pracy i psychologii organizacji.* Gdynia: Akademia Marynarki Wojennej.

Bartkowiak, G., & Krugiełka, A. (2018). Job crafting wśród nauczycieli szkół podstawowych i gimnazjów. *Prace Naukowe Uniwersytetu Ekonomicznego we Wrocławiu*, 512, 13–25.

Bennet, D. (2022) Remote workforce, virtual team tasks, and employee engagement tools in a real-time interoperable decentralized metaverse. *Psychosociological Issues in Human Resource Management, 10*(1), 78. https://doi.org/10.22381/pihrm10120226.

Berg, J. M., Dutton, J. E., & Wrześniewski, A. (2013). Job crafting and meaningful work. *Purpose and meaning in the workplace* (pp. 81–104). https://doi.org/10.1037/14183-005

Berg, J. M., Wrześniewski, A., & Dutton, J. E. (2010). Perceiving and responding to challenges in job crafting at different ranks: When proactivity requires adaptivity: Adapting to challenges in job crafting. *Journal of Organizational Behavior, 31*(2–3), 158–186. https://doi.org/10.1002/job.645.

Bindl, U. K., Unsworth, K. L., Gibson, C. B., & Stride, C. B. (2019). Job crafting revisited: Implications of an extended framework for active changes at work. *Journal of Applied Psychology, 104*(5), 605–628. https://doi.org/10.1037/apl0000362.

Dale, S. (2015). Heuristics and biases: The science of decision-making. *Business Information Review, 32*(2), 93–99. https://doi.org/10.1177/0266382115592536.

Glinka, B. & Kostera, M. (2016). Archetypy, opowieści archetypiczne i metafory. In Glinka, B. & Kostera M. (red.). *Nowe kierunki w organizacji i zarządzaniu*, (2nd ed, pp. 155–170). Warszawa: Wolters Kluwer.

Hollensen, S., Kotler, P., & Opresnik, M. O. (2023). Metaverse—the new marketing universe. *Journal of Business Strategy, 44*(3), 119–125. https://doi.org/10.1108/jbs-01-2022-0014.

Hu, Q., Taris, T. W., Dollard, M. F., & Schaufeli, W. B. (2020). An exploration of the component validity of job crafting. *European Journal of Work and Organizational Psychology, 29*(5), 776–793. https://doi.org/10.1080/1359432x.2020.1756262

Kapica, Ł., & Baka, Ł. (2021). What is job crafting? Overview of theoretical concepts for work formation, *Medycyna Pracy, 72*(4), 423–437. http://medpr.imp.lodz.pl.

Karunathilaka, G. S. (2022). Virtual team adaptation: Management perspective on individual differences. *Businesses, 2*(2), 118–128. https://doi.org/10.3390/businesses2020008.

Kasprzak, E., Michalak, M., & Minda, M. (2017). Kwestionariusz kształtowania pracy–KKPracy. Polska adaptacja narzędzia. *Psychologia Społeczna, 12*(4), 43.

Katzenbach, J. R., & Smith, D. K. (2015). *The wisdom of teams: Creating the high-performance organization*. Boston, Massachusetts: Harvard Business Review Press.

Kilty, T. J., & Burrows, A. C. (2022). Integrated STEM and partnerships: What to do for more effective teams in informal settings. *Education Sciences, 12*(1), 58. https://doi.org/10.3390/educsci12010058.

Kooij, D. T., van Woerkom, M., Wilkenloh, J., Dorenbosch, L., & Denissen, J. J. (2017). Job crafting towards strengths and interests: The effects of a job crafting intervention on person–job fit and the role of age. *Journal of Applied Psychology, 102*(6), 971. https://doi.org/10.1037/apl0000194.

Krawczyk-Bryłka, B. (2016). Virtual team building—rules and challenges. *Zeszyty Naukowe Uniwersytetu Szczecińskiego. Studia Informatica, 40*, 99–111. https://doi.org/10.18276/si.2016.40-09.

Krugiełka, A. (2019). *Modeling CSR in relation to the internal client*. Poznań: Publishing House of the Poznań University of Technology.

Lencioni, P. M. (2012). *The five dysfunctions of a team: Team assessment*. John Wiley & Sons.

Magen-Nagar, N., & Shonfeld, M. (2018). The impact of an online collaborative learning program on students' attitude towards technology. *Interactive Learning Environments, 26*(5), 621–637.

Moore, T. J., Johnston, A. C., & Glancy, A. W. (2020). STEM integration. In *Handbook of research on STEM education* (pp. 3–16). New York: Routledge.

Obuchowski, K. (2002). *Galaktyka potrzeb. Psychologia dążeń ludzkich*. Poznań: Profit and S-KA.

Paletz, S. B., Chan, J., & Schunn, C. D. (2017). The dynamics of micro-conflicts and uncertainty in successful and unsuccessful design teams. *Design Studies, 50*, 39–69.

Pyszka, A. (2015). Modele i determinanty efektywności zespołu. *Studia Ekonomiczne*, 230, 36–54.

Rubin, I. M., Plovnick, M. S., & Fry, R. E. (1978). Task-Oriented Team Development. New York: McGraw-Hill.

Salas, E., Goodwin, G. F., & Burke, C. S. (2008). *Team effectiveness in complex organizations: Cross-disciplinary perspectives and approaches*. New York: Routledge.

Tims, M., Bakker, A. B., & Derks, D. (2012). Development and validation of the job crafting scale. *Journal of Vocational Behavior, 80*(1), 173–186. https://doi.org/10.1016/j.jvb.2011.05.009.

Wrześniewski, A., & Dutton, J. E. (2001). Crafting a job: Revisioning employees as active crafters of their work. *Academy of Management Review, 26*(2), 179–201. https://doi.org/10.5465/amr.2001.4378011.

Wrześniewski, A., LoBuglio, N., Dutton, J. E., & Berg, J. M. (2013). Job crafting and cultivating positive meaning and identity in work. In *Advances in positive organizational psychology* (Vol. 1, pp. 281–302). Leeds: Emerald Group Publishing Limited.

Yeh, C., Jo, G. D., Ko, Y.-J., & Chung, H. K. (2023). Perspectives on 6G wireless communications. *ICT Express, 9*(1), 82–91. https://doi.org/10.1016/j.icte.2021.12.017.

Zhang, F., & Parker, S. K. (2019). Reorienting job crafting research: A hierarchical structure of job crafting concepts and integrative review. *Journal of Organizational Behavior, 40*(2), 126–146. https://doi.org/10.1002/job.2332.

10 Challenges and opportunities for cultural diversity in managing research and educational institutions in the economic age of 5.0

Justyna Bagińska, Paulina Graczyk, Anna Maria Wiśniewska, and Agata Włodkowska

The modern globalized world is characterized by an increasing mobility of societies, which, in turn, reinforces the role and importance of cultural diversity and soft competences. This holds particularly true for the management of companies, which increasingly employ workers from a variety of often distant cultures. Educational institutions, including universities, are unique entities. On the one hand, they function as research and educational institutions that educate young people from diverse cultures and religions. On the other hand, they operate as enterprises which, despite their specific characteristics, require management. Thus, this cognitive and intriguing aspect has been the focal point of discussion. The Vistula Group of Universities, the subject of this text in the context of Poland, is an exceptional entity. It is a private university, not a state university. The GUV can therefore be treated as a private undertaking, which additionally includes economic and higher education legislation. Second, AFiB Vistula is one of the most internationalized universities in Poland, where students from more than 100 countries study.

As per The Law on Higher Education and Science (Part II, Article 7.1), the system of higher education and science is composed of: (1) higher education institutions; (2) federations of entities of the higher education system and science, hereinafter referred to as "federations"; (3) the Polish Academy of Sciences (PAN); (4) scientific institutes of PAN; (5) research institutes, acting on the basis of the Act of 30 April 2010 on research institutes; (6) international scientific institutes; (7) Łukasiewicz Center and institutes operating within the Łukasiewicz Research Network; (8) other entities conducting mainly scientific activities on an independent and continuous basis (Law on Higher Education and Science, 2018).

DOI: 10.4324/9781003502272-11

Based on the POL-on register, in the academic year 2021/22 there were 362 universities in Poland. In the academic years 2010/2011–2019/2200, the number of students decreased from 1841.3 thousand to 1204.0 thousand, whereas an increase to 1218.2 thousand students was observed from the academic year 2020/2021. Systematic decreases were also observed in the number of graduates (GUS, 2021, 2022).

One of the Poland's oldest non-public universities is the University of Vistula, established in 1992 as the second non-public university in the country. It is one of the pillars of the Vistula Group of Universities, which includes Vistula University in Warsaw, Wroclaw Business University of Applied Sciences in Wrocław, Vistula School of Hospitality in Warsaw and Olsztyn University of Applied Sciences. Since 2019, it is part of Vistula University in Pultusk (About the University).

Vistula, which is a case study of this text, is based in Warsaw—the capital of Poland and a metropolis inhabited by nearly 2 million people. It represents the largest labor market in Poland, offering high wages, standard of living and education at the highest level in the best universities in the country. The city boasts a high level of security, making it attractive for students and graduates. The Wrocław Academy of Business in Applied Sciences is located in the capital of Lower Silesia—Wrocław. Ranking as the third largest city in Poland with more than 20 universities, which are vital scientific centers influencing the social, economic, and cultural life of the capital of Lower Silesia. For several years Wrocław has been distinguished from other cities in terms of modern business services, high technology, and IT industries.

The staff engaged in management, administrative, teaching and research departments hail from several countries. The VU and WAB employ 393 lecturers, with approximately 10% originating from outside Poland, including Azerbaijan, Belgium, Belarus, Spain, India, Japan, Nigeria, Macedonia, Ukraine, the USA, Uzbekistan, Turkey, and Italy. 80% of instructors conduct their teaching in English.

The VU and WAB have approximately 11,000 students representing 100 countries, including approximately 7,000 at Vistula University alone. Foreign students make up 60% of the total student body. The high internationalization of the university is its hallmark. Students present the traditions, cuisines, and culture of their countries. This is evidence of openness and sensitivity to cultural diversity.

According to the Annual Prospects Report since 2017, one of the GUV universities—Vistula University ranked first among non-public universities in terms of internationalization (Perspektywy University Ranking, 2022). It is also currently at the forefront in terms of both internationalization and employability of graduates based on high-quality education.

Literature review

The exploration of cultural diversity has been the focus of many studies and scientific publications. They are implemented, among others, in the framework of cultural studies, political sciences, and sociology and management. Each discipline emphasizes and analyzes different aspects of this topic.

Diversity management in management literature is defined as creating and maintaining a friendly working environment for all employees, through respect and sensitivity for their diversity. It encompasses aspects such as gender, race/ethnicity, age, as well as cognitive abilities such as problem-solving skills and communication styles (Barney, 1991). Elwira Gross-Gołacka adds aspects such as family structure, position, geographical location, and values. (2017). Diversity is the result of the diversity of personal characteristics of employees in an organization, while diversity management is a certain management process in which the potential of each employee is fully exploited (Thomas, 1991). Variety can be likened to a "double-edged sword" as it can serve as both, a performance barrier and an activity for increasing value (Kemper, Bader, & Froese, 2016).

Managing diversity is not just about leveling the playing field for individual members of a group or giving preference (although this is by the way), but about recognizing that diversity broadly understood improves the quality of the organization as a whole. It is not solely about minorities or women (Thomas Jr., 1992). Effective diversity management within a multicultural organization allows for an increase in the level of employee innovation and, consequently the organization's achievement of a competitive advantage on the market. It also facilitates the creation of good conditions for cooperation in many dimensions.

Reviewing the literature, certain scholars (Flynn et al., 2001; Mäkelä, Andersson & Seppälä, 2012; Stahl & Tung, 2014) contend that cultural and linguistic diversity in the workplace can act as a prominent source of conflict. This is attributed, among other factors, to communication difficulties, different behavioral norms or communication codes, but also to management errors. Cultural diversity can also have a positive impact on the development and creativity of the team, including their learning., This is highlighted in the work of researchers such as James G. March, Anne Bartel-Radic and Jennifer A. Chatman and Francis J. Flynn, and Wioletta J. Karna and Agnieszka Knap-Stefaniuk, (Bartel-Radic, 2006; Chatman & Flynn, 2001; March, 1991; Karna & Knap-Stefaniuk, 2018).

In the context of this topic, the article Ely and Thomas (2001) and their classification of perspectives of diversity are particularly important. According to their analysis, "the impact of cultural diversity on group functioning is influenced by what we call the group's 'diversity perspective': group members' normative beliefs and expectations about cultural diversity and its role in their work group" (Ely & Thomas, 2001, p.234). The authors distinguish: (1) integration and learning perspective, (2) access and legitimacy perspective, (3) and discrimination and fairness perspective. According to the first, cultural diversity is a resource, a source of development for a company, if it is recognized and effectively used for the accomplishment of the tasks and missions of the entity concerned and the achievement of additional benefits. The second perspective is based on the recognition that the subject's environment does not function in a vacuum but is culturally diverse. This makes the organization, for pragmatic reasons (including reaching new customers), try to adapt or match the diversity at the level of the company's employees. In this perspective, competence or creative resources arising from the cultural diversity of employees are overlooked. The third and final perspective of discrimination and fairness assumes that a culturally diverse team serves as evidence of fair treatment of workers (Hofstede, Hofstede, & Minkov, 2010)

Methodology

We are witnessing the escalating importance of Industry 5.0, for which, in addition to digital and technical competences, so-called soft skills, i.e., multicultural communication, emotional intelligence, leadership, self-awareness and critical thinking, are particularly vital. The text focuses on reconstructing and understanding how cultural diversity influences the management of a company specific to a private university. Vistula University and University of Business served as exemplars within this context. Quantitative research was utilized in the field of university staff within three groups: management, teaching and research staff and administrative staff. This approach facilitated the capture of opinions of a significant group of employees and enabled it to be statistically described in terms of research questions. An online questionnaire was used to obtain the data, using the online survey tool, which contains both closed questions (yielding quantitative data) and open questions, allowing respondents to freely speak on a given subject (yielding qualitative data). A request to complete the survey was sent to a randomly selected group of management, administrative and research and teaching staff employed at Vistula University and Wroclaw Business University of Applied Sciences, whose addresses are in the database. Excluded from the survey were the Main School of Tourism and Hospitality Vistula, Olsztyn University Józef Rusiecki and the Aleksander Gieysztor Academy in Pułtusk due to a relatively small representation of employees and students from outside Poland compared to other entities. 52 people completed the online survey. All have been completed in full. The contributions to the survey then underwent statistical analysis.

The following research questions were raised:

- What are the strengths and weaknesses of culturally diverse teams?
- What are the chances and challenges of managing a specific organization such as a private university?
- For which group is cultural diversity the most important and the least important?

We assume that the cultural diversity we face at the level of staff management, research and education services requires the "elusive soft skills" mentioned above, and poses a number of challenges for both managers, administrators, and academics. For each of these groups, cultural diversity has a different meaning and impact on them in different ways. For academics, the positive aspects of working in a multicultural environment create a range of opportunities and the positive aspects outweigh the negative consequences. Management and administrative staff are less affected by these benefits.

Test results

The studies involved 52 people aged between 24 and 81, including 32 women and 20 men. The majority of the respondents had Polish citizenship, the remaining Azerbaijani, Ukrainian, and Belarusian citizenship. Considering the professional group of 27 academic teachers, 20 administrative staff and 13 management staff. It should be noted that some employees had more than 1 position.

8 out of 10 respondents work in multicultural teams. This is most relevant for administrative staff (95%). One question was how to understand multiculturalism. The answers were, understandably, diverse, taking into account the different elements of the concept. Respondents commonly described multiculturalism as living and working in a culturally, ethnically, and religiously diverse environment. The answers were positive, highlighting the advantages of multiculturalism: openness, curiosity, broadening horizons, discovering novelties, cognitive qualities, greater tolerance. Participants in the survey are aware of the origin of their colleagues. The most frequently mentioned were Ukraine, Turkey, other former Soviet republics, South Asia, and Sub-Saharan Africa.

An overwhelming majority of respondents (79%) are familiar with the culture of the countries or countries where their colleagues originate from. This suggests that working in an intercultural team significantly increases the knowledge of the culture of other countries and promotes the exchange of knowledge on this subject. Importantly, 8 out of 10 respondents involved take into account the holiday schedule of all employees. A substantial 93% of participants consider the coworkers' diet when organizing meetings; this is true for all the academics surveyed to the highest degree. Most respondents (71.5%) did not happen to assign a person from their team negative traits resulting from the stereotyping of a given nation. Moreover, half of the respondents believe that they should raise awareness of the culture of the country or countries where their colleagues come from. Two-thirds of managers feel the greatest need in this respect. The least identified issue in this question is ("hard to say") administrative staff (42%).

The question of more people from different cultures who should work in a given team yielded diverse responses, These responses in context are supplemented by the interviewees from further questions of the survey: the central concern is not about the a need to increase the number of people from different cultures, but centers on identifying specific skills and competences these people will contribute to a given team.

At the core of our article lie the strengths and weaknesses of a culturally diverse team. Research findings reveal that few respondents see the weaknesses of such teams, and that the examples given in the question are challenges that must be tackled such as. Effective integration program, effective communication, understanding, tolerance, respect. What has been condemned most often as the weaknesses of such a team is a different sense of time and punctuality, a superior-subordinate relationship, and the resulting differences in approach to the performance of duties, the understanding of instructions, or the question of compliance with obligations and deadlines. Respondents also pointed out that some people communicate with each other in their native languages, which can be incomprehensible to other team members who are present. This fosters a sense of alienation and can create barriers. In the light of the statements made by the respondents, the least prominent issue (least frequently observed) appears to be discrimination based on gender and religion.

As per the respondents, the greatest challenges of working in a multicultural team are primarily cultural and linguistic barriers. These encompass issues of cultural sensitivity, the need for multilingual communication (using more than one foreign language in speech and writing, translation of documents), issues of effective communication, different definitions of authority, rights and responsibilities, the problem of stereotypes. It is also a matter of celebration at different times and the associated availability of staff and students. It was important for the management to enforce the work they were contracted to, the question of organizing meetings, a different sense of time and responsibility of colleagues. In addition, academics were concerned with the different levels of preparation of students for the curriculum (substantive and linguistic disparities), the need to take into account cultural specificities and diversity when preparing and implementing teaching activities, the different approaches of students to discipline, different interpretations of the term "deadline," or the reconciliation of different experiences of students resulting from differences in their age (e.g. 16 and 19 years), and different perspectives of the world. For administrative staff, these were issues of language barriers on the part of students, translation of documents or difficulties in accepting the rules in force in Poland (e.g., failure to respect office hours, degrees and titles, forms of politeness of hierarchy, age) and legal issues (visas, differences in law concerning the rules of study).

The strengths of a multicultural team in terms of opportunities are, in the opinion of respondents, primarily the ability to capture a broader perspective and move beyond Eurocentrism. This includes heightened linguistic and cultural competences among team members, greater creativity, the potential to foster international cooperation and increased prestige of the university.

In the context of the topic being studied, it is important that training on multiculturalism is organized in the universities being studied. Every second respondent participated. These were management staff (57%) and academics (55.5%). 42% of administrative staff also participated. 9 out of 10 people surveyed who have taken part in such training courses, regardless of their job position, use the knowledge gained from them in practice. This attests to the relevance and practical dimension of such training programs. Two-thirds of all respondents see a constant need to attend such workshops or training. This is predominantly observed among the management board (78.5%).

Conclusions and recommendations

Research has demonstrated that multicultural groups yield more opportunities than challenges, contributing to understanding other cultures, broadening horizons, enhancing creativity, and grasping a broader perspective, including moving beyond Eurocentrism. In the context of a specific institution such as a university, these are key elements that can be used in research and scientific activities. Interestingly, respondents identified opportunities in the challenges suggested by the author. According to the respondents, the challenges of working in an intercultural team are, among others, a different sense of time, the relationship of a superior—subordinate and the resulting differences in the approach to the performance of duties and the understanding of commands. Different groups respondents drew attention to different aspects.

In conclusion, respondents emphasize the necessity for regular intercultural training or workshops, advocating for language training for employees, soft skills workshops, as well as conflict resolution or negotiation sessions. The methodological and stereotyped preparation of administrative staff and teaching staff for the growing number of students from different cultural backgrounds is deemed indispensable. Given geopolitical, civilizational, and demographic changes, we must be prepared to accept the primacy of multiculturalism over homogeneity. Multiculturalism should not be feared, it is not a threat and an opportunity for development, especially in institutions such as universities.

References

Barney, J. (1991). Firm resources and sustained competitive advantage. *Journal of Management, 17*(1), 99–120. https://doi.org/10.1177/014920639101700108.

Bartel-Radic, A. (2006). Intercultural learning in global teams. *Management International Review, 46*(6), 647–678. https://doi.org/10.1007/s11575-006-0121-7

Ely, R. J., & Thomas, D. A. (2001). Cultural diversity at work: The effects of diversity perspectives on work group processes and outcomes. *Administrative Science Quarterly, 46*(2), 229–273. https://doi.org/10.2307/2667087.

Flynn, F. J., Chatman, J. A., & Spataro, S. E. (2001). Getting to know you: The influence of personality on impressions and performance of demographically different people in organizations. *Administrative Science Quarterly, 46*(3), 414–442. https://doi.org/10.2307/3094870.

Gross-Gołacka, E. (2017). *Diversity management. Towards diverse human resources in the organization*. Warsaw: Difin.

GUS. (2021). Szkolnictwo wyższe w roku akademickim 2020/2021 (wyniki wstępne)—Główny Urząd Statystyczny. <https://stat.gov.pl/files/gfx/portalinformacyjny/pl/defaultaktualnosci/5488/8/7/1/szkolnictwo_wyzsze_w_roku_akademickim_2020-2021.pdf> Accessed 15.8.23.

GUS. (2022). Szkolnictwo wyższe w roku akademickim 2021/2022 (wyniki wstępne)—Główny Urząd Statystyczny. < https://stat.gov.pl/obszary-tematyczne/edukacja/edukacja/szkolnictwo-wyzsze-w-roku-akademickim-20212022-wyniki-wstepne,8,8.html> Accessed 14.01.23.

Hofstede, G., Hofstede, G. J., & Minkov, M. (2010). *Cultures and organizations, software of the mind, intercultural cooperation and its importance for survival*. New York: Mc Graw Hill Education.

Karna, W. J., & Knap-Stefaniuk, A. (2018). Challenges in managing employees in multicultural environment. *Marketing i Zarządzanie, 51*, 143–151. https://doi.org/10.18276/miz.2018.51-14.

Kemper, L. E., Bader, A. K., & Froese, F. J. (2016). Diversity management in ageing societies: A comparative study of Germany and Japan. *Management Revue, 27*(1–2), 29–49. https://doi.org/10.5771/0935-9915-2016-1-2-29.

Law on Higher Education and Science (2018). Act of 20th July 2018. Published in Warszawa by Government Printing Office. https://lexlege.pl/ustawa-z-dnia-20-lipca-2018-r-prawo-o-szkolnictwie-wyzszym-i-nauce/

Mäkelä, K., Andersson, U., & Seppälä, T. (2012). Interpersonal similarity and knowledge sharing within multinational organizations. *International Business Review, 21*(3), 439–451. https://doi.org/10.1016/j.ibusrev.2011.05.003.

March, J. G. (1991). Exploration and exploitation in organizational learning. *Organization Science, 2*(1), 71–87. https://doi.org/10.1287/orsc.2.1.71J.

Perspektywy University Ranking 2022. (2022), <https://ranking.perspektywy.pl/2022/ranking/ranking-uczelni-niepublicznych> Accessed 13.01.23.

Stahl, G. K., & Tung, R. L. (2015). Towards a more balanced treatment of culture in international business studies: The need for positive cross-cultural scholarship. *Journal of International Business Studies*, *46*(4), 391–414. http://dx.doi.org/10.1057/jibs.2014.68.

Thomas, R. R. (1991). *Beyond race and gender: Unleashing the power of your total workforce by managing diversity*. New York: Amacom. https://doi.org/10.1002/hrdq.3920030413.

Thomas, R. R., Jr. (1992). Managing diversity: A conceptual framework. In: S.E. Jackson (Ed.), *Diversity in the workplace: Human resources initiatives* (pp. 306–317). New York: The Guilford Press.

11 Personalistic ethics—an axiological dimension of Management 5.0

Krzysztof Nowakowski, Łukasz Skowron, and Ewa Mazur-Wierzbicka

Introduction

The ongoing socio-economic changes are characterized by how digital technology influences business management. An analysis of articles on management highlights the widespread use of the "Business 5.0" term, particularly within the context of IT companies. This term describes the economic transformation resulting from artificial intelligence, interactive multimedia, and faster data transmission and processing. The evolving landscape of competition compels companies to reevaluate, enhance, and restructure their business processes. Product life cycles are shrinking, with innovation emerging as the paramount determinant of success. Consumers now demand products and services of the highest quality that also fulfill environmental standards.

Corporate social responsibility encompasses sustainability, environmental stewardship, and the provision of products and services that are safe for consumers (Langley, 2020). To meet these expectations, Management 5.0 leverages human capital—namely, the knowledge and skills of employees—in various aspects of enterprise strategy implementation. Establishing adaptable structures that align with the dynamic market environment necessitates perpetual learning and the adoption of novel approaches to work organization. In decentralized companies, where tasks are executed through cooperation and mutual trust, ethical employees capable of self-regulation and critical self-assessment are indispensable. Typically, these individuals possess high levels of education and self-esteem and engage in creative and unconventional work. Consequently, managers are more inclined than ever to prioritize ethics that cultivate self-discipline and customer satisfaction.

Ethical viewpoints are formalized through moral codes and directives, which emanate from theories comprising concepts and assertions underpinning these principles. Normative corporate ethics aims to offer counsel and direction on appropriate employee conduct (Jones et al., 2005). This chapter is driven by the observed trend of managers devoting increased attention

DOI: 10.4324/9781003502272-12

to ethical predicaments arising from the consequences of information technology use. The concepts of liberalism, utilitarianism, and certain facets of capitalist ethics are explained in detail. A pivotal aspect of the analysis is personalistic ethics.

Subsequently, a case study of a chosen educational institution has been presented, along with respondents' standpoints on the ethical dimension of work and the significance of modern technologies. The analysis outcomes served to assess the ethics of Management 5.0. The conclusion outlines crucial recommendations for cultivating a culture of strong ethics and self-esteem in the digital era.

Ethics of capitalism in the context of selected philosophical and social concepts

Ethical considerations have been and continue to be integral to numerous theoretical concepts. Socrates believed that virtuous behavior arises from understanding what such behavior entails. According to him, comprehending fairness and embodying fairness are synonymous (Tatarkiewicz, 2022). For contemporary managers, this serves as a suggestion to foster ethical attitudes through specialized training programs. Socrates' concept of ethical intellectualism emphasizes that acquiring knowledge is tantamount to leading a virtuous and contented life.

The exploration of morality and the examination of how moral principles impact society were also subjects addressed by Plato. He delineated various facets of the soul and assigned distinct virtues to each; wisdom represented the virtue of reason, and fortitude was linked to an impulsive soul, while self-control was ascribed to the desiring soul. These virtues were all subordinated to the fourth—righteousness—which maintains equilibrium among all the other virtues inherent to the human soul. Plato offered a framework for understanding the influence of different emotions and the means of governing them while highlighting the benefits of a harmonious life. His idealism shaped ethical theory by proposing that tangible and intangible goods follow hierarchical structures, with ideals of spiritual beauty occupying the pinnacle.

The third eminent philosopher of the classical period was Aristotle. In his framework, intellectual virtues like wisdom and reason exist alongside ethical virtues such as generosity, moderation, and bravery (Arystoteles, 2010). According to Aristotle, a balanced mode of behavior, known as the "golden mean," can be found in every realm. Living in a virtuous way entails satisfying spiritual and existential needs in equilibrium. Hence, an excessive preoccupation with wealth and material possessions distances individuals from spiritual values and a genuine comprehension of the world around them. An implication for workers and entrepreneurs is the counsel to eschew extremes and strike a harmony between personal and professional life (Megone & Robinson, 2002).

The ethical and economic doctrine intertwined with Christianity was elucidated by the Catholic philosopher Thomas Aquinas (Szacki, 2006). He criticized excessive wealth accumulation and advocated for supporting the impoverished through donations and other philanthropic endeavors. A prominent Dominican figure denounced usury and the lending of money at exorbitant interest rates, leading to the categorization of trade within less ethical spheres. Morally, work was seen as a means to counteract vanity and fulfill existential needs. An essential ethical guideline for entrepreneurs was the endorsement of the "fair price," one that aligned with the value of goods or services. Craftsmen and farmers were expected to serve the collective, rather than merely boosting individual consumption and wealth. Tending to the land was esteemed as a worthy pursuit for a Christian, while obedience to feudal lords was deemed prudent and a mark of embracing the temporal world.

The evolution of the market economy generated a demand for financial services and capital, and the expansion of international trade transformed the behaviors of many Europeans. As economic changes unfolded, ethical perspectives regarding the role and significance of work underwent a transformation. Economic history literature underscores the impact of Protestant denominations on shaping capitalist attitudes. It is believed that October 31, 1517, marked the beginning of the Reformation, when Luther presented his 95 theses in Wittenberg, challenging the Catholic Church's practices. The Reformation redefined the understanding of a Christian's vocation, extolling qualities like diligence, frugality, stability, and entrepreneurship. The ability to amass material possessions began to be seen as a manifestation of divine grace, and success in one's chosen field was construed as fulfilling a calling. Calvinism's adherents embraced the notion of predestination, believing it endowed them with the capacity to enhance their skills (Weber, 2002).

Work ceased being seen solely as a penance for original sin; instead, it became a way to demonstrate faith. Protestantism dismantled moral barriers to the activities of bankers, pawnbrokers, and other financial professionals. Profiting from capital garnered societal approval and offered an ideological basis for the emergence of early corporations. The roots of contemporary economic ethics go back to the morality of Protestantism.

The "spirit of capitalism" is often attributed to a pivotal concept of Adam Smith. His theory posits that humans are essentially "economic animals" (homo oeconomicus), driven by the pursuit of maximizing personal benefits. Entities engage in market activities when the gains outweigh the associated costs. Entrepreneurs adhering to this principle seek novel avenues for growth, offering innovative products, technologies, unearthing untapped resources, and modernizing work practices.

The market mechanism has driven progress, with competition fostering modernization. Fundamental ethical tenets of liberalism encompass the following: individual liberty, which opposes practices like serfdom and forced labor; economic freedom, coupled with a stance against state institutions regulating market interactions; trade freedom, advocating for the dismantling of barriers hindering the movement of goods, services, and capital across borders. As per the author of "An Inquiry into the Nature and Causes of the Wealth of Nations,"—published in 1776 (Smith, 2007)—the source of prosperity lies in the production of goods and services rather than the wealth accumulated through colonial expansion as asserted by mercantilists or agriculture as advocated by the physiocrats.

During the late 17th and early 18th centuries, analysts of market societies held the perspective that autonomous individuals could forge ethical social contracts. According to Locke, the social compact aimed to safeguard legal ownership and civil liberties, encompassing economic, cultural, and political freedoms. Locke underscored the equality of all citizens under the law and the division of state authority into legislative and executive branches. He asserted that the government's responsibility was to adhere to regulations, uphold the tenets of the social contract, and subject itself to the scrutiny of citizens through elections (Locke, 2015). These principles laid the foundation for the ethics of the social contract.

The progenitor of secular normative ethics is the "Introduction to the Principles of Morality and Legislation," published in 1789. Bentham asserted that human beings are driven by pursuing pleasure and avoiding discomfort (Bentham, 1958). Accordingly, actions that enhance overall happiness are deemed correct, while those leading to unhappiness are deemed wrong. Public institutions bear the responsibility of contributing to the establishment of favorable living conditions. Bentham associated the concept of good with utility, which aimed to maximize material or immaterial benefits. The utility assessment should consider factors like intensity, duration, certainty, and uncertainty of outcomes, along with their scope and distant impact (Provis, 2012). Mill, a follower of Bentham, argued that individuals could act altruistically for their pleasure. Economically, utilitarians supported the free market, viewing the interplay of supply and demand as a mechanism to negotiate mutual gains and remove transactional restrictions. Utilitarians perceived laws as a result of consensus among diverse interest groups.

The notion of ethical individualism was introduced by Kant, the author of "Critique of Pure Reason" (1781), "Critique of Practical Reason" (1788), and "Critique of the Power of Judgment" (1790). Kant's concept emerged as a counterpoint to utilitarianism and religious ethical systems. Kant posited that actions are morally commendable when stemming from a free and voluntary will that is driven by ethical intent. Such actions are governed by obligations rooted in law. The categorical imperative for human behavior is encapsulated in the rule: "Act only according to that maxim whereby you can at the same time will that it should become a universal law." This means adhering to principles that apply equally to all members of society. A second norm of ethical conduct prescribes: "Act in such a way that you treat humanity, whether in your own person or in the person of any other, never merely as a means to an end, but always at the same time as an end." (Kant, 2017). These moral imperatives function similarly to fundamental laws in science. They underscore the inherent value of life, advocating for holistic interactions between individuals. Treating workers as mere tools or means is unethical, as it contradicts another principle: "Act only according to that maxim whereby you can at the same time will that it should become a universal law of nature." Since Kant's works, including the "Metaphysics of Morals" (Kant, 2022), subjectivity has emerged as a central theme in ethical deliberations.

Personalism as a philosophy of direction

The considerations outlined above underscore that ethical guidance revolves around safeguarding the human individual's integrity and moral consciousness within their professional endeavors. Consequently, a novel approach to analyzing the management process involves adopting the personalistic paradigm (Schwartz, 2017). This multifaceted concept underscores the significance of cultivating ethical awareness to attain complete personal maturity (Hill, 2018).

Several pivotal "schools" of personalism can be identified. Phenomenological and historical personalism is exemplified by figures like Scheler, Ingarden, Stein, Pannenberg, Rosenzweig, and Guardini. The existentialist perspective finds representation in the works of Marcel, Jaspers, Brunner, Berdyaev, Szestov, Tillich, Pratt, Macintosh, Harkness, and Garnett. Neotomist personalism encompasses thinkers such as Maritain, Wust, Gilson, Nédoncelle, Woroniecki, Sawicki, Granat, Gogacz, Krąpiec, Jan Rodziński, Szostek, and Wielgus. The religious-philosophical variant resonates through the works of Wojtyła, Tischner, Cohen, Ebner, Buber, and Teilhard de Chardin. Personalism psychosociology finds its proponents in Laberthonnière, Durkheim, and Wundt. The absolutist perspective is championed by Caird, Green, Royce, Taylor, Calkins, and Hocking. Panpsychic personalism is evident in the works of Ward, Stern, Tennant, Carr, Whitehead, and Hartshorne (Bartnik, 2000). Due to space constraints, delving into every facet of personalism here is impractical. However, a comprehensive analysis of select texts allows for extrapolating the core tenets of personalism into the realm of management.

The drive to humanize work is palpable among proponents of the "behavioral school." This inclination was spearheaded by Mayo, whose research at the Hawthorn Corporation in 1927 debunked the conventional management concept and underscored the significance of social relationships in enhancing labor productivity. This marked a shift from viewing workers as mere components within the organizational structure. Mayo's research revealed that employees yearned for engagement in their work and meaningful connections with their supervisors. The implications were clear: Beyond ensuring technical efficiency, management must cultivate a positive workplace atmosphere and foster constructive relationships. This novel approach to governance was termed "human relations."

The significance of addressing workers' needs was further emphasized by Maslow, who, in his work "A Theory of Human Motivation," outlined a hierarchy of needs and provided a compelling rationale for fulfilling existential and social desires (Shafritz & Ott, 2001).

McGregor, another luminary in the psychological approach to management analysis, authored a paper under the evocative title: "The Human Side of Enterprise" in 1957. In this influential work, McGregor emphasized the necessity of considering employees' personalities and relationships with their tasks. Delving into the significance of professional growth, he introduced the concepts of X and Y-type profiles. The former model characterizes employees as needing supervision and control from managers, portraying them as self-centered and minimally motivated toward work. Conversely, the Y personality type embodies individuals capable of independent tasks which embrace the organization's culture. Managers overseeing such subordinates can grant them autonomy and responsibility (Shafritz & Ott, 2001). An intriguing organizational concept emerged in 1981 through Ouchi's work titled "The Z Organization," outlining a participatory management style.

Direct communication between employees and managers stands as a cornerstone of a company's culture. Ethical matters gain heightened importance in the presence of differing attitudes and behaviors and conflicts stemming from diverse professional experiences (Thomas, 2011). The personalistic approach takes into consideration the multifaceted commitment of employees to the company's objectives. Notably, since the 1980s, companies have begun implementing recommendations stemming from psychological and sociological research. This has led to enhanced company performance, facilitated by consultations and participatory management practices, giving rise to a novel Organization Development (OD) model. According to French and Bell, OD involves applying behavioral sciences theory and sociological research methods to foster a culture of teamwork. It aims to shift operational principles from a mechanistic to an organic organizational model, aligning with the concepts outlined in "Mechanistic and Organic Systems."

The advent of the digital age has introduced challenges in the realm of computer technology applications. A distinctive attribute of enterprises in this new century is Management 5.0, which signifies a focus on automating processes and integrating ICT solutions. Leadership in the digital era necessitates ethical responsibility in decision-making and the harmonization of task teams (Wasieleski & Weber, 2019).

The emergence of cyber-economics has heightened interactivity in interactions with customers, suppliers, and distributors. Employees' innovation and operational efficacy have become pivotal factors in determining market success. Business 5.0 harnesses AI (Artificial Intelligence), Machine Learning, and other techniques to optimize performance. Substituting human labor with machines compels a reevaluation of the individual's role and significance within the workplace. From a personalist standpoint, paramount inquiries revolve around self-esteem, responsibility for personal development, and self-realization (Paliwal, 2006).

Methodology—case study analysis

The analysis of the axiological dimension of Management 5.0 delves into the extent of integration between moral expectations and the utilization of ICT (Information and Communications Technology) within management practices. It also explores the influence of this technology on the role and significance of interaction in the workplace. Furthermore, the study encompasses feedback on the ethical implications of ICT adoption. The multifaceted exploration of leadership performance prompted the formulation of inquiries directed at the staff of Warsaw University of Applied Sciences (WPANS). The research project was executed by distributing an electronic survey link. Responses were collected anonymously, with the survey open from November 6 to December 4, 2022. Of the 137 employees to whom the survey was directed, 94 responded, constituting 68.6% of the study population. These outcomes are indicative of the chosen organization and reflect the viewpoints of the employed individuals.

WPANS, selected for this survey due to its utilization of ICT for educational purposes and employee communication, relies on key IT tools like the Cisco Web application and the e-Wszechnica portal. These ICT solutions facilitate synchronous and asynchronous learning (e-learning), teleconferencing, and continuous communication among teaching and management staff.

Demographically, the respondents comprised 31.2% men (29) and 68.8% women (64). The predominant age group was 51 and above (46.2%; 43 individuals), followed by those aged 41–50 at 29.0% (27 individuals). The third-largest cohort was aged 31–40 (18.3%; 17 individuals). Individuals under the age of 30 represented 6.5% (6 participants). The majority of respondents (79.6%; 74) resided in large cities (over 250,000 inhabitants), while 11.8% (11 individuals) were from small towns with populations up to 50,000. Medium-sized urban areas (50,000–250,000 inhabitants) were home to 3.2% (3 individuals), and there were five respondents (5.4%) from rural areas.

WPANS staff exhibited a solid professional foundation, with 47.8% (44 individuals) possessing doctoral education and 51.1% (47 individuals) holding higher education degrees with master's qualifications. Regarding occupation, 76.3% (71 individuals) identified themselves as belonging to the educational sector with humanistic training. The legal and administrative category was represented by 11.8% (11 individuals), while other professions included military and police (5.4%; 5 individuals), as well as economic and trade roles (4.3%; 4 individuals).

The sample primarily comprised highly educated individuals, with the majority serving as educators across various educational tiers (74.2%; 69 individuals). Respondents included senior, middle, and lower-level managers, constituting 18.3% (17 individuals), while office workers accounted for 4 (4.3%) participants. Concerning the total duration of their employment since inception, a significant majority had worked for over 11 years (88.2%; 82 individuals). It is worth noting that for specific questions, the provided answers needed to align with the total number of respondents due to data gaps.

Importance of digital technology for development and personal fulfillment at work

The majority of publications concerning technology highlight the impact of ICTs in enhancing task efficiency. An approach rooted in personalism within management analysis necessitates the application of humanist criteria. In his article titled "The Need for Economic Personalism," Gronbacher (1998) outlines several principles of economic personalism. The interpretation of ethical management principles is as follows: individual subjectivity is the ultimate goal in ontological and epistemological contexts (principle: the person's centrality). Employees who remain open to their surroundings enrich their inner lives (principle: subjectivity and autonomy). Each employee possesses inherent dignity and uniqueness (principle: human dignity). Given people's social nature, the working community becomes pivotal for professional development (principle: the person within a community). Managers should contribute added value to their work lives, influencing colleagues positively—the principle: participation and solidarity (Gronbacher, 1998). In alignment with this paradigm, WPANS staff were posed with various questions about the impact of digital technology on their professional lives. Findings revealed that 48.4% (45 individuals) believe that digital technology usage diminishes the quality of interpersonal relationships. Conversely, 18.3% (17 individuals) held the opposing view, while 33.3% (31 individuals) remained undecided. This outcome suggests that ICT contributes to an atomization process. According to respondents, the substitution of direct interpersonal contact with communication mediated by ICT software weakens social bonds. Employees allocate less time for discussions and shared experiences, focusing instead on managing applications and email.

Another phenomenon noted by respondents was the strengthening of a trend toward centralized management. In response to a query about the increasing or decreasing centralization of management through digital technology usage, a notable 36.5% (34 individuals) asserted that IT (Information Technology) amplifies centralization. A significantly smaller proportion (11.8%; 11 individuals) indicated a decrease in this trend. More than half of WPANS employees (51.6%; 48 individuals) remained undecided on this matter.

In light of the obtained results, it is essential to consider the trajectory of changes ushered in by the expansion of information networks. Technological advancements have facilitated the spatial diversification of organizational structures while also providing tools for monitoring and controlling employees on an unprecedented scale. A new economic order is shaped by a technology where individual subjectivity wanes. This perspective was echoed by 37.6% (35 individuals) of respondents who disagreed with the notion that digital technology enhances the subjective treatment of employees. A slightly larger percentage was represented by undecided responses (39.8%; 37 individuals). Positive views on the subjective treatment of employees due to IT usage amounted to 22.6% (21 individuals).

It is essential to highlight the trend toward objectifying individuals in the workplace. The utilization of chatbots capable of listening and interacting, the demand for technical proficiency in using computer applications, and the assumption that technology can resolve all issues contribute to undervaluing the personal worth of each individual. Automating the provision of educational services necessitates a reconfiguration of the dynamics between educators and students, professors and learners, as well as mentors and employees. In the economic context of 5.0, innovation and proactive, innovative actions are the most valuable components of work. Therefore, updating existing knowledge becomes a prerequisite for deliberate and responsible synchronous and asynchronous education through the Internet. Of the respondents, 55.4% (51 individuals) highlighted the potential for enhanced self-actualization through digital technology. On the contrary, 21.8% (20 individuals) expressed a negative perspective on this matter, while 22.8% (21 individuals) remained neutral.

The process of acquiring new knowledge entails enriching current experiences and cultivating effective multimedia relationships. As per the responses, 36.5% (34 individuals) of participants believe that the incorporation of digital technology enhances their job satisfaction. Conversely, 23.7%

(22 individuals) held a differing perspective, while 39.8% (37 individuals) chose not to express an opinion on the matter. Operating within a networked environment can contribute significantly to enhancing personal experiences and overall fulfillment. Surveyed employees showcased a positive appraisal of various facets of cyberspace that contribute to individual growth and a deeper understanding of organizational principles and goals. An intriguing ethical analysis revolves around the question: "Do you believe digital technology bolsters or weakens work ethics?" The results indicated that 50.5% (47 individuals) chose not to express an opinion on the matter, 25.8% (24 individuals) endorsed the notion of digital technology reinforcing work ethics, while 23.7% (22 individuals) held the opposing view.

While the application of standardization and web activity monitoring certainly enhances discipline among employees, it is essential to bear in mind that within educational institutions, work ethics also encompass the responsibility for organizing learning processes and using them to attain professional standards among students and teachers.

Summary

The roots of personalistic ethics can be traced back to early psychological studies that delved into the significance of human needs and social connections for driving economic development. Over time, personalism took various trajectories, some intertwined with religious concepts while others followed separate paths. Exploring personal integrity has illuminated that heightened moral awareness correlates with a more substantial alignment between professed beliefs and actual behavior.

In today's context, several distinct spheres of ethical inquiry stand out. These encompass a critical analysis of individual behaviors among employees and managers, ethical audits evaluating the rules and procedures of organizations, scrutiny of the interactions between corporations and the broader social landscape (embracing the ethos of Corporate Social Responsibility or CSR), evaluation of the moral foundations of economic systems, and more specific investigations such as assessing companies for conflicts of interest, discriminatory practices, and the implementation of ESG (Environmental, Social, and Governance) strategies (O'Sullivan et al., 2012).

The advent of the 5.0 economy, coupled with the rapid expansion of digital technology, ushers in fresh challenges that transcend the confines of the economic sphere and extend into the moral domain. This holds particularly true for the emerging paradigm of learning organizations that wield influence over all participants within the digital landscape. The analyses presented within this article center on an educational institution whose staff members are distinguished by their higher educational backgrounds and conscientious work ethos. Findings reveal that respondents perceive IT as a factor that tends to centralize management, thereby failing to foster a subjective approach toward employee relations actively. Consequently, the hypothesis of heightened management involvement has been debunked. This case study counters prevalent notions propagated in many publications advocating for personalized employee treatment.

According to the study's author, the quality of human interactions is paramount and deserving heightened attention. The risk of detachment from work and the erosion of social bonds are tangible concerns as perceived by surveyed individuals.

Contemporary pedagogical processes benefit from IT tools, which have seamlessly integrated into the workflows of educators, lecturers, trainers, and coaching professionals. Media and computer applications have enabled the dissemination of educational services beyond traditional classroom confines. Survey participants notably appreciated the advantages brought by digital technology, citing an enhanced sense of job satisfaction. The opportunities and challenges identified within Management 5.0 necessitate further research and in-depth analysis, mainly focusing on larger workforce collectives.

References

Arystoteles. (2010). *Etyka wielka. Poetyka.* Warszawa: Wydawnictwo Naukowe PWN.

Bartnik, C. (2000). *Personalizm.* Warsaw: Wydawnictwo OK Tomasz Wiater.

Bentham, J. (1958). *Wprowadzenie do zasad moralności i prawodawstwa.* Warsaw: Wydawnictwo Naukowe PWN.

Gronbacher, G. (1998). The need for economic personalism. *The Journal of Market & Morality, 1*(1), 1–34.

Hill, A. (2018). *Business. Christian ethics for the marketplace.* Downers Grove, Ill.: Inter Varsity Press.

Jones, C., Bos, R., & Parker, M., (2005). *Business ethics. A critical approach.* New York: Routledge.

Kant, I. (2017). *Uzasadnienie metafizyki moralności.* Wydawnictwo Marek Derewiecki, Kęty, Poland.

Kant, I. (2022). *Metafizyka moralności.* Warszawa: Wydawnictwo Naukowe PWN.

Langley, Q. (2020). *Business and the culture of ethics.* Business Expert Press LLC.

Locke, J. (2015). *Dwa traktaty o rządzie.* Warszawa: Wydawnictwo Aletheia.

Megone, C., & Robinson, S. (Eds). (2002). *Case histories in business ethics.* New York: Routledge.

O'Sullivan, P., Smith, M., & Esposito, M. (Eds). (2012). *Business ethics. A critical approach: Integrating ethics across the business world.* New York: Routledge.

Paliwal, M. (2006). *Business ethics.* New Age International Ltd. Publishers, New Delhi, India.

Provis, C. (2012). *Individuals, groups and business ethics.* Routledge, New York.

Schwartz, M. S. (2017). *Business ethics. An ethical decision-making approach.* Chichester, UK: Wiley Blackwell.
Shafritz, J. M., & Ott, J. S. (2001). *Classic of organization theory.* Boston, MA: Harcourt College Publishers.
Smith, A. (2007). *Badania nad naturą i przyczynami bogactwa narodów.* Warszawa: Wydawnictwo Naukowe PWN.
Szacki, J. (2006). *Historia myśli socjologicznej.* Warszawa: Wydawnictwo Naukowe PWN.
Tatarkiewicz, W. (2022). *Historia filozofii. Tom 1.* Warszawa: Wydawnictwo Naukowe PWN.
Thomas, R. M. (Ed). (2011). *Teaching ethics. Volume Two: Business ethics.* Suffolk, UK: Ethics International Press Ltd.
Wasieleski, D. M., & Weber, J. (Eds). (2019). *Business ethics.* Bingley, UK: Emerald Publishing Limited.
Weber, M. (2002). *The protestant ethic and the "Spirit" of capitalism: And other writings.* New York: Penguin Books.

12 Agility and creativity as a determinant of efficient use of ICT

Hubert Gąsiński, Magdalena Kaczkowska-Serafińska, Maria Kocot, and Artur Kwasek

Introduction

The development of the concept of agility has become the modern enterprise's response to the emergence of uncontrollable changes in the market environment resulting from rapid digitalization. Creativity remains essential, signifying the ability to think innovatively and the determination to foster innovation. To thrive amidst such turbulent conditions, a company must cultivate the capacity to address the new challenges of the business environment strategically. This necessitates using ICT tools (integrated within agility frameworks) that ensure the utmost timeliness and depth of data and effective communication.

The volatile market environment compels employees to cultivate the necessary attributes for swift responsiveness to emerging risks and capitalizing on market opportunities. Hence, employees must possess agility and creativity, which encompass the ability to implement and leverage ICT tools.

Theoretical agility and creativity of the organization

Today's dynamic business reality dictates that every organization must devise strategies to endure challenging and turbulent market conditions. Organizations now function within a dynamic market environment that compels the integration of IT solutions across all operational domains, owing to exceedingly tumultuous shifts in the market landscape. These shifts present formidable challenges for modern organizations (Zhen et al., 2021). Additionally, these difficulties are made worse by the speed at which innovation and technology are developing, the ongoing digitalization process, and the elevated expectations of customers for personalized offerings (Stverkova & Pohludka, 2018).

Hence, it is imperative for organizations to adopt comprehensive strategies to fortify their market position (Todorovych, 2020). This includes

DOI: 10.4324/9781003502272-13

enabling the efficient utilization of IT tools within the enterprise's IT environment. An approach that holds promise in this regard is the adept implementation of organizational agility principles.

Within the relevant literature, organizational agility has garnered numerous definitions. Frequently, it is understood as the ability to endure and navigate a competitive, turbulent, and unpredictable environment (Goldman et al., 1995; Sahota, 2012). This challenging environment underscores the imperative for swift and efficient responses to market fluctuations (Almahamid et al., 2010; Goldman et al., 1995; Gunasekaran, 1998; Hormozi, 2009; Kidd, 1994; Leberecht, 2016; Meredith & Francis Bessant et al., 1999; Narasimhan et al., 2006; Rigby, 2000; Sajdak, 2014; Sahota, 2012; Sanchez & Nagi, 2001; Teece, 2007; Trzcieliński, 2007; Walczak & Skalik, 2010; Yang & Liu, 2012; Zhang & Sharifi, 2000). Consequently, organizations must fulfill customers' market demands by devising offerings tailored to their individualized needs (Narasimhan et al., 2006; Yang & Liu, 2012).

Organizational agility is also understood as encompassing proactive initiatives, adaptability within swiftly evolving business landscapes, flexibility, and rapid responsiveness (Zhang & Sharifi, 2000). Cultivating these attributes empowers organizations to fortify their market standing by intelligently and proactively identifying opportunities while mitigating emerging risks (Almahamid et al., 2010; Kidd, 1994). The uncontrolled shifts in the market environment due to ongoing digitalization necessitate the development of agile behaviors among employees and entire organizations. The organization's agility consequently permeates various levels of its functioning.

Furthermore, while scrutinizing an organization's operations in the context of modern business environments, it's paramount to recognize its existence within the era of Industry 5.0 (Bessant et al., 1999; Leberecht, 2016). Consequently, to bolster its market position, leveraging IT tools for efficient management is indispensable (Rigby, 2000; Sanchez & Nagi, 2001; Teece, 2007).

The agility of workers is closely intertwined with creative endeavors (Luecke, 2005; Mroziewski, 2010; Strużycki, 2004). Creativity involves the process of conceiving and expressing novel ideas to address problems or fulfill needs. As such, creativity serves as a pivotal factor in generating innovation. The constituents of creativity encompass knowledge, creative thinking, and motivation (Bessant et al., 1999; Sanchez & Nagi, 2001).

In the literature, creativity signifies anchoring a company's operations in forward-thinking, envisioning growth and expansion. The company's objective transcends mere "survival"; it aims to evolve and enhance its market value (Ren et al., 2001; Rowe & Nejad, 2009; Tsourveloudis & Valavanis, 2002).

Creative actions manifest in various dimensions (Hoek et al., 2001):

- Innovation: Pioneering novel ideas and approaches,
- Openness of Mind: Cultivating a receptive mindset to new concepts,
- Systematic Employee Development and Knowledge Enrichment: Fostering employee growth and deepening knowledge,
- Creation of Higher-Value Products and Services: Developing offerings of superior quality and value,
- Creative Decision-Making: Formulating innovative decisions,
- Enhancing Organizational Effectiveness: Amplifying the efficiency of organizational operations,
- Cultivating Agile Traits Among Workers: Instilling characteristics of agility in employees.

Consequently, it can be inferred that agility is intimately intertwined with creativity. The latter remains a pivotal determinant of agility.

Today's organization and the challenges of the Economy 5.0

The dynamic process of digital transformation, deeply integrated into the era of sustainable development, is often referred to as the era of Society 5.0 and Economy 5.0. This transformation instigates specific trends that compel contemporary organizations to evolve with agility. Companies are compelled to confront cutting-edge technologies, which encompass a variety of IT tools (Borowiecki et al., 2021).

These tools significantly influence the caliber of an organization's offerings. The gradual advancement of digitalization mandates the introduction of innovations that ensure and fortify the organization's established market position. Economy 5.0 has introduced a premier IT solution that permeates nearly every aspect of production. This includes developing novel products and fully integrated value chains that are made possible by the skillful application of cutting-edge IT tools. The organization's processes have been computerized, enabling production to be precisely customized to intricately match customers' individual needs. Consequently, the methodologies governing business practices and the operational dynamics of entire market organizations and structures have undergone dynamic shifts. These transformative processes are spurred not only by innovative business models but also by cutting-edge technologies such as artificial intelligence (Zhen et al., 2021).

In this intricate reality, modern organizations operate. Its members must adjust to market demands and, as a result, cultivate suitable agile qualities that can successfully meet the demands of digitization.

Modern enterprise computing and efficient use of IT tools

In scientific literature, the term "IT" has been ascribed various definitions. It is commonly described as the technology employed to store, transfer, and process data, information, knowledge, and ultimately wisdom (Sallnäs & Björklund, 2020; Szkudlarek & Milczarek, 2014). IT signifies the resources an enterprise utilizes to manage the information necessary for fulfilling its mission. This encompasses a collective of users, information systems, and management methodologies (Turban et al., 2006). IT constitutes a distinct portion of the computerized information system (Pearce, 2012), often referring to computer and software technologies.

Information technology encompasses hardware and computers, computer networks encompassing software, systems, and utilities, along with the methods of their utilization. In practice, the term "information technology" is frequently abbreviated to "IT," and variations like "information technology" or "information technologies" can be found in the literature (Pearce, 2012).

Information and Communication Technologies (ICT) encompasses all elements associated with the electronic collection, storage, and processing of information, existing within the ICT sector. The ICT sector, in turn, constitutes a segment of the economy comprised of enterprises primarily engaged in producing goods and services that facilitate the electronic recording, processing, transmission, reproduction, or display of information (Seweryn, 2017).

Information and communication technologies, owing to their versatile nature and ever-expanding capabilities, play a pivotal role in all facets of a company's operations. They constitute a novel and dynamically evolving realm of knowledge, interweaving with various technologies (telecommunications, software, and hardware) to achieve the following:

- processing, which involves the application of methods and procedures to transform information without causing its destruction or consumption,
- acquiring, which encompasses generating information, including that which may not be consciously recognized,
- selection, which entails the process of choosing valuable and necessary information for further processing while discarding irrelevant data,
- analyzing, which provides a means to navigate complex realities and comprehend them effectively,
- processing, which involves generating new information based on previously collected and stored data,
- storage, which involves placing selected data within virtual memory structures,

- management, which serves as a means to access information effectively, and encompasses control over information processes to optimize them,
- dissemination, which ensures that information reaches as many recipients as possible.

The core of an organization's functioning lies in operating within cyberspace, facilitated by computer networks, where the time required for information transmission and decision-making must be exceedingly short. The enhanced efficiency of enterprise operations owes much to the employment of information technologies. Leveraging substantial information resources accelerates management processes and improves the quality of numerous operations (Oleksiejczuk & Oleksiejczuk, 2009).

Balancing organizational agility, creativity, and effective ICT use in polish enterprises: empirical findings

We conducted primary research to achieve our research goals. We used a survey method and sent out online questionnaires to participants in February 2022. We followed the standards of the Computer-Assisted Web Interviewing (CAWI) technique. The results were analyzed using the SPSS Statistics software.

Our research group included 745 people from different age groups, selected randomly. You can find the respondents' demographic information in Table 12.1.

In the context of the article's objectives, it was pivotal to ascertain the domains in which respondents employ ICT tools (with an emphasis on three key areas). The visualization of this data is illustrated in Table 12.2.

Additionally, the study aimed to gauge respondents' perceptions of the significance of ICT in their work environments. Respondents notably emphasized the role of technology in enhancing productivity, streamlining tasks, and expediting performance. A concise overview of these responses is encapsulated in Table 12.3.

Continuing on, let's elucidate the factors contributing to the enhancement of digital competence. The foremost catalysts encompass the promise of personal growth, financial incentives, and the empowerment of self-reliance. A comprehensive breakdown of these motivating factors is provided in Table 12.4, which offers descriptive statistics.

Identifying agile and creative traits within the study participants has gained paramount significance. These undoubtedly encompass commitment, credibility, open-mindedness, and competence. Detailed data concerning this matter is laid out in Table 12.5, which provides descriptive statistics.

Table 12.1 Sociodemographic data of respondents

Age	*Number*	*%*
Under 20	174	24
21–30	449	60
31–40	69	9
41–50	46	5
Over 50	10	1
Total	**745**	
Sex		
Female	329	45
Male	416	55
Total	**754**	100
Domicile		
Village	141	19
City with a population of up to 20,000	92	12
Town with 21–50,000 inhabitants	79	11
Town with 51–200,000 inhabitants	49	7
City with more than 200,000 inhabitants	384	51
Total	**745**	100
Material status		
Very good	106	14
Good	405	55
Average	218	29
Bad	16	2
Total	**745**	100
Professional activity		
Unemployed	89	12
Employed full-time	453	61
Employed part-time	127	17
Owns a business	41	5
Engaged in agricultural farming	7	1
Engaged in both full-time employment and business activities	28	4
Total	**745**	100

Source: Own study according to the studies conducted.

The study subsequently focused on the behaviors exhibited by agile and creative participants within the workplace. Those engaged in the study demonstrated leadership qualities, goal attainment, and the ability to manage project teams.

Discussion

Based on the conducted research, the goal was to ascertain the relationship between organizational agility, creativity, and the effective utilization of ICT. A structural model was estimated using the maximum likelihood

Table 12.2 Areas of use of ICT tools

Area of use	*Frequency*	*Percentage*
Manufacturing	92	4.1%
Services	297	13.3%
Logistics	150	6.7%
Finance	223	10.0%
Human resources management	112	5.0%
Sales	322	14.4%
Promotion	163	7.3%
Marketing	245	11.0%
Administration	195	8.7%
ICT support	68	3.0%
Training	161	7.2%
Research	48	2.1%
Other	159	7.1%
Total	**2235**	**100.0%**

Source: Own study based on the conducted research.

Table 12.3 The role of ICT in the workplace

Essential in the workplace	*212*	*9.5%*
Streamlines task execution	532	23.8%
Increases productivity	566	25.3%
Helps accomplish tasks	487	21.8%
Enhances speed	416	18.6%
Is unnecessary	22	1.0%
Total	2235	100.0%

Source: Own study based on the conducted research.

Table 12.4 Descriptive statistics

Mean	7.9
Median	8
Standard deviation	1.5
Minimum	1
Maximum	10
Mode	8
1st Quartile	7
2nd Quartile	8
3rd Quartile	9
Variance	2.3
Square root of variance	1.5

Source: Own study based on the conducted research.

Table 12.5 Descriptive statistics

Mean	7.2
Median	7
Standard deviation	1.7
Minimum	1
Maximum	10
Mode	8
1st Quartile	7
2nd Quartile	7
3rd Quartile	8
Variance	2.9
Square root of variance	1.7

Source: Own study based on the conducted research.

method to achieve this. There were no grounds to reject the null hypothesis that the residual values of the empirical and theoretical matrices are equal to zero ($\chi2 = 1065.87$; $p = 0.009$). The Root Mean Square Error of Approximation (RMSEA) value of 0.085 indicates that the model fits the data well.

Apart from unobservable endogenous and exogenous variables listed below, the structural model estimated by the maximum likelihood method includes endogenous observable variables (presented in Table 12.6).

Unobservable endogenous variables

Z1: For what purpose do you use ICT tools in your workplace?
Z2: Do you consider ICT technology to be...
Z3: What potentially motivates you to enhance your digital competencies?
Z4: Is your... taken into account where you work (or used to work)?
Z5: In the projects you undertake...

Unobservable exogenous variables

e1, e2, e3, e4, e5, e6, e7, e8, e9, e10, e11, e12, e13, e14, e15, e16, e17, e18, e19, e20, e21, e22, e23, e24, e25, e26, e27, e28, e29, e330 33, e34, e35, 36, e37, e38, e39, e40, e41

The non-standardized and standardized model factors are summarized in Tables 12.7 and 12.8.

The above interpretations are valid under the assumption that the values of the remaining variables remain constant. The coefficients' values describe both the direction (positive/negative) and the strength of the explanatory variable's impact on the explaining variable. Standardized coefficients can be employed to compare the magnitude of effects across different explanatory variables. Non-standardized factor values are contingent upon the measurement units of the variables (Domański, 1990; Kline, 2005).

Table 12.6 Endogenous observable variables

X1: Production	X21: Independence
X2: Services	X22: Professional situation
X3: Logistics	X23: Material situation
X4: Finance	X24: Life situation
X5: Human resources management	X25: Prospects for development
X6: Sales	X26: Social affiliation
X7: Promotion	X27: Want to evaluate yourself
X8: Marketing	X28: Competence
X9: Administration	X29: Innovation
X10: ICT support	X30: Creativity
X11: Training	X31: Openness of mind
X12: Research	X32: Commitment
X13: Other	X33: Dedication
X14: Is essential in the workplace	X34: Taking risks
X15: Improves task execution	X35: Reliability
X16: Increases work efficiency	X36: You can be a leader
X17: Facilitates task completion	X37: You achieve your goals
X18: Increases operational speed	X38: You achieve your goals in the time schedule
X19: Is unnecessary	X39: You achieve your goals in the planned budget schedule
X20: Money	X40: You can implement several projects simultaneously
	X41: You can manage your project team

Source: Own elaboration.

Based on the standardized coefficients of the model, it was found that for the variable Z1: "What purpose do you use ICT tools for in your workplace?," the strongest influence comes from variables: X6: Sales, X2: Services, and X8: Marketing. In contrast, the weakest influence comes from variable X12: Research.

Based on the standardized coefficients of the model, it was found that for the variable Z2: "Do you consider ICT technology to be...?," the strongest influences are from variables: X16: Increases work efficiency, X15: improves task execution, while the weakest influence comes from variable X19: "is unnecessary" and X14: "is indispensable in the workplace."

Based on the standardized coefficients of the model, it was found that for the variable Z3: "What potentially motivates you to enhance your digital competencies?," the strongest influences come from variables: X25: Development perspective and X21: Independence, while the weakest influence comes from variable X26: Social affiliation and X24: Life situation.

Based on the standardized coefficients of the model, it was found that for the variable Z4: "Is your input taken into account where you work (or used to work)?," the strongest influences come from variables: X32: Commitment, X28: Competence, while the weakest influence comes from variable X34: Taking risks and X29: Innovation.

Table 12.7 Unstandardized coefficients of the model

Variables	*Estimated parameter value*	*Estimation error*	*Critical value*	*p-value*
X1	0.2576	0.105	22.86	***
X2	0.83168	0.104	17.62	***
X3	0.41952	0.071	19.17	***
X4	0.62376	0.084	19.66	***
X5	0.31372	0.105	23.2	***
X6	0.9016	0.107	23.22	***
X7	0.45632	0.093	20.76	***
X8	0.6854	0.122	20.4	***
X9	0.54556	0.108	19.66	***
X10	0.19044	0.102	20.32	***
X11	0.4508	0.671	18.93	***
X12	0.13432	0.68	19.01	***
X13	0.44528	0.742	19.52	***
X14	0.68448	0.104	16.63	***
X15	0.7268	0.378	15.86	***
X16	0.391	0.109	18.18	***
X17	0.51796	0.079	18.27	***
X18	0.65412	0.088	18.3	***
X19	0.19872	0.109	18.18	***
X20	0.55752	0.097	18.2	***
X21	0.56856	0.084	18.27	***
X22	0.50968	0.122	18.18	***
X23	0.46552	0.108	18.27	***
X24	0.40664	0.105	22.86	***
X25	0.59984	0.104	17.62	***
X26	0.3358	0.071	19.17	***
X27	0.42688	0.084	19.66	***
X28	0.552	0.105	23.2	***
X29	0.4278	0.107	23.22	***
X30	0.4738	0.093	20.76	***
X31	0.51888	0.122	20.4	***
X32	0.59892	0.108	19.66	***
X33	0.50692	0.102	20.32	***
X34	0.33948	0.675	19.05	***
X35	0.5428	0.68	19.01	***
X36	0.48392	0.74	19.5	***
X37	0.575	0.104	16.63	***
X38	0.50416	0.373	15.82	***
X39	0.45816	0.109	18.06	***
X40	0.40756	0.079	18.27	***
X41	0.4186	0.088	18.3	***

Note: ***denotes $p < 0.001$, Source: Own elaboration.

Based on the standardized coefficients of the model, it was found that for the variable Z5- "In the projects you undertake...?," the strongest influences come from variables: X37: You achieve planned goals and X38: You achieve goals within the scheduled time, while the weakest influence comes from

Table 12.8 Standardized coefficients of the model

Variables	*Estimated parameter value*
X1	0.28
X2	0.904
X3	0.456
X4	0.678
X5	0.341
X6	0.98
X7	0.496
X8	0.745
X9	0.593
X10	0.207
X11	0.49
X12	0.146
X13	0.484
X14	0.744
X15	0.79
X16	0.425
X17	0.563
X18	0.711
X19	0.216
X20	0.606
X21	0.618
X22	0.554
X23	0.506
X24	0.442
X25	0.652
X26	0.365
X27	0.464
X28	0.6
X29	0.465
X30	0.515
X31	0.564
X32	0.651
X33	0.551
X34	0.369
X35	0.59
X36	0.526
X37	0.625
X38	0.548
X39	0.498
X40	0.443
X41	0.455

variable X40: You can handle multiple projects simultaneously and X41: You can manage project teams.

ICT's impact on work efficiency can be described as substantial. Consequently, businesses should prioritize developing and modernizing this technology while fostering trust, given employees' keen interest in enhancing their digital competencies. Agility and organizational creativity assume crucial roles as catalysts for improving employee attributes and enabling them to utilize IT tools effectively. This concept is expounded in the author's theoretical model, which illustrates the influence of social activity on business efficiency.

Consequently, the proficient utilization of ICT is closely tied to cultivating organizational agility and agile attributes. Creativity falls within the realm of agility and is pivotal in determining the effective application of ICT. Agile organizations adeptly employ IT tools in sales, services, and marketing. However, enhancing employees' digital proficiency is a prerequisite for effectively utilizing ICT. As a result, company management should bear this in mind and consider organizing training programs to enhance such qualifications. A firm's market influence and competitiveness can be strengthened by this important information and the presented statistical relationships.

References

Almahamid, S., Awwad, A., & Adams, A. (2010). Effects of organizational agility knowledge sharing on competitive advantage; An empirical study in Jordan. *International Journal of Management, 27*(3), 10–12.

Bessant, J., Francis, D., Meredith, S., Kaplinsky, R., & Brown, S. (1999). Developing manufacturing agility in SMEs. *International Journal of Technology Management, 22*(1/2/3), 28. https://doi.org/10.1504/ijtm.2001.002953.

Borowiecki, R., Olesiński, Z., & Rzepka, A. (2021). Evolution of organization management in light of Economy 4.0 challenges. In Duda, J., & Gąsior, A. (Eds), *Industry 4.0: A Glocal Perspective* (1st ed.). New York: Routledge. https://doi.org/10.4324/9781003186373.

Domański, C. (1990). *Testy statystyczne*. Warszawa: Państwowe Wydawnictwo Ekonomiczne.

Goldman, S. L., Nagel, R. N., & Preiss, K. (1995). *Agile competitors and virtual organizations: Strategies for enriching the customer*. New York: Van Nostrand Reinhold.

Gunasekaran, A. (1998). Agile manufacturing: Enablers and an implementation framework. *International Journal of Production Research, 36*(5), 1223–1247. https://doi.org/10.1080/002075498193291.

Hormozi, A. M. (2009). Agile manufacturing: The next logical step. *Benchmarking: An International Journal, 8*(2), 132–143. https://doi.org/10.1108/14635770110389843.

I. van Hoek, R., Harrison, A., & Christopher, M. (2001). Measuring agile capabilities in the supply chain. *International Journal of Operations & Production Management, 21*(1/2), 126–148. https://doi.org/10.1108/01443570110358495.

Kidd, P. T. (1994). *Agile manufacturing: Forging new frontiers, reading*. Woburn, MA: Addison-Wesley.

Kline, R. B. (2005). *Principles and practice of structural equation modeling* (2nd ed.). New York: The Guilford Press.

Leberecht, T. (2016). Designing the strategy. Bet on agility. *Harvard Business Review Poland, 166–167*, 3, 17.

Luecke, R. (2005). *Managing creativity and innovation*. Konstancin Jeziorna: MT Biznes sp. z o.o.

Meredith, S., & Francis, D. (2000). Journey towards agility: The agile wheel explored. *The TQM Magazine, 12*(2), 137–143. https://doi.org/10.1108/09544780010318398.

Mroziewski, M. (2010). *Styl zarządzania jako instytucjonalny czynnik kreowania kapitału przedsiębiorczości organizacyjnej. Koncepcja ewolucyjno-normatywna*. Gdańsk: Wydawnictwo Uniwersytetu Gdańskiego.

Narasimhan, R., Talluri, S., & Mahapatra, S. K. (2006). Multiproduct, multicriteria model for supplier selection with product life-cycle considerations. *Decision Sciences, 37*(4), 577–603. https://doi.org/10.1111/j.1540-5414.2006.00139.x.

Oleksiejczuk, E., & Oleksiejczuk, A. (2009). Rola technologii informacyjnej w zarządzaniu oraz jej wpływ na kształtowanie się społeczeństwa informacyjnego. *Przedsiębiorczość-Edukacja*, *5*, 57–68.

Pearce, J. M. (2012). The case for open source appropriate technology. *Environment, Development and Sustainability, 14*(3), 425–431. https://doi.org/10.1007/s10668-012-9337-9.

Ren, J., Yusuf, Y. Y., & Burns, N. D. (2001). Organizational competitiveness: Identifying the critical agile attributes using principal component analysis. In *16th International Conference on Production Research, ID*. The International Foundation for Production Research (IFPR), Prague (Vol. 588, p. 29).

Rigby, K. (2000). Bullying in schools: Guidelines to effective action. *Professional Reading Guide for Educational Administrators, 21*(1), 28–36.

Rowe, G., & Nejad, M. H. (2009). Strategic leadership: Short-term stability and long-term viability. *Ivey Business Journal, 73*(5), 6–11.

Sahota, M. (2012). *An agile adoption and transformation survival guide*. New York: Working with Organizational Culture.

Sajdak, M. (2014). Agile response of modern enterprises to new environmental challenges. *Studia Oeconomica Posnaniensia, 11*, 3–13.

Sallnäs, U., & Björklund, M. (2020). Consumers' influence on the greening of distribution–exploring the communication between logistics service providers, e-tailers and consumers. *International Journal of Retail & Distribution Management, 48*(11), 1177–1193.

Sanchez, L. M., & Nagi, R. (2001). A review of agile manufacturing systems. *International Journal of Production Research, 39*(16), 3561–3600. https://doi.org/10.1080/00207540110068790.

Strużycki, M. (Ed.). (2004). *Corporate governance*. Warsaw: Difin.

Stverkova, H., & Pohludka, M. (2018). Business organizational structures of global companies: use of the territorial model to ensure long term growth. *Social Science, 7(12)*, 98.

Szkudlarek, P., & Milczarek, A. (2014). Rola społeczeństwa informacyjnego w kreowaniu zrównoważonego rozwoju. *Ekonomia i Środowisko*, 3(50), 209–220.

Teece, D. J. (2007). Explicating dynamic capabilities: The nature and microfoundations of (sustainable) enterprise performance. *Strategic Management Journal, 28*(13), 1319–1350. https://doi.org/10.1002/smj.640.

Todorovych, K. (2021). *Books: Becoming more agile*. Novi, Mich.: IMA. https://www.sfmagazine.com/articles/2021/october/books-becoming-more-agile/?psso=true

Trzcieliński, S. (2007). *Agile enterprise: Concepts and some results of research*. Poznań: IEA Press.

Tsourveloudis, N. C., & Valavanis, K. P. (2002). On the Measurement of enterprise agility. *Journal of Intelligent & Robotic Systems, 33*, 329–342. https://doi.org/10.1023/A:1015096909316.

Turban, E., McLean, E. R., Leidner, D. E., & Wetherbe, J. C. (2006). *Information technology for management: Transforming organizations in the digital economy*. New York: John Wiley and Sons.

Walczak, M., & Skalik, J. (Eds.). (2010). *Comparison of traditional and agile project management approaches*. Wrocław: University of Economics in Wrocław.

Yang, C., & Liu, H.-M. (2012). Boosting firm performance via enterprise agility and network structure. *Management Decision, 50*(6), 1022–1044. https://doi.org/10.1108/00251741211238319.

Zhang, Z., & Sharifi, H. (2000). A methodology for achieving agility in manufacturing organisations. *International Journal of Operations & Production Management, 20*(4), 496–513. https://doi.org/10.1108/01443570010314818.

Zhen, J., Xie, Z., & Dong, K. (2021). Impact of IT governance mechanisms on organizational agility and the role of top management support and IT ambidexterity. *International Journal of Accounting Information Systems, 40*, 100501. https://doi.org/10.1016/j.accinf.2021.100501.

13 Employee involvement in a volatile Society 5.0 landscape

Mariana Petrova, Sultan Ramazanov, and Ludmiła Stemplewska

Introduction

This chapter addresses matters pertaining to employee involvement within an unpredictable environment, highlighting the influence of selected factors on increasing employee engagement. Consequently, this facilitates the establishment of conditions for enhancing organizational functionality and fostering growth within the context of Society 5.0. The chapter defines and identifies factors that trigger changes in employee involvement and underscores shifts in awareness concerning the persistent emergence of unforeseeable circumstances within the work environment.

The relationship between employee engagement levels and organizational effectiveness is mainly due to businesses' constant pursuit of increased financial, organizational, and sales performance in an effort to gain customers' favor. Although there may not be a clear definition of involvement in academic literature, its essence can be connected to a person's behavior in the workplace. This demeanor, which consists of cognitive, emotional, and behavioral elements, is shaped by the unpredictability of the organizational environment and the extent to which these changes intersect with the challenges employees are accustomed to facing.

The essence of employee involvement

Employee involvement is defined as a specific attitude toward work (Juchnowicz, 2012). It consists of three different components: emotional, cognitive, and behavioral. Involved employees, according to Juchnowicz, maintain a positive attitude toward the organization (or work), focus on tasks, complete them with passion, and take actions that are advantageous to the business.

Attention should be drawn to the fact that engagement centers on the mental relationship between employees and the organization. It is divided into organizational and professional attachments. The former represents employees' attitudes resulting from positive social exchanges in

DOI: 10.4324/9781003502272-14

the workplace. It can be observed in various relationships with the organization, team, or superiors. Professional attachment pertains to engagement in a specific profession, involving a particular set of competencies and behaviors in accordance with the requirements of the job (Meyer & Herscovitch, 2001).

As a multi-dimensional category posing challenges during research, employee involvement is related to many essential employee behaviors, e.g., turnover, job satisfaction, and citizenship behaviors (Johnson, Groff, & Taing, 2009).

The following research trends were outlined in the literature (Gallagher & Parks, 2001):

1 emphasis on employee engagement with the employer organization (authors exploring this context strive to clarify the concept's essence, provide a definition, depict its dimensions or nature, and endeavor to develop a model that organizes the causes, relationships, and benefits of organizational engagement).
2 research encompassing theoretical and empirical investigations demonstrating engagement's different goals. As a result, commitment to working conditions includes a personal commitment to work as an employment commitment, involvement in one's job, and commitment to one's position and line of work.

Mutual relationships change over time while maintaining trust, loyalty, and mutual commitment as long as both parties adhere to specific rules (Saks, 2006). Engagement is a mutually beneficial type of relationship where both the employer and employee take actions toward each other that extend beyond formal obligations (Pech & Slade, 2006).

Organizational engagement, which includes other types of engagement (such as engagement in the work being done, engagement in the profession being pursued, and interpersonal engagement in the workplace environment), is the most significant from a management perspective. From the perspective of an employer, the most valuable type of engagement entails making changes and taking ownership of them, identifying problems and offering solutions, showcasing innovation, and looking for new professional challenges.

Alternatively, behavioral indicators of employee engagement can be encapsulated as a triad (Guryn, 2009)

Behavioral indicators of employee engagement can be captured in the form of a triad (Guryn, 2009):

- **speaks** (which refers to speaking positively about the organization in various social circumstances),

- **remains** (which signifies consciously connecting one's future with the organization),
- **acts** (which implies investing additional effort into one's work).

Even in challenging situations, employees remain engaged and loyal, and consistently deliver high-quality work (Berłowski, 2010). An essential aspect is the observation of engagement at an individual level. According to Saks (2006), work engagement has a positive relationship with organizational commitment, civic engagement, and job satisfaction.

Determinants of employee involvement

Numerous conceptualizations of employee engagement issues point to the crucial importance of employee engagement in achieving the organization's objectives. The literature emphasizes the correlation between employee involvement and productivity, profitability, innovation, and personal safety variables. It is, therefore, not surprising that managerial staff are increasingly interested in employee involvement and reliable methods of measurement (Rudawska, 2011).

The Gallup-Sharecare Well-being Index is a reliable and comprehensive instrument consisting of five dimensions of well-being (Roy et al., 2018):

- Objectives (a positive attitude toward everyday activities and motivation to achieve goals),
- Relationships (having supportive relationships and experiencing love in one's life),
- Finances (economic comfort, which minimizes stress and provides an appropriate sense of security),
- Community (a positive attitude toward one's place of residence, a sense of security, and community pride),
- Physical dimension (having good health and sufficient energy to perform daily tasks).

Equitable, just, and supportive employment relationships form the foundation of a worker's sense of psychological security. Research by Saks (2006) has demonstrated that employees' perceptions of organizational support correlate positively with their commitment to work. In contrast, the perception of support from supervisors is linked to higher levels of engagement. Additionally, the degree of employee involvement and active participation in the work process are positively correlated with the perception of fairness, which significantly impacts both. Employee success hinges on comprehensive support, which includes appropriate role assignments. These factors include effective performance management, suitable delegation of responsibilities, empowerment to complete tasks, and adequate training (Wójcik, 2009).

The business management must have a positive attitude to increase employee engagement. The main reason for its insufficient involvement is attributed to a lack of trust between employers and employees. Disengagement results from employees' distrust toward their superiors and their lack of belief in what they are told, which develops a crisis in the relationship between managers and their staff.

Pech and Slade (2006) have distinguished four groups of factors that are potential causes of a lack of employee engagement:

1 external environmental variables: instability and uncertainty,
2 psychological factors: a lack of meaning, an absence of identification, a lack of trust, a sense of being underestimated, unmet desires, a sense of injustice, a lack of interest, stress, and anxiety,
3 organizational factors: reorganization, unfavorable working conditions, poor management and leadership, excessive red tape, a lack of resources, acceptance of and tolerance for subpar performance, and the complexity of the job,
4 other contributing factors: drug abuse, skill deficits, indolence, illnesses, and interpersonal issues.

Many variables affect employee engagement, and not all employers have control over them. It should be emphasized that engagement is a relatively long-lasting employee condition that results in a specific behavior that meets the employer's expectations. A high level of commitment is fundamental to achieve better results with the same resources.

An engaged employee displays focus, energy, and job satisfaction. This positive state often results from the employer providing the necessary support, understanding, and awareness of their role in fostering engagement.

In our study, respondents emphasized their commitment to the work process. Notably, 37% of workers said they were somewhat committed, compared to 29% who thought they were firmly committed. On the other hand, 19% do not believe they are sufficiently engaged in their work, and a smaller percentage of respondents (12%) noted that they are unlikely to be involved. A mere 3% reported a lack of engagement in their work.

These findings reflect the psychological state of employees. A significant portion of employees desire to work with passion, while a smaller group indicates a lack of engagement. Various reasons could underlie these sentiments, including fear of job loss, which might lead to increased engagement in some employees and decreased commitment or even depressive states in others.

Enhancing employee involvement is tied to a positive attitude toward the organization and its values. Engaged employees perform tasks that benefit the company and their colleagues, seeking personal fulfillment through their work.

For some employees, competence, and experience bolster involvement, while for others, these factors might weaken their commitment due to perceived fear and stress.

Mobilizing a person's energy in times of danger triggers the body's fight-or-flight responses. Fears about the future can lead to heightened involvement or, conversely, a withdrawal from working life due to a sense of helplessness, potentially culminating in mental health challenges.

The current economic and political situation highlights that the media and interpersonal discussions focus on the impacts of the pandemic and the war in Ukraine, causing stress regarding well-being. It's not feasible to isolate oneself from this unpredictable reality, intensifying societal anxiety by adding another layer of uncertainty.

The fear of job loss has become a pervasive social concern, narrowing perspectives. This apprehension frequently paralyzes individuals and obscures opportunities concealed within this stressful situation.

Economic crises have historically led to significant job losses, raising questions about managing such challenging conditions and mitigating job insecurity anxiety in individuals and companies.

The survey revealed that 39% of respondents fear losing their jobs, while 13% are terrified. A mere 17% of those surveyed have no opinion on the matter. Conversely, a minority of surveyed workers (12%) are unlikely to feel fearful about job loss, and 1% are confident that their jobs are secure in the real world.

Increasingly, individuals value work environments that foster positive relationships and interpersonal interactions. The period of isolation has underscored that while workers are enthusiastic about performing tasks from home, they also yearn for meaningful connections and enduring positive relationships with others.

Proper engagement in work cannot be achieved if both the worker and the employer fail to make the necessary efforts to achieve it. An employer is responsible for maintaining an adequate level of commitment from its employees, necessitating the pursuit of appropriate solutions.

One such solution is to strive to create a positive working atmosphere, instill loyalty, stimulate creativity, and foster autonomy in decision-making, all aligning with the company's values. Caring for working conditions is also crucial. Balancing all aspects of an employee's life becomes significant for managers, who must engage with employees individually.

Passion and enthusiasm at work often evoke similar emotions in other employees. Research findings indicate that a substantial proportion of workers engage with and approach their jobs with passion and enthusiasm. A staggering 73% of respondents demonstrate strong passion and enthusiasm for their work, while only 20% admit to having low levels of passion and enthusiasm in the workplace.

Conclusions

The current environment creates conditions for organizations to take action to increase employee involvement, enabling them to adapt quickly to changing realities. Developing a sense of mutual trust, attending to others' needs, and exercising leadership are requirements.

Poor employee involvement can result from errors originating from the organizational side and incorrect attitudes of managers. However, there are exceptions where the responsibility lies with the employee who waits for someone else to solve their problems and only complains about the negatives.

Employees fall into one of three groups: (1) those who take charge of their own lives, work, think, and achieve their self-set goals; (2) those who perform well and accomplish both company and loosely defined personal goals under the influence of a positive organization and working environment; and (3) those who rely on others, complain all the time, expect others to take care of them, and then blame others for the adverse events that occur in their lives.

The question of whether organizations should constantly work to increase employee engagement levels is another finding when looking at employee engagement levels. If an organization chooses people who are the right fit for specific roles (those willing to work arduously, creatively, devotedly, and diligently), then increasing employee involvement is a sensible goal.

Inequalities between nations, generations, sexes, or language minorities are meant to be eliminated by the new values that innovation will bring about. Delivering goods and services that are suited to individual needs is another objective of these values. Therefore, as conceptualists emphasize, the society of the future is not about a world run and governed by robots and artificial intelligence. Instead, it ought to put each person at the center of attention. This society aims to create a place where people respect one another, where generational divides are broken down, and where everyone can live an active and fulfilling existence.

People, things, and systems will all be connected in Society 5.0. Managers now understand the importance of ongoing knowledge acquisition. Such a need and orientation to enhance employees' knowledge in various industries are evident. Interdisciplinary training is becoming more vital as managers demand multifunctional employees.

The advancement of technology has given everyone quick access to various kinds of information. Consequently, some individuals are becoming more educated and focused on personal development. It's important to highlight the growing number of highly qualified candidates. Employees possess diverse qualifications. For a manager to effectively communicate with employees, merely acquiring existing competencies within generally available knowledge and studies is insufficient. Managers must develop themselves daily, choosing current and applicable knowledge to manage manufacturing agents effectively.

References

Berłowski, P. (2010). Zaangażować sercem. *Personel i Zarządzanie, 3*, 58–61.

Gallagher, D. G., & Parks, J. M. (2001). I pledge thee my troth... contingently: Commitment and the contingent work relationship. *Human Resource Management Review, 11*(3), 181–208.

Guryn, H. (2009). Czy warto mierzyć zaangażowanie pracowników. *Personel i Zarządzanie, 4*.

Johnson, R. E., Groff, K. W., & Taing, M. U. (2009). Nature of the interactions among organizational commitments: Complementary, competitive or synergistic?: Interactions among commitments. *British Journal of Management, 20*(4), 431–447. https://doi.org/10.1111/j.1467-8551.2008.00592.x.

Juchnowicz, M. (2012). *Employee involvement. Methods of evaluation and motivation.* Warsaw: Polish Economic Publishing House.

Meyer, J. P., & Herscovitch, L. (2001). Commitment in the workplace: Toward a general model. *Human Resource Management Review, 11*(3), 299–326. https://doi.org/10.1016/s1053-4822(00)00053-x

Pech, R., & Slade, B. (2006). Employee disengagement: Is there evidence of a growing problem? *Handbook of Business Strategy, 7*(1), 21–25. https://doi.org/10.1108/10775730610618585

Roy, S., Hasan, A., Biswas, R. K., & Bhaumik, S. (2018). Impact of employee engagement on employee performance: Moderating role of emotional intelligence. *International Journal of Productivity and Performance Management, 67*(7), 1361–1377. https://doi.org/10.1108/IJPPM-06-2017-0195

Rudawska, A. (2011). Motywowanie do zaangażowania w organizację oraz życie społeczne i rodzinne. *Journal of Management and Business Administration. Central Europe, 19*, 75–85.

Saks, A. M. (2006). Antecedents and consequences of employee engagement. *Journal of Managerial Psychology, 21*(7), 600–619. https://doi.org/10.1108/02683940610690169.

White, B. (2013). *Employee engagement research update.* Hamilton, NJ: Blessing White.

Wójcik, M. (2009). Zaangażowany poszukiwany. *Personel i Zarządzanie*, 1, 36–39.

14 Best practices in sustainability communication and reporting among the world's largest companies in the realm of Industry 5.0

Marta Drozdowska, Małgorzata Leśniak-Johann, and Kamila Pihur

Introduction

Technology stands as a pivotal force propelling transformative shifts within industries and economies. The emergent concept of Economy 5.0 epitomizes this evolution. Utilizing these transformative dynamics and distributing their benefits to the larger community is a central goal of Industry 5.0 (Hirica, 2021). A comprehensive literature review shows that the productivity- and profit-centric paradigms of Economy 4.0 are not up to par with sustainable development's requirements (Ghobakhloo et al., 2022). Industry 4.0's ongoing evolution deviates more and more from its initial goals of promoting social equity and sustainable development in favor of digitalization and the incorporation of artificial intelligence to enhance production efficacy and adaptability (Battini et al., 2022).

This trajectory of development and globalization has simultaneously increased prosperity and exacerbated regional disparities. The result is the formation of vulnerable pockets in various regions (Huang et al., 2022). To put the ideas of Economy 5.0 into practice, the definition of industry needs to be broadened to include aspects that are tied to social structure and concrete steps toward sustainability (Sharifzadeh, 2022).

A 2022 study by a team of academics (Song et al.) compared how Fortune Global Top 500 companies interacted with the Sustainable Development Goals (SDGs) the United Nations established in 2015. This analysis drew upon publicly available information published from November 1, 2019, to February 15, 2020. Among the sampled group of 500 companies, 304 have forayed into the SDG framework, incorporating relevant content on their official platforms. Notably, 32.6% of these businesses align their current business activities with the SDGs without undertaking a strategic

DOI: 10.4324/9781003502272-15

realignment. A further 22.8% have devised actions or strategies that are aligned with specific SDGs. However, the adoption of the SDGs framework is still in its infancy, as 39.0% of Fortune 500 entities have yet to furnish any SDG-related context online (Song et al., 2022).

The novel concept of Economy 5.0 transcends the mere production of goods and services, encompassing domains of human-centricity, sustainability, and resilience (Xu et al., 2021). The human-centric approach repositions basic needs and individuals at the center of the production process within industries (Nahavandi, 2019). Integral to developmental paradigms, sustainability directs attention to resources and the environment, while resilience safeguards crucial community elements (Lu et al., 2021). The 2015 agreement on the 17 Sustainable Development Goals (SDGs) is aligned with these transformations and seeks to strengthen governance in this domain (Persson et al., 2016).

To achieve sustainability, multinational corporations and brands pursue various distinct and heterogeneous communication strategies. In a 2021 study, the research team under the direction of Nishitani et al. discovered that organizations with a proactive attitude toward the SDGs are more likely to amplify sustainability initiatives through successful implementation. This dynamic hinges on the interplay between stakeholder influence, the proactive company approach toward SDGs, and the ensuing reinforcement of sustainable development initiatives.

This study has a dual purpose: first, to examine the extent to which corporations with the world's highest revenues pursue sustainable development. The second objective of the authors is to describe exemplary practices in sustainable development based on accepted criteria that include social impact, environmental considerations, and financial aspects.

Materials and methods

The research employed data from the Global Fortune 500 and the Forbes Top 100 Most Sustainable Companies of 2022. Additionally, it drew from the strategic communication and reported sustainable development endeavors of selected companies, all contributing to achieving the research objectives.

The research methodology encompassed the following sequential stages:

- building a ranking database (the initial phase involved creating a comprehensive database with appropriate rankings),
- comparison and analysis of databases (a meticulous comparison of the database content was conducted to ascertain the extent of overlap between the world's top 500 revenue-generating companies and the 100 most sustainable corporations globally,

- an exhaustive examination of the communication strategies and reporting mechanisms related to sustainable development initiatives within the highest-ranking, most sustainable corporations; this was conducted using a set of predetermined criteria, namely social impact, environmental repercussions, and economic ramifications.

Global 100: the world's most sustainable corporations

The Corporate Hunts organization compiles the Global 100 list of the world's most sustainable corporations. The methods employed are based on a set of up to 25 key performance indicators (KPIs). The metrics used to compile the Global 100 World's Most Sustainable Corporation Ranking encompass four main domains: environmental, social, governance, and economic. Environmental metrics include energy, greenhouse gas (GHG), water, waste, volatile organic compound (VOC), nitrogen oxide (NOx), sulfur oxide (SOx) productivity, and sustainable investment. Social metrics track injuries, fatalities, employee turnover, and paid sick leave. Governance metrics evaluate sustainability pay linkage, non-male representation in executive management and board positions, racial diversity on boards, suppliers' sustainability scores, and corporate engagement with lobbying activities aligned with the goals of the Paris Agreement. Economic metrics encompass CEO-to-employee pay ratios, percentage tax paid, pension fund quality, and sanction deductions (Staff, 2022).

The list includes publicly listed companies with a minimum gross revenue of $1 billion in $PPP currency. Companies from all industries and geographical regions are automatically considered before screening out companies from specific sectors or with identified egregious practices. A taxonomy has been developed to assess the contributions of businesses to sustainable transitioning, incorporating revenue mapping and alignment with the United Nations Sustainable Development Goals. This methodology is aligned with the segment reporting guidelines established by global accounting standard-setting bodies. It provides a complementary reporting framework for conventional environmental, social, and governance (ESG) metrics (Staff, 2022).

The scope of the collected data is extensive, encompassing various specific facets that shed light on numerous pressing issues. These issues span from the effectiveness and efficiency of utilizing environmental resources to the management of the workforce, gender disparities, pay inequities, the representation of minorities, and even the fines paid by corporations. The data extracted from these diverse metrics served as the foundation for generating a comprehensive ranking list. This was achieved through the allocation of weights to different metrics and the subsequent calculation of result percentages for companies relative to their peers within a specific industry

(Staff, 2022). By adding up all the different sub-indices, a composite indicator was made. This composite indicator was then employed to establish a ranking that ranges from A+ (indicating the highest position) to D- (denoting the lowest position).

Six companies were meticulously selected for comprehensive analysis due to their dual ranking in The Global Fortune 500 and Forbes' Top 100 Most Sustainable Companies of 2022. These distinguished firms comprise Apple, Tesla, Alphabet Inc., Cisco Systems, HP Inc., Unilever, and HP Enterprise C.O. A thorough examination was directed toward the communication channels of these six entities.

The analysis focused on the predominant communication channels employed to engage with their customers and stakeholders. These channels comprised the official website, methods used to explain sustainable development approaches, and the company's mission, vision, values, focus areas, goals, and commitments (as per the adopted terminology). Moreover, the study included assessments of sustainable reports, influential social media platforms including Instagram, Facebook, YouTube, and Twitter, and their discussions on sustainability from November 2021 to October 2022. It also encompassed evaluations of crucial industry involvements, strategies for promoting sustainable products, and exemplary instances of best practices in sustainable development.

This comprehensive analysis spanned key domains of sustainable development initiatives, aligning seamlessly with the 17 Sustainable Development Goals outlined by the United Nations in 2018.

Results

Global business leaders and sustainable development

The Fortune Global 500 rankings for 2022 encompass the world's 500 largest companies, evaluated based on their revenue. A distinct geographical concentration of these major companies is evident across three global regions: Southeast Asia (primarily China), North America (USA), and Europe (European Union and UK). A noteworthy 29% of these companies (145) originate from China, marking the most significant quantitative representation globally, while 25% hail from the USA. Despite the larger number of Chinese companies, US-based companies exhibit higher profitability rates.

Consistently for another year, there remains minimal representation from the world's most prosperous companies within the developing nations of Latin America, alongside a nearly negligible presence of firms headquartered in Africa. Predominantly, companies are concentrated in various industries such as finance (109), energy (68), technology (34), and engineering and construction (16).

Only six top 500 companies have secured spots on the prestigious Global 100 list: Apple Inc., Alphabet Inc., HP Inc., Unilever PLC, Tesla Inc., and Cisco Systems Inc. These predominantly consist of US firms operating in the IT, telecommunications, and automotive sectors. The sole UK representative, Unilever PLC, operates within the chemical industry (see Table 14.1). While Apple and Alphabet hold the leading positions in both rankings, the remaining entities listed occupy roughly half of that ranking (refer to Table 14.1).

The inclusion of these 100 most sustainable global corporations is a substantial distinction, underscoring their adherence to comprehensive reporting standards across environmental, social, management, and economic metrics. Notably, the majority of the world's top 500 corporations do not provide such detailed insights into their activities, even though many do communicate their commitment to environmentally friendly practices through their communication channels. According to Staff (2022), "The World's Most Sustainable Corporations," the majority of the companies in the Global 100 ranking are from nations with modest economies, primarily Denmark, Sweden, Finland, Canada, and France.

Environmental metrics have been meticulously gathered and compiled for the examined companies, ensuring comprehensive coverage. The presented percentages indicate their respective positions in relation to the sectors under consideration. Each of the six businesses has demonstrated commitments to energy, water, waste management, coal, and clean investments. It is notable, however, that only Apple, Cisco Systems, and HP undertake actions across all of these domains, demonstrating comparable levels of commitment. Cisco Systems emerges as the leader among them.

Regarding clean revenue, Tesla and Apple have taken the lead. This specifically pertains to the products they offer, which are categorically identified within the applicable taxonomy as low-carbon products.

Social metrics were collected from three of the six analyzed companies, specifically Cisco Systems, HP, and Unilever. Among these, HP and Unilever are clear leaders, showcasing low employee turnover rates and workplace accidents.

The management metrics scrutinized within the ranking often overlap with other ESG reporting frameworks, particularly within the social dimension. Issues related to gender and race equality within boards and managerial positions are frequently addressed. The Global 100 most sustainable companies, especially Unilever, Cisco Systems, and HP, exhibit noteworthy performances. Notably, Cisco Systems received the best overall rating (the B category, 60%–65%). In contrast, other scrutinized businesses achieve B- ratings (55%–60%).

Table 14.1 Most sustainable companies among the 500 largest in the world

Company	*Industry*	*Main seat*	*Country*	*Place in Global 500 ranking*	*Place in G100 ranking*	*Revenue ($M)*
Apple Inc	Telephones and telecom equip manufacturing	Cupertino	US	7	48	365,817
Alphabet	IT services except telecom and hosting	Mountain View	US	17	36	257,637
HP Inc	Computers and peripherals manufacturing	Palo Alto railway station	US	202	50	63,487
Unilever PLC	Personal products (retail chemical)	London	UK	205	78	62,006
Tesla	Cars and trucks manufacturing, including parts	Austin	US	242	52	53,823
Cisco systems	Telephones and telecom equip manufacturing	San Jose	US	274	28	49,818

Source: Own elaboration based on Fortune (2022).

Focus areas of sustainability

All companies surveyed proclaimed their commitment to sustainable development. They all publish their sustainability activity reports, share their activities on social media, and have bookmarks on official websites dedicated to diversification development. Tesla is the exception here. These companies' missions either explicitly relate to sustainable development (e.g., Tesla's mission is to "accelerate the transition to sustainable energy") or encompass broader goals (e.g., Google's mission is to "organize the world's information and make it universally useful"). Some businesses establish distinct Corporate Social Responsibility (CSR) or sustainability initiatives that revolve around their core business objectives. For example, Cisco's CSR Mission is to "power an inclusive future and create equitable access to opportunity." Companies' key areas extend beyond their day-to-day operations. There is a clear commitment not only to the business environment and customers but also to local communities, people who are left out (people in poor countries, the elderly, and people with disabilities), and environmental activities, such as campaigns and financial support for protecting species, preserving forests, fighting climate change, cleaning up water pollution, and managing waste. The economic impact is the least talked about. Companies tend to focus on the supply chain and only a few other things, like economic opportunity or empowerment.

Communication of sustainability in accordance with SDG 2030

All the companies subjected to research effectively conveyed their unwavering dedication and active participation in SDG 2030 (see Table 14.2). Cisco emerges as the leader, with the highest number of references to SDGs, by articulating actions related to 14 specific SDGs.

The only SDG that does not appear as a Focus area in any report is ZERO HUNGER. However, three SDGs are consistently communicated across all surveyed companies, namely:

1 Affordable and Clean Energy: this is particularly highlighted through technological innovations in manufacturing, the advancement of zero-emission technologies, reduction of greenhouse gas emissions, and the augmentation of renewable energy availability.
2 Responsible Consumption and Production: this is demonstrated by responsible supply chain management and sourcing practices, consideration of human rights and working conditions within the supply chain, management of operational waste, and adoption of circular design principles and lifecycle management approaches.
3 Climate Action: this is underscored by commitments to reduce carbon footprint, enhance environmental and climate change management and reporting protocols, and expand the accessibility of renewable energy resources.

It is pertinent to note that while the aforementioned SDGs find comprehensive representation in communication efforts, there is a notable absence of any specific reference to SDG Zero Hunger in the focus areas covered within any of the reports.

Certain SDGs appear to hold significant importance for companies. For instance, Cisco and HP strongly emphasize SDG 8: Decent Work and Economic Growth. This is evident through their commitment to racial equity, business ethics, human rights, working conditions within the supply chain, fostering digital inclusion, and nurturing talent. On the other hand, Alphabet and Cisco concentrate their efforts on SDG 11: Sustainable Cities and Communities. Their focus entails enhancing environmental benefits through more sustainable workplaces and communities, addressing critical

Table 14.2 Contribution of the sustainable development goals 2030

	SDG2030	*Apple*	*Tesla*	*Alphabets*	*Unilever*	*Cisco*	*HP*
1	No poverty			2	1	3	
2	Zero hunger				1		
3	Good health and well-being		1		1	1	
4	Quality education		1	1		3	2
5	Gender equality		1		1	1	2
6	Clean water and sanitation	1	2		1	2	1
7	Affordable and clean energy	1	1	1	1	1	1
8	Decent work and economic growth			2	1	6	4
9	Industry innovation and infrastructure	1	1			2	
10	Reduced inequalities			1	1	3	2
11	Sustainable cities and communities	1		4		5	2
12	Responsible consumption and production	1	1	1	1	3	5
13	Climate action	1	1	2	1	1	6
14	Life below water	1					2
15	Life on land	1		1	1		1
16	People, justice and strong institutions		1			2	1
17	partnership for goals				1	3	2

Source: Own elaboration based on Alphabet Inc. (2020); Apple (2022); Cisco (2021); HP (2021); Tesla (2021); and Unilever (2021).

human needs and disaster relief, fostering economic empowerment, and ensuring environmental protection.

Communication sustainability in social media

All the examined companies effectively communicated their sustainability initiatives through various social media platforms. Notably, Unilever stands out as the most proactive participant. Unilever engages with three of the four major social media platforms—YouTube, Facebook, and Twitter—dedicating significant portions of its presence to addressing various dimensions of sustainability. Unilever's YouTube channel features distinct sections such as "What planet are you on?," "How we're Acting for a healthier planet," "Our Clean Future," "Explainers," "Futuremakers," and "Unilever Heroes." These dedicated channels cover a broad spectrum of sustainability topics, including innovative approaches to reducing environmental impact, participation in #COP27 events, trends within the health and well-being sector, net-zero endeavors, renewable resource adoption, biodiversity conservation, support for local communities, initiatives to combat food waste, and more.

YouTube emerges as the preferred platform for communicating sustainability. With the exception of Tesla, all companies showcase their commitment to sustainability in a clear and well-defined manner, demonstrating strong dedication to their sustainable objectives. Unilever, in particular, shines as a standout company, with sustainability taking a prominent position within its communication strategy.

In contrast, Facebook appears to be the least utilized platform for sustainability communication. Among the companies, Apple and Tesla exhibit minimal engagement on this platform, primarily employing it for basic communication and promotional purposes. Two companies, Unilever and Cisco, consistently and prominently convey their unwavering commitment to sustainability through their Facebook presence.

Apple and Tesla are notably less active in promoting their sustainable development activities through social media than the other companies. Apple exclusively utilizes YouTube for this purpose, while Tesla's social media presence lacks a distinct and robust focus on sustainability.

Several trends are discernible in the realm of sustainability communication via social media:

1 Direct Relevance: Companies often engage with issues that directly impact them. For instance, Cisco Systems champions women in technology, HP focuses on equipping teachers with tech skills, and Unilever delves into areas like biodiversity, food waste reduction, and health and well-being trends;
2 Reporting and Success Highlighting: Companies share their sustainability journey through reports and critical achievements. Tesla utilizes Instagram to present its Impact Report, while Alphabet uses Facebook for similar purposes;
3 Event Calendar Alignment: Corporations align with significant dates and events to emphasize their commitment. Examples include Earth Day, Pride Day, Coming Out Day, Tolerance Day, and Hunger and Homelessness Awareness Week. Alphabet, Cisco, HP, and Unilever all participate in these initiatives;
4 Employee Engagement: Companies communicate bottom-up initiatives that involve their workforce. This ranges from employee volunteering to charitable events such as business runs and Clean Beach Week. Cisco's Bee Downtown initiative and Unilever's diverse employee engagement categories—like Sustainability Storyteller, Impactful Social Entrepreneur, Planet Hugger, Impact Unlocker, and Pet Lover—exemplify this trend;

5 NGO Collaborations and Sustainable Initiatives: Collaboration with non-governmental organizations and support for sustainable projects are prevalent. HP's partnership with WWF for global forest protection and Unilever's involvement with COP27 are notable instances. Cisco's efforts to aid Ukraine exemplify corporate engagement in crisis response;
6 Informative Communication: Often, communication is informational rather than promotional. Unilever's Myth Buster series on Twitter—a platform to dispel misconceptions such as the idea that processing soy diminishes its nutritional value—exemplifies this educational approach.

In summary, the landscape of sustainability communication on social media is dynamic and diverse. Companies are strategically aligning their efforts, leveraging their influence to address pertinent issues, showcasing their achievements, fostering employee participation, collaborating with NGOs, and educating their audiences. This multifaceted approach reshapes how sustainability is perceived and championed in the digital era.

Discussion

Based on the survey findings, it's evident that only six companies from The Global Fortune 500 managed to secure positions among the 100 most sustainable companies of 2022, as recognized by Forbes. These noteworthy companies include Apple Inc., Alphabet Inc., HP Inc., Unilever PLC, Tesla Inc., and Cisco Systems Inc. However, this limited representation highlights a substantial opportunity for fostering sustainable practices within some of the world's largest corporations, particularly those in the energy, engineering, and IT sectors. The challenge at hand involves steering these businesses toward what can be termed "5.0," an ambitious endeavor that frequently demands a fundamental shift in operational philosophy.

Even companies ranked among the top 100 most sustainable corporations frequently fail to maximize the communication potential associated with such recognition. Only Cisco acknowledges this aspect across its information channels among the identified companies. This observation is unexpected, given that membership in this elite group implies adherence to stringent reporting standards. In industries embracing the concept of 5.0, such as IT, telecommunications, and the automotive industry, companies' actions regarding sustainable development are especially relevant.

It is worth noting that all six surveyed companies have embraced reporting their sustainable development initiatives through various social media platforms. Among these platforms, YouTube emerges as the favored choice for conveying sustainability-related endeavors, while Facebook garners the least attention for this purpose.

The survey findings underline the gap in effectively capitalizing on sustainable practices among the corporate giants, emphasizing the potential for substantial transformation across industries. The journey toward 5.0 necessitates a robust commitment to sustainability and a reimagining of operational paradigms. This underscores communication's pivotal role in this transformative process through various channels, especially social media.

The majority of the social media content that the analyzed companies publish focuses on popular and socially acceptable sustainable development initiatives. These actions include joint waste cleanups, trends in reducing food waste, and promoting gender equality.

However, in their sustainable development content, the analyzed companies do not provide information about critical environmental aspects such as pollution, greenhouse gas emissions, or the environmental impacts associated with their production processes. Instead, they focus on content that can positively influence and support the company's promotional and marketing endeavors.

Drawing from the conducted analyses, several recommendations for reporting and communicating sustainable development activities can be identified. These recommendations include:

1 Initiating a comprehensive reporting of activities by the world's largest companies (ranked by revenue), particularly Chinese firms, with a significant presence on The Global Fortune 500 list. This approach could indirectly encourage participation in global supply chains for products and services, where non-financial reporting of Environmental, Social, and Governance (ESG) aspects is expected to expand, especially in regions like Europe.
2 Placing a greater emphasis on addressing and reporting social issues within enterprises as a pivotal component of sustainable development and the 2030 Agenda. Key aspects such as working conditions, workers' rights, gender equality, and racial equality require special attention, as they represent significant challenges. The current level of reporting in this domain remains incomplete among the surveyed companies.
3 Taking more audacious actions and setting trends in communicating sustainable development initiatives while incorporating educational content into social media campaigns.
4 Expanding the range of information dissemination activities to encompass diverse communication channels. This expansion should not be confined solely to the most popular platforms, like social media. The objective is to amplify the reach of undertaken activities and enhance customer awareness about the companies' initiatives.
5 Encouraging prominent companies to engage in sectors of the economy that do not directly align with their core business functions. Expanding

sustainability initiatives into domains unrelated to the company's primary industry can attract a broader audience for its efforts.

These companies have a substantial opportunity to enhance their approach to sustainable development reporting and communication. By incorporating these recommendations, they can leverage their influence and resources to drive more comprehensive and impactful sustainable practices across various sectors of the economy.

References

Alphabet Inc. (2020). *Alphabet sustainability bond framework 2020.* abc.xyz. https://abc.xyz/assets/investor/static/pdf/SustainabilityBondFramework2020.pdf.

Apple. (2022). *Apple environmental progress report.* apple.com. https://www.apple.com/environment/pdf/Apple_Environmental_Progress_Report_2022.pdf.

Battini, D., Berti, N., Finco, S., Zennaro, I., & Das, A. (2022). Towards Industry 5.0: A multi-objective job rotation model for an inclusive workforce. *International Journal of Production Economics, 250*, 108619. https://doi.org/10.1016/j.ijpe.2022.108619.

Cisco. (2021). *United Nations (UN) sustainable development goals.* https://www.cisco.com/c/m/en_us/about/csr/esg-hub/governance/frameworks/unsdg.html.

Fortune. (2022). *Global 500*, Fortune. Available at: https://fortune.com/ranking/global500/2022 Accessed 08.4.24.

Ghobakhloo, M., Iranmanesh, M., Mubarak, M. F., Mubarik, M., Rejeb, A., & Nilashi, M. (2022). Identifying industry 5.0 contributions to sustainable development: A strategy roadmap for delivering sustainability values. *Sustainable Production and Consumption, 33*, 716–737. https://doi.org/10.1016/j.spc.2022.08.003.

Hirica, A. (2021). Industry 5.0—Are designers leading the way? *Design Management Review, 32*(4), 12–17. https://doi.org/10.1111/drev.12275.

HP. (2021). *Sustainable impact report.* hp.com. https://h20195.www2.hp.com/v2/GetDocument.aspx?docname=c07539064.

Huang, S., Wang, B., Li, X., Zheng, P., Mourtzis, D., & Wang, L. (2022). Industry 5.0 and Society 5.0—Comparison, complementation and co-evolution. *Journal of Manufacturing Systems, 64*, 424–428. https://doi.org/10.1016/j.jmsy.2022.07.010.

Lu, Y., Adrados, J. S., Chand, S. S., & Wang, L. (2021). Humans are not machines—anthropocentric human-machine symbiosis for ultra-flexible smart manufacturing. *Engineering, 7*(6), 734–737. https://doi.org/10.1016/j.eng.2020.09.018.

Nahavandi, S. (2019). Industry 5.0—a human-centric solution. *Sustainability, 11*(16), 4371. https://doi.org/10.3390/su11164371.

Nishitani, K., Nguyen, T. B. H., Trinh, T. Q., Wu, Q., & Kokubu, K. (2021). Are corporate environmental activities to meet sustainable development goals (SDGs) simply greenwashing? An empirical study of environmental management control systems in Vietnamese companies from the stakeholder management perspective. *Journal of Environmental Management, 296*, 113364. https://doi.org/10.1016/j.jenvman.2021.113364.

Persson, Å., Weitz, N., & Nilsson, M. (2016). Follow-up and review of the sustainable development goals: Alignment vs. internalization. *Review of European, Comparative & International Environmental Law, 25*(1), 59–68. https://doi.org/10.1111/reel.12150.

Sharifzadeh, M. (2022). *Industry 4.0 vision for energy and materials: Enabling technologies and case studies.* Hoboken, NJ: John Wiley & Sons, Inc. https://doi.org/10.1002/9781119695868.

Song, L., Zhan, X., Zhang, H., Xu, M., Liu, J., & Zheng, C. (2022). How much is global business sectors contributing to sustainable development goals? *Sustainable Horizons, 1*, 100012. https://doi.org/10.1016/j.horiz.2022.100012

Tesla. (2021). *Impact report 2020.* Tesla.com. https://www.tesla.com/ns_videos/2020-tesla-impact-report.pdf.

Unilever. (2021). *Unilever annual report and accounts.* Unilever. Available at: https://www.unilever.com/files/92ui5egz/production/61ebc6542e967e6fb5a8d5ee05a79238c8f6e4f7.pdf. Accessed 17.8.23.

United Nations. (2018). *The sustainable development goals report.* New York: United Nations. https://sdgs.un.org/2030agenda.

Xu, X., Lu, Y., Vogel-Heuser, B., & Wang, L. (2021). Industry 4.0 and Industry 5.0—Inception, conception and perception. *Journal of Manufacturing Systems, 61*, 530–535. https://doi.org/10.1016/j.jmsy.2021.10.006.

15 Business evolution

Emerging challenges for companies in achieving zero-carbon performance

Piotr F. Borowski

Introduction

The global impact of climate change has prompted nations and economies to actively seek ways to diminish their ecological footprint. Across various sectors, a systematic process of transformation is underway, presenting both economies and businesses with the formidable task of achieving climate neutrality by 2050. Nations and economies grapple with profound challenges, encompassing investment, societal, and climate-related hurdles, while businesses are primarily confronted with the need for technological overhaul. This dynamic shift toward cleaner energy sources and the implementation of the Green Deal has far-reaching effects, propelling innovation within diverse industries, facilitating the decarbonization of the energy sector, and enhancing overall energy efficiency. The ambitious target of reducing greenhouse gas emissions by a minimum of 55% by 2030 necessitates a substantial increase in the utilization of renewable energy and heightened energy efficiency. Fundamental to this endeavor is the imperative to curtail energy consumption, a measure pivotal in reducing emissions and cutting energy expenditures for both consumers and industries (GLT, 2023). Within the European Union, including Poland, the comprehensive adoption of the Green Deal and the integration of low-carbon solutions are imperative and warrant widespread implementation. Furthermore, the process of electrification demands significant investments in network infrastructure, energy storage, and hydrogen technology. Energy companies are confronted with the dual challenge of adapting to technological advancements and embracing structural transformations. To effectively engage with eco-friendly energy, heightened participation necessitates the adoption of inventive solutions anchored in emerging technologies and digitalization, accompanied by a series of strategic investments (Borowski, 2021). In Poland, the direction of decarbonizing and implementing energy produced from renewable sources is essential. Wind energy, photovoltaics, and the hydropower sector, with high flexibility and storage capacity, are crucial

DOI: 10.4324/9781003502272-16

and complementary components of the energy system. Furthermore, the process of decarbonizing Poland, predominantly through a substantial integration of offshore wind power, stands as the strategy that boasts the most cost-effective approach. This assessment considers both initial investments and ongoing operational expenses. In addition to facilitating the process of decarbonizing, renewable energy sources play a pivotal role in safeguarding energy sovereignty.

Fossil fuel phase-out

Transitioning away from fossil fuels serves the collective interests of Europe, addressing both climate concerns and the imperative of ensuring the security of raw material supply, along with supply stability and price equilibrium (Borowski, 2022a; Mason et al., 2022; Piggot et al., 2019). Escalating costs of imported raw materials result in diminished societal income, thus impacting the overall quality of life and exerting repercussions on the broader European economy. Over recent years, the energy landscapes of Poland and Europe have been undergoing profound shifts, marked by a decline in the proportion of traditional coal-based energy in favor of emerging technologies, notably renewable sources. Furthermore, this transformation entails a shift from centralized production within extensive Combined Heat and Power (CHP) plants to decentralized technologies, anchored in concepts like prosumers. The renewable energy sector stands out as one of the economy's most rapidly expanding domains, generating novel, reliable, well-compensated, and pioneering employment opportunities (Sadorsky, 2012). Prominent conventional energy corporations are broadening their production scope and directing investments toward renewable energy sources. These enterprises exhibit dynamic investments in the advancement of renewable energy systems, thus diversifying the overall energy portfolio (Standar et al., 2022).

Renewable energy

Both large corporations and individual consumers are increasingly becoming active participants in the electricity market (Shi et al., 2022). The necessity of investing in constructing their own power plants has become evident not only for consumers utilizing micro-installations but also for the category known as business prosumers (self-producers). These prosumers have recently been disproportionately affected by elevated wholesale energy prices, further compounded by capacity fees. Despite the presence of support systems for energy-intensive industries, they continue to shoulder the brunt of the escalated energy price surge. This impact is particularly pronounced in sectors with high end-product electricity costs, such as metal, chemical, wood, plastics industries, among others (Instytut Energii Odnawialnej, 2022). Within this evolving landscape, established energy consumers are now transitioning into the realm of energy producers.

Photovoltaics

Global photovoltaic production experienced a remarkable upsurge of nearly 180 TWh in 2021, marking a record-breaking increase of 22%. This boost propelled the worldwide energy output from photovoltaic panels beyond the 1000 TWh threshold. Across numerous nations, photovoltaics are emerging as the most cost-effective choice for electricity generation, thereby significantly influencing the sector's growth trajectory and anticipated investments in the upcoming years. The momentum of renewable energy expansion is also palpable in Europe, notably in the photovoltaic sector. In July 2021, The European Commission introduced a proposal to elevate the renewable energy target for 2030 from 32% to 40%, subsequently proposing an increase to 45% in May 2022. To align with the 2030 goals and in response to the energy crisis precipitated by Russia's incursion into Ukraine, many European countries have already prolonged their supportive frameworks for photovoltaics to accelerate capacity expansion (IEA, 2023). Addressing the energy crisis arising from insufficient gas supplies to European nations could be achieved by augmenting the proportion of renewable energy in the energy mix (Niemeyer & Meyers, 2022) or revisiting the utilization of fossil fuels (Borowski, 2022a).

In Poland, the photovoltaic market is projected to sustain its momentum in the forthcoming years. The revised forecast anticipates that a photovoltaic capacity of 20,000 MW could be achieved as soon as 2025, with the cumulative installed capacity potentially reaching up to 28,500 MW by 2030. To ensure the continued advancement of photovoltaics, the removal of administrative and network hindrances is imperative. Furthermore, establishing regulations and legal frameworks that streamline network access is crucial (Instytut Energii Odnawialnej, 2022).

Wind energy

Despite experiencing another favorable year for wind power, marked by a new installed capacity of 94 GW globally in 2021, the pace of wind power development remains insufficient. To guarantee a secure and robust global energy transition, the scope of its expansion must be broadened. At the present rate of installation, it is projected that only 75% of the necessary global wind power, as stipulated by the 1.5°C and zero emissions trajectory outlined in the 2050 roadmap, will be attained by 2030. This shortfall would lead to an inability to meet the climate targets (Bath & Lee, 2022).

The cumulative installed capacity across Europe is experiencing steady growth. Over the past decade, it has expanded to exceed 200 GW. Presently, the most expansive onshore wind farm on the continent is the Fântânele-Cogealac wind farm in Romania, comprising 240 turbines with a collective capacity of 2.5 MW each (Menear, 2020). In contrast, the largest offshore wind farm both in Europe and globally is the Walney Extension wind farm in the United Kingdom (Ronergy, 2022), boasting a capacity of 659 MW, facilitated by 200 turbines. The cumulative wind power production has surged to 426 TWh. This notable surge in production has positioned the wind industry as a substantial component of Europe's energy mix, and it currently holds the distinction of being the paramount renewable energy source, surpassing even hydropower (Fernández, 2023).

On land, wind energy possesses inherent potential to serve as a dual solution for both the climate crisis and the economic challenges (MENA, 2021). Fresh investments in onshore wind energy present an avenue toward a more environmentally friendly energy mix, reduced energy costs, and cleaner air. Similar to its European counterparts, Poland should expeditiously transition to zero-emission, distributed renewable sources, with wind energy emerging as the prime candidate for substantial development and the dynamic expansion of fresh generation capacity. Moreover, the swift advancement of wind energy facilitates emissions-free electricity production for households and accelerates the electrification of heating, transportation, and industrial sectors. The cost-effectiveness of wind-produced energy within the market will effectively decarbonize the Polish economy, aiding in meeting emission targets and sustaining competitiveness in the global arena. Nurturing energy-intensive sectors within Poland will hinge upon the utilization of renewable energy sources. To ensure the ongoing growth of industries like steel and heavy manufacturing, it's crucial to implement the most competitively priced energy technologies, including wind energy. This is especially vital considering the imminent move away from carbon in the steel sector, which will significantly amplify its electricity requirements (TPA Poland, 2021).

Wind energy has been on a sustained upward trend for years. The expanding installed capacity of wind farms coupled with increasing production volumes substantiates this trend. This progression is evident both in technological advancements, such as larger and more efficient production units, as well as in production growth through the introduction of new capacity and a heightened generation from wind sources. Historically, wind energy development has predominantly occurred on land. However, a recent observable shift is the extension of its reach onto seas and oceans. Forecasts projecting the costs associated with generating new generations of turbines underscore wind energy's emergence as an appealing alternative to conventional energy sources (dise.org.pl, 2019).

Hydropower engineering

The systematic warming of the climate observed over recent decades has been closely linked to alterations in the extensive hydrological cycle. Crucial factors contributing to climate change encompass human activities, deforestation, and industrial operations, which collectively disrupt Earth's water cycle—a cycle that should perpetually replenish water from oceans into the atmosphere, subsequently as precipitation onto land, then through rivers and lakes, before ultimately returning to seas and oceans. Concurrently, climate change elevates atmospheric water vapor levels and introduces greater unpredictability to water availability. It's worth noting that during flood events (Borowski, 2022b), a significant portion of rainwater rapidly flows through elevated rivers into saltwater seas and oceans, leading to a scenario where surplus precipitation doesn't contribute to freshwater storage (Borowski, 2020). The adverse ramifications of climate change manifest in heightened occurrences of floods, heatwaves, and forest fires. Such changes result in more intense rainfall in specific regions (e.g., Pakistan floods—August/September 2022), while other areas experience heightened drought severity (e.g., California drought and summer 2022 fires) (UNICEF, 2022; U.S. Drought Monitor, 2023). Europe is starting to confront challenges regarding freshwater accessibility, with Poland offering a poignant example of the complex hydrological predicament within the continent. Thus, Poland aptly exemplifies the intricate interplay between water availability and climate change impacting Europe's present circumstances (Borowski, 2022b). Moreover, Poland's freshwater resources are limited, with an annual availability per capita ranging from 1400 to 1600 m3 (according to varying sources), marking one of the lowest figures across Europe. This, despite water consumption being approximately double the OECD average. Poland is particularly vulnerable to water deficit, with projections indicating a potential up to 30% increase by 2050 (Climatechangepost, 2022).

Despite water access challenges in certain nations, hydropower stands as a widely embraced environmentally friendly technology in Europe. While assessing the environmental impact of hydroelectric power, it's essential to consider research indicating that water reservoirs and hydroelectric power plants also contribute to greenhouse gas emissions (Borowski, 2022b). Hydroelectric reservoirs can give rise to methane and carbon dioxide emissions across diverse climatic regions, attributed to the decomposition of allochthonous or autochthonous organic matter. This natural process fosters methane generation in anaerobic conditions or extensive water bodies with substantial depths. However, when contrasted with the carbon dioxide emissions stemming from fossil fuel energy production, the carbon footprint associated with hydropower remains significantly lower (Borowski, 2022b; Quaranta et al., 2022). Across European nations, the annual production (installed capacity) of hydropower varies, ranging from 33,391 MW in Norway, 2,385 MW in Poland, 97 MW in Belarus, to 4 MW in Estonia.

In 2021, new hydroelectric plants were inaugurated in both Norway and Turkey. The hydropower report by the International Energy Agency (IEA, 2021) forecasts a roughly 8% surge in Europe's total installed capacity by 2030, propelled by greenfield hydropower initiatives as well as the enhancement and expansion of preexisting infrastructure across the continent. Hydropower is built upon well-established technologies, boasting an overall efficiency surpassing 80% and potentially reaching up to 90%. In terms of efficiency, hydraulic turbines outperform photovoltaic panels by a factor of around five and surpass wind technologies by approximately threefold (dise.org.pl, 2019).

Gap between countries in terms of installed RES capacity

The gap in countries' economic standing, socio-economic circumstances, inclination to innovate and invest, and inherent natural factors such as climate and geographical positioning have discernible implications for the adoption and utilization of renewable energy sources in energy production. A comprehensive analysis of energy production via renewable sources among the top ten most advanced nations in this domain warrants a comparison of the gaps between these countries concerning their installed capacities. To facilitate this assessment, the following DI distance indicator was employed:

$$DI = 1\text{-}ICCnICCp$$

where DI stands for Distance Index

ICC_n – installed capacity of the next country

ICC_p—installed capacity of the previous country

Referring to Table 15.1, the largest disparity in photovoltaic energy production is found between Italy and Germany, with a margin of 0.61. In contrast, the narrowest gap occurs between the Netherlands and France, as well as Turkey and Ukraine, both registering a mere 0.03 difference. Consequently, Germany holds a significant lead in photovoltaic development globally, with the 0.61 disparity indicating that Italy would need to double its production to align with German photovoltaic output. Similarly, Germany maintains a considerable advantage in wind energy, with a 0.57 distance separating it from the subsequent nation, Spain. However, the differentiation between Sweden and France, as well as Poland and Denmark, is minuscule, at just 0.01. This establishes Germany as a frontrunner in solar and wind energy production among European nations. In the domain of hydropower, Norway emerges as the predominant player. Notably, Table 15.1 underscores the marginal differences between individual countries in the group

Table 15.1 Gap between countries in terms of installed renewable energy sources (RES) capacity

Solar energy		*Wind energy*		*Water energy*	
Country	*DI*	*Country*	*DI*	*Country*	*DI*
Germany	1.00	Germany	1.00	Norway	1.00
Italy	0.61	Spain	0.57	Turkey	0.06
Spain	0.30	United Kingdom	0.10	France	0.19
France	0.08	France	0.31	Italy	0.11
Netherlands	0.03	Sweden	0.01	Spain	0.10
United Kingdom	0.04	Italy	0.06	Switzerland	0.17
Ukraine	0.41	Turkey	0.26	Sweden	0.02
Turkey	0.03	Netherlands	0.35	Austria	0.11
Belgium	0.16	Denmark	0.07	Germany	0.24
Poland	0.05	Poland	0.01	Portugal	0.35

Source: Own elaboration.

of the ten most advanced hydropower nations, ranging from 0.02 to 0.24. Only Portugal and Germany present a more noticeable gap, standing at 0.35. Among these countries, no significant outliers stand out in terms of hydropower performance when compared to their counterparts. This distribution of installed hydropower capacity is fundamentally shaped by each country's water availability and topography, leading mountainous regions to exhibit notably higher installed capacities in contrast to their lowland counterparts.

Innovative energy carriers

Hydrogen

The forthcoming surge in the hydrogen economy necessitates the establishment of an entire value chain framework and the development of comprehensive infrastructure (Falcone et al., 2021). This notably involves constructing new renewable energy source (RES)-based generation capacities, encompassing biomass and organic solid waste, to facilitate hydrogen production plants and their low-carbon source derivatives (Abdalla et al., 2018; Aziz et al., 2021). Moreover, the hydrogen economy mandates advancements in processes and technologies, including electrolyzer installations, networks for hydrogen distribution, pertinent transport and transmission infrastructure, hydrogen storage facilities, refueling networks, and the creation of fuel cells for applications across energy, heating, transport, and other economic sectors. Given its inherent attributes, hydrogen is poised to supplant fossil fuels, aligning with initiatives like the Polish hydrogen strategy. It can substitute for coke and natural gas in industrial furnaces, thereby contributing to industrial decarbonization. Hydrogen can be produced from electricity and then converted back into electricity through fuel cells, rendering it an energy carrier and storage solution, heralded as a highly promising chemical energy storage medium that can be reconverted into heat and electricity. Hydrogen holds potential not only for large-scale industrial and energy setups but also for end-users. Additionally, hydrogen will serve as a foundation for generating synthetic fuels, replacing crude oil for challenging applications. A crucial caveat, however, is that hydrogen production should adhere to innovative and environmentally friendly methodologies, epitomized as green hydrogen. Presently, less than 2% of global hydrogen production relies on "clean technologies." To realize the envisioned zero-emission economy, it is imperative to ensure the production and provision of green hydrogen sourced from renewable energy sources. The hydrogen sector is currently witnessing the emergence of Hydrogen Valleys, pioneering full-fledged hydrogen economies. A Hydrogen Valley can be defined as a geographical enclave (city, region, or industrial zone) where numerous hydrogen applications converge into an integrated ecosystem. Essentially, a Hydrogen Valley constitutes a project—often funded by local, national, and international resources—that amalgamates various industrial and research endeavors spanning the complete hydrogen value chain, encompassing production, transportation, distribution, storage, and end-use (Garcia-Navarro, 2021). These Hydrogen Valleys, through their holistic approaches, lay the groundwork for crafting regional "hydrogen mini-economies" by synergizing hydrogen supply and demand to enhance scalability, optimize asset utilization, and curtail expenses. In an ideal scenario, this linkage spans the entirety of the hydrogen supply chain: from production and storage to distribution and final utilization by residents, consumers, manufacturing firms, or public transportation systems. Presently, nearly 40 Hydrogen Valleys exist globally, predominantly concentrated in Germany, with specific figures for individual countries outlined in Table 15.2.

Currently, there are almost 40 Hydrogen Valleys in the world, predominantly found in Germany, with specific figures for individual countries outlined in Table 15.2.

The most significant Hydrogen Valley, with a daily production of 3180 T/day, operates in Rotterdam, the Netherlands. On the other end of the spectrum, the smallest Hydrogen Valley is situated in Fukushima, Japan, with a capacity of 0.5 tons per day (Garcia-Navarro, 2021). In Poland, however, the Hydrogen Valleys are still in the planning phase. The intention is to establish at least five, but not exceeding seven. These Polish hydrogen valleys are envisioned as integral components of the broader European

Table 15.2 Number of hydrogen valleys by country

Main location	*Number of hydrogen valley*
Germany	5
China	3
France	3
Netherlands	3
Spain	3
United States	3
Australia	2
Italy	2
United Kingdom	2
Belgium	2
Austria	1
Republic of Chile	1
Denmark	1
French Guiana	1
Japan	1
Portugal	1
Romania	1
Slovakia	1
Thailand	1
Total	38

Source: Own study based on (Clean Hydrogen Partnership, 2023).

Hydrogen Ecosystem. The Polish Hydrogen Valley Innovation Ecosystem will encompass pioneering industrial projects and substantial multi-year investment initiatives, slated to be executed within designated geographic regions. These hydrogen valleys will provide a platform for R&D and investment projects, fostering collaboration among local, national, and international partners. To harness Poland's scientific and technological potential in hydrogen technologies, the establishment of a dedicated unit is planned. This unit's responsibilities will primarily encompass coordinating tasks and project implementation, initiating novel solutions, and promoting education and knowledge dissemination related to hydrogen (Instytut Energii Odnawialnej, 2022).

Renewable energy study results

To propagate knowledge about environmentally sustainable energy and foster the adoption of innovative approaches, it is imperative to systematically execute educational campaigns and initiatives aimed at raising awareness about renewable energy sources. Entrepreneurs, whether embarking on new ventures or already established, should possess comprehensive insight into the diverse array of potential solutions. Within the context of this study, primary research was conducted through survey methodologies, focusing on understanding the comprehension of renewable energy sources (RES) and the practical implementation of these solutions among young entrepreneurs. The survey was conducted in November 2022 on 121 young people from 22 countries who have experience running a business or intend to open their own soon. The study involved 68 men and 46 women; seven respondents did not answer about their gender.

The age spectrum of respondents spanned from 17 to 27 years. Participants were queried about their acquaintance with renewable energy sources (RES). When asked about their basic knowledge on renewable energy matters, 90% of respondents affirmed their familiarity with RES. Within the study cohort, 82% expressed a perspective that RES yields advantageous outcomes. A noteworthy 95% of participants emphasized the significance of climate protection. In the scenario where implementing RES solutions would entail supplementary expenses, 70% of respondents indicated their willingness to absorb such costs. In terms of gender-based distinctions, 94% of women expressed readiness to assume additional expenses associated with RES, while this figure stood at 83% for men. This implies that women might exhibit greater openness to shouldering the incremental costs linked to RES than men.

The study participants expressed a potential desire to install renewable energy sources such as photovoltaics, hydropower, or wind energy in their households. By far, the largest group of respondents were those who would have chosen photovoltaic panels. On average, approximately one in five respondents expressed interest in hydroelectric power installations and wind turbines.

Summary

The findings from the studies detailed in this chapter underscore that companies are progressively embracing renewable energy sources for energy generation and displaying a genuine eagerness to invest in novel solutions. Furthermore, certain European nations stand out as frontrunners in solar and wind energy production. Notably, Germany boasts an impressive installed capacity of 58.4 GW for solar energy and 63.7 GW for wind energy, while Norway takes the lead in hydropower with a capacity of 33.3 GW. The survey data highlights the paramount importance of climate protection for young entrepreneurs, with 95% recognizing its significance. This demographic is also willing to embrace RES-based solutions, even if it involves additional costs, as evidenced by the 70% affirmative response. Among young entrepreneurs, photovoltaics emerges as the most favored solution, garnering the preference of 61% of respondents. The adoption of green hydrogen stands as another avenue to curtail environmental impact.

The growing popularity of hydrogen production and utilization is reflected in the proliferation of hydrogen valleys (currently numbering 38 globally), which set the stage for cultivating regional hydrogen mini-economies.

References

Abdalla, A. M., Hossain, S., Nisfindy, O. B., Azad, A. T., Dawood, M., & Azad, A. K. (2018). Hydrogen production, storage, transportation and key challenges with applications: A review. *Energy Conversion and Management, 165*, 602–627. https://doi.org/10.1016/j.enconman.2018.03.088.

Aziz, M., Darmawan, A., & Juangsa, F. B. (2021). Hydrogen production from biomasses and wastes: A technological review. *International Journal of Hydrogen Energy, 46*(68), 33756–33781. https://doi.org/10.1016/j.ijhydene.2021.07.189.

Bath, A., & Lee, J. (2022, April 4). *Global wind report 2022*. Global Wind Energy Council. https://gwec.net/global-wind-report-2022/.

Borowski, P. F. (2020). Nexus between water, energy, food and climate change as challenges facing the modern global, European and Polish economy. *AIMS Geosciences, 6*(4), 397–421. https://doi.org/10.3934/geosci.2020022.

Borowski, P. F. (2021). Digitization, digital twins, blockchain, and Industry 4.0 as elements of management process in enterprises in the energy sector. *Energies, 14*(7), 1885. https://doi.org/10.3390/en14071885.

Borowski, P. F. (2022a). Mitigating climate change and the development of green energy versus a return to fossil fuels due to the energy crisis in 2022. *Energies, 15*(24), 9289. https://doi.org/10.3390/en15249289

Borowski, P. F. (2022b). Water and hydropower—challenges for the economy and enterprises in times of climate change in Africa and Europe. *Water, 14*(22), 3631. https://doi.org/10.3390/w14223631.

Clean Hydrogen Partnership. (2023). *Hydrogen Valleys*. H2 Valley map | H2Valleys. https://h2v.eu/hydrogen-valleys.

Climatechangepost. (2022). *Fresh water resources in Poland*. Climatechangepost.com. https://www.climatechangepost.com/poland/fresh-water-resources/

dise.org.pl. (2019). *Współpraca konwencjonalnych źródeł węglowych i wielkoskalowego OZE*. dise.org.pl. https://dise.org.pl/raport-2019-oze.pdf.

Falcone, P. M., Hiete, M., & Sapio, A. (2021). Hydrogen economy and sustainable development goals: Review and policy insights. *Current Opinion in Green and Sustainable Chemistry, 31*, 100506. https://doi.org/10.1016/j.cogsc.2021.100506.

Fernández, L. (2023). *Wind energy in Europe*. Statista. https://www.statista.com/topics/3415/wind-energy-in-europe/#topicOverview.

Garcia-Navarro, J. C. (2021). *What is a hydrogen valley?*. Hydrogen Central. https://hydrogen-central.com/what-is-a-hydrogen-valley/.

GLT. (2023). *Where does our electricity come from?*. https://www.germanledtech.de/en/news/where-does-our-electricity-come-from.

IEA. (2021). *Renewable electricity – renewables 2021 – analysis*. IEA. https://www.iea.org/reports/renewables-2021/renewable-electricity?mode=market&region=World&publication=2021&product=Total.

IEA. (2023). *Solar*. IEA. https://prod.iea.org/energy-system/renewables/solar-pv.
Instytut Energii Odnawialnej. (2022). *Raport—Rynek Fotowoltaiki w Polsce 2022*. Raport"Rynek Fotowoltaiki w Polsce 2022"—EC BREC Instytut Energetyki Odnawialnej | Fotowoltaika. https://ieo.pl/pl/raport-rynek-fotowoltaiki-w-polsce-2022.
Mason, L. R., Melton, C. C., Gray, D., & Swallow, A. L. (2022). Climate change, social work, and the transition away from fossil fuels: A scoping review. *Sustainability, 14*(12), 7086. https://doi.org/10.3390/su14127086.
MENA. (2021). Poland : Onshore wind energy in poland—report and assumptions of the amendment to the act. *MENA Report*, May.
Menear, H. (2020, July 16). *Is Facebook building the Netherlands' Biggest Data Centre?* Data Centre Magazine. https://datacentremagazine.com/data-centres/facebook-building-netherlands-biggest-data-centre.
Ministerstwo Klimatu i Środowiska. (2023). *Polska Strategia Wodorowa do Roku 2030- Ministerstwo Klimatu I środowiska—portal gov.pl*. Ministerstwo Klimatu i Środowiska. https://www.gov.pl/web/klimat/polska-strategia-wodorowa-do-roku-2030.
Niemeyer, L., & Meyers, K. (2022, May 1). *A new kind of "mining" has arrived in the Ohio Valley. what will crypto mean for the region?* NKyTribune. https://nkytribune.com/2022/05/a-new-kind-of-mining-has-arrived-in-the-ohio-valley-what-will-crypto-mean-for-the-region/.
Piggot, G., Boyland, M., Down, A., & Torre, A. R. (2019). Realizing a just and equitable transition away from fossil fuels. *Development, 2016*, 202033.
Quaranta, E., Georgakaki, A., & Letout, S. (2022). *Clean Energy Technology Observatory, Hydropower and pumped hydropower storage in the European Union: Status report on technology development, trends, value chains and markets : 2022*. Urząd Publikacji Unii Europejskiej. **https://data.europa.eu/doi/10.2760/256255.**
Ronergy. (2022). *History of wind energy in Europe—ronergy services*. Ronergy Services—Especializados en el mantenimiento eólico. https://ronergy.com/en/history-of-wind-energy-in-europe/.
Sadorsky, P. (2012). Modeling renewable energy company risk. *Energy Policy*, https://doi.org/10.1016/j.enpol.2010.06.064.
Shi, M., Wang, H., Xie, P., Lyu, C., Jian, L., & Jia, Y. (2022). Distributed energy scheduling for integrated energy system clusters with peer-to-peer energy transaction. *IEEE Transactions on Smart Grid, 14*(1), 142–156. https://doi.org/10.1109/tsg.2022.3197435.
Standar, A., Kozera, A., & Satoła, Ł. (2022). the importance of local investments co-financed by the European union in the field of renewable energy sources in rural areas of Poland. *Energies, 14*(2), 450. https://doi.org/10.3390/en14020450.
TPA Poland. (2021). *Raport "Lądowa Energetyka Wiatrowa w polsce"*. TPA Poland. https://www.tpa-group.pl/pl/w-oczekiwaniu-na-nowy-wiatr-na-ladzie-premiera-raportu-ladowa-energetyka-wiatrowa-w-polsce/
UNICEF. (2022). *Devastating floods in Pakistan*. UNICEF. https://www.unicef.org/emergencies/devastating-floods-pakistan-2022.
U. S. Drought Monitor. (2023). *U.S. drought monitor*. https://droughtmonitor.unl.edu/CurrentMap/StateDroughtMonitor.aspx?CA.

Index

Note: **Bold** page numbers refer to tables.

For Product Safety Concerns and Information please contact our EU representative GPSR@taylorandfrancis.com
Taylor & Francis Verlag GmbH, Kaufingerstraße 24, 80331 München, Germany

www.ingramcontent.com/pod-product-compliance
Ingram Content Group UK Ltd.
Pitfield, Milton Keynes, MK11 3LW, UK
UKHW022353190926
475702UK00015B/2262
9781032819693